The Investor's Toolbox

How to use spread betting, CFDs, options, warrants and
trackers to boost returns and reduce risk

by Peter Temple

HARRIMAN HOUSE LTD

3A Penns Road
Petersfield
Hampshire
GU32 2EW
GREAT BRITAIN

Tel: +44 (0)1730 233870
Fax: +44 (0)1730 233880
email: enquiries@harriman-house.com
website: www.harriman-house.com

First edition published in Great Britain in 2003
Second edition published in Great Britain in 2007

Copyright Harriman House Ltd

The right of Peter Temple to be identified as author has been asserted
in accordance with the Copyright, Design and Patents Act 1988.

ISBN 1-905641-04-4
978-1-905641-04-8

British Library Cataloguing in Publication Data
A CIP catalogue record for this book can be obtained from the British Library.

Printed and bound by Cambridge Printing, University Printing House, Cambridge.

About the author

Peter Temple has been working in and writing about financial markets for the last 36 years. After an 18 year career in fund management and stockbroking, he became a full time writer in 1988.

His articles appear in the *Financial Times*, *Investors Chronicle* and a range of other publications. He has written more than a dozen books about investing, mainly aimed at private investors.

He and his wife live in part of a converted bobbin mill in the Lake District National Park.

Acknowledgements

Any author writing a factual book relies on a diverse range of contacts both for information and for the benefit of their experience. Many individuals helped with both editions of this book.

Philip Jenks embraced the original idea of this book and backed it when – during depressed times for investment publishing – few other publishers wanted to take on new projects. Myles Hunt at Harriman House has taken up the baton and has been instrumental in producing the second edition.

Stephen Eckett deserves special mention for firming up many of the disjointed ideas I originally had about what this book should cover into a firm coherent plan, and for some useful and detailed comments on the finished manuscript of both editions.

I have been writing on a regular basis about derivatives in one form or another since the mid 1990s. Tony Drury, at that time a publisher of financial books, commissioned my first book on the subject. This book, *Traded Options – a Private Investor's Guide*, was first sponsored by LIFFE (as it was then called, before Euronext came on the scene) and ProShare. It has been a consistent seller over 11 years and three editions. Tony Hawes and several other LIFFE employees contributed greatly to my initial education about the options market. Jonathan Seymour at LIFFE provided some specific help with screenshots related to LIFFE products in the first edition of *The Investor's Toolbox*, and re-used in this edition. Ian Tabor at LIFFE also provided help on this edition.

Staying on options, I have talked to a number of futures and options brokers over many years. John Paul Thwaytes, Bill Newton and James Bateman at ODL Securities and MyBroker are long standing contacts, as are Bruce Williams at Renzburg, John Newman (now at Natexis Metals), and Frank Freeman and Julia Williams at Sucden. All of them have had some input into the book. James Bateman provided some specific help with screenshots in Chapter 9 of the first edition.

On spread betting I have dealt personally through Cantor Index for some time, and David Buik was a mine of information on the various articles I have written on the subject, as well as dealing with a number of specific queries relating to the first edition of this book. In the course of compiling the first edition, Brian Griffin at CMC Markets spent time with me and was of immense help in getting me to understand the mechanics of their approach to spread betting and also understanding how CFDs work.

I originally came across exchange-traded funds in the course of researching a lengthy article on investment funds for a Pearson publication. Adam Seccombe and several other colleagues at BGI were of considerable help in getting me to understand the nuances of these novel and highly effective ways of investing. Esther Nass-Fetzmann has helped with more recent queries, particularly on the subject of metals-related ETFs.

Technical analysis is a vital component of using these products successfully. In terms of understanding technical analysis and market timing, I owe a considerable debt to long-standing contacts David Linton and Jeremy du Plessis at Updata, Martin Stamp at Ionic Information, and particularly John Ingram at Winstock Software.

Steve Hunter at Ultra Financial Systems has spent a considerable time talking to me about market timing theories and I have also used Nigel Webb's Optimum option pricing software as an example in many books and articles because of the clear and simple way it deals with this complex topic. Peter Hoadley's OptionStrategy software has also been invaluable in getting my own mind around some of the more complex strategies explained in the later parts of this book. I have never met either Peter Hoadley or Nigel Webb, but their efforts have been of great help to me, whether they have realised it or not.

I have written on these subjects over many years in a variety of publications, with the forbearance of a long list of editors.

Matthew Vincent, Rosie Carr and Richard Anderson at *Investors Chronicle* have commissioned articles from me on stock futures, traded options, and technical analysis software. Emma Lou Montgomery and Richard Beddard at Interactive Investor have allowed me free range writing about a number of the ideas covered in this book, and specifically on hedging, portfolio strategy and exchange traded funds.

Deborah Hargreaves, Kevin Brown and Rob Budden at the *Financial Times* have commissioned articles on a range of the investment concepts and techniques included in this book. They too have my thanks for thus making me keep my knowledge up to date in these areas.

Finally, my wife Lynn has contributed to both editions of this book with her usual diligence. The appendices on information sources and further reading are primarily her work, as is the glossary of web addresses. She has read the manuscript with some care from the standpoint of an ordinary private investor to make sure I did not lapse too often into the jargon it is all too easy to use when talking about derivative products.

Any errors or lack of clarity that remain are entirely my own doing.

Peter Temple
September 2006

Contents

Preface

What the book covers

This book is intended to be a simple practical guide to how you can use some of the newer investment products like spread betting, binary betting, contracts for difference, covered warrants and exchange-traded funds, as well as older ones like futures and options, to help your investing. In different ways, each of these products allows you either to:

- boost the returns you get in exchange for taking on greater risk;
- hedge your bets in exchange for slightly lower returns;
- use much less capital to achieve the same market exposure; or
- move money into and out of a range of markets and sectors efficiently.

I believe they are tools that all investors need to know about and be able to use when the occasion demands it. They should help you confront successfully any lengthy period of trendless or volatile markets.

While the past three years has seen a generally strong upward trend in stock markets, this is not bound to continue. Periodic volatility is the natural order of things. Interestingly enough – despite what appears to have been a bull market – recent years have also seen increased use by private investors of many of the tools described in this book. That's proof that they work, and can be applied, in all market conditions.

Who the book is for

I wrote the first edition of this book primarily for private investors like you and me. The second edition follows exactly the same pattern. There is no advanced mathematics or fancy formulas to master. It is a practical guide for those who already have some experience of investing in shares, but who want to take their investing strategies on to the next level.

I hope as well that finance students and individuals who are just embarking on a career in the financial markets may find it a useful way of getting to grips quickly and easily with some of the concepts they will be expected to master in great detail as their careers progress.

How the book is structured

Chapter 1

This is a light-hearted look at the **history** of the derivatives markets, how they have developed, and which individuals have been the key players. I explain the link between the older derivatives, like futures and options, and newer concepts like spread betting and contracts for difference.

Chapter 2

Chapter 2 provides a quick run-through of the **basic mechanics** of futures, options, and warrants and the other tools that are similar to them. We'll cover basic principles like the fact that in using these techniques you are dealing in a contract rather than the underlying asset, the idea of cash settlement, expiry dates, time value, volatility, fair-value, shorting and margin. These are basic concepts that also apply to newer products like spread betting and contracts for difference.

We'll also run through the types of security and commodity that can be traded through the futures and options markets in their various guises, including interest rates, stock market indices, shares, and commodities. Ordinary investors can trade interest rate or gold futures through the medium of these markets. You don't need to be a professional to use them – as long as you have a view, a trading plan, and an awareness of risk.

Chapter 3

Here we take a look at **futures** in more detail, examining the nuts and bolts of how futures contracts work. Among the topics discussed are margin, differences in margin requirements because of volatility, the way futures markets are structured with different expiry months, how to trade futures, and the theory behind index futures. There won't be any complicated maths or algebra to cope with. It'll be strictly how the market works in practice.

Chapters 4 and 5

These chapters cover **contracts for difference (CFDs)** and **spread betting** in detail. We'll see how spread betting, for example, is simply a different way of trading futures contacts, and how CFDs and spread betting differ in terms of their tax treatment, the way margin is levied, and the capital commitments required. Most importantly we'll look at the basic differences between these two ways of trading and how they might affect you as an investor. What you need to make sure is that you use the type of product that's right for you. These chapters will tell you how to make that decision. The chapter on spread betting also includes an all-new section on binary betting, effectively a way of taking a 'fixed odds' bet on the short term course of the stock market.

Chapter 6

This chapter looks at **options** in more detail. We'll let you into the secret of working out the right price for an option. One of the things we'll focus on here is the crucial importance of volatility and how it determines the type of trade that might be best at any one time. We'll also look at some of the principles behind popular option strategies. These are key building blocks, but they are not that difficult to grasp. You can use options for speculation, hedging, and to yield extra income from your existing shares, and we'll show how the market works in practice.

Chapter 7

Here we dissect the new market for **covered warrants** in London. This is a close cousin of the options market - but with some important differences. We'll also take a peek at the historical perspective of the Continental European covered warrants markets and how they have grown. Their example alone suggests that this is a market that, once better understood, could be very popular with investors. This chapter shows how covered warrants tie in with older-established derivative products and points up the precise ways in which they are superior.

Covered warrants have developed considerably since the first edition of The Investors Toolbox was written, and newer developments like certificates – warrants that work like index trackers - are also explored in this new edition.

Chapter 8

Exchange-traded funds (ETFs) have been hugely popular in the USA because of their cheapness and because they provide an easy way of getting exposure to the market quickly and efficiently. This could be something you need at specific points in the future roller-coaster ride that the market will provide.

We will look at the ETFs on offer in the UK, US and other markets where they are traded, and how precisely they work. One important attribute is that in buying and selling ETFs you are avoiding the risks associated with specific stocks, and opening up simple market timing strategies.

We all tend to overestimate our stock picking ability. ETFs give us a way of focusing single-mindedly on what and where we want our overall market exposure to be, avoiding the distractions of profit warnings, dividend cuts, accounting irregularities and management changes.

As with covered warrants, the ETFs market has also changed considerably in the past three years. These new developments, especially the development of bond and commodity ETFs, are fully covered in this new edition.

Chapter 9

It's no good knowing about all of these new everyday derivatives without understanding how to access them and use them for yourself. Chapter 9 looks in turn at **how to deal** in each of the markets. We'll look at issues like the dealing vocabulary, the bid-offer spreads you can expect, commission charges and other costs, how to choose a broker and what they will and won't let you do, and how much money you need to have to be able play in each of the markets.

Accessing these markets isn't as convoluted as you might think. One important point is that many spread betting and CFD firms are really a 'one-stop shop' way of dealing. You can, for example, deal in futures and options through spread betting. For ETFs and covered warrants you can use your existing broker, provided the firm is up to speed with these new techniques. We'll give you a guide to the all-important ticker symbols for covered warrants and ETFs, which are similar to those on shares. We'll also do some cost comparisons on the most economical derivative to use to get the exposure you want for the risk you want to run.

Chapters 10 and 11

If you've got this far you should understand which derivatives you want to use and what they can do for you. In Chapters 10 and 11 we really get down to the nitty-gritty of practical trading with some examples of **strategies**. In the futures area, we'll look at trading methods like cash extraction trades (which economise on your use of capital), relative value trades, and pairs trading, and we'll give some worked examples.

We'll also examine how you can use put and call options and warrants to give effect to your view of the market. Again we'll have worked examples of some popular strategies like *long calls*, *long puts*, *straddles*, *strangles* and *spreads*. Don't be put off by the jargon: you'll soon be familiar with it.

Last but not least, in this chapter we'll show you how to use options and warrants for hedging your portfolio against a fall in the market and how to use covered call option writing to generate portfolio income in stable markets.

Chapter 12

Many investors fall foul of the stock market as a whole, and derivatives in particular, because they lack a coherent plan and a broad understanding of the way their assets should be diversified. In Chapter 12 we'll cover the basics of **money management and trading techniques**.

We'll tell you:

- How to formulate a trading strategy using ETFs, futures, options and warrants;

- How to use technical analysis to time your trades and work out the realistic profit potential of a trade;

- How to make use of market timing software; and -

- How to use option valuation software for options and covered warrants, including the theory behind it and how to use it for 'what if' modelling of trading scenarios.

This brings us to one general point about the book. If, after a first reading, you decide you only want to use one particular type of derivative in your trading, you need to read, or re-read, not only the chapter on that particular product, but also the appropriate section of Chapter 9 on dealing methods, and the appropriate parts of Chapters 10 and 11 to suss out the right strategies to use. Chapter 12 is a must, whatever you deal in.

Appendices

Finally, in the appendices to the book there is a directory of brokers and other service providers that can help you take your first steps in the derivatives market, a detailed look at sources of information on derivatives, a glossary of web addresses and some places to go for further reading.

This has been fully revised to take account of web site redesigns and new publications in the period since the first edition was published.

Supporting web site

The web site supporting this book can be found at:

www.harriman-house.com/toolbox

Introduction

The D-Word

Covered warrants, certificates, CFDs, ETFs, futures and options, spread betting and binary betting. The jargon can be puzzling. But what all of these new and different ways of trading have in common is that they are everyday derivatives. And they are tools that can be used just as effectively by private investors as by the professionals.

Don't be put off by the D-word. The D in derivatives needn't stand for danger. This book is here to help you understand these tools and use them in a way that suits your investing style. Used properly they can help improve your returns and control the risks that you run.

Many investors lost plenty of money through investing in equities in the later stages of the bull market that ended in early 2000. If they had used some of the tools we'll explore in this book, they could have limited and even offset their losses. That's why they are worth taking seriously.

Three years on from the publication of the first edition of this book it has become clear that my question as to whether we were set for a long period of modest returns was, perhaps, premature.

In fact mid-2003 just about marked the start of a new bull phase which, depending on your viewpoint, is either simply a rally in a much longer bear market that has only just begun, or the start of the next golden age of stock market prosperity.

The point remains that stock markets are unpredictable and, if you want to sleep at nights, you need some way of counteracting the volatility to which they are inevitably prone, and ways of moving money into and out of the market quickly as circumstances dictate.

Are we set for a long period of modest returns?

Though I've researched the equity market and the stocks within it in one form or another for over thirty-five years, I still find it hard to pinpoint exactly when a new uptrend or downtrend in the market will begin. In fact no one really knows.

I asked the question at the heading of this section three years ago and if you had invested in UK small company stocks and emerging markets at that time, the answer to it – until recently - would have been 'no'. There have been some big returns earned in these areas, and even in something as basic as gold bullion, since then. But it doesn't alter the fact that over long periods, as the table later in this chapter shows, the returns from equities as a whole are relatively modest.

What if the market now 'reverts to the mean' and there is a period of underperformance to make up for the good times we've had over the past few years? If so, the best that investors can hope for from their holdings in shares or bonds is single digit percentage gains on average, and possibly a fair degree of volatility in those returns. Some years will be good and some will be bad, and the percentage changes and swings from peak to trough and back again could be quite substantial. This is the normal condition of investing.

To show what I mean, have a look on the next page and see what has happened to Japan's stock market index in the aftermath of their bubble market in the 1980s. Even after it descended sharply from its peak, the Nikkei spent 10 years oscillating between 15,000 and 22,000. Recently it's recovered a little way from a low point considerably less than this. The idea that it will get back to its 1989 high any time soon is frankly bizarre.

Now compare this to the action of major Western markets before and since the market lows in 2003. The US NASDAQ market indices probably bear the closest resemblance to the Nikkei. Although it may not have seemed like it at the time, broader market benchmarks like the FTSE100 and the US Standard & Poors 500 did not reach such extreme valuations.

Figure (i) – Charts of Nikkei, Nasdaq and FTSE

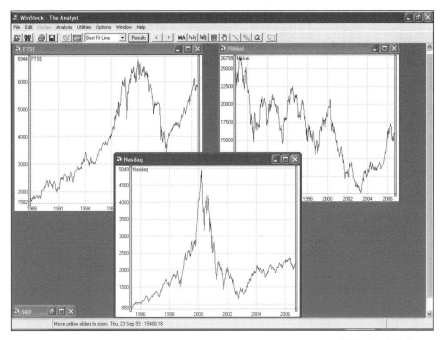

The central point is that the bull market of the 1990s was the exception, the like of which had not been seen since the 1920s and, notwithstanding generally rising share prices over the last three years, has not been since seen since and probably will not be seen for another generation or two. Excluding bubbles like this, the normal market pattern is for uptrends to last just short of three years and for bear markets to be nasty, but brief, perhaps lasting just under two years. However, there have also been sometimes quite long periods during which the markets have gone sideways.

Look at the table opposite and see what Barclays Capital says about the long-term inflation-adjusted returns from different types of investment, and what happened in periods of market stagnation in the past.

The message from this is that the returns experienced in equities for much of the 1990s were a flash in the pan, and that the long-term real gains from equities are almost always a single figure percentage. In stagnant markets they are likely to be plus or minus low single figures. And if returns over the last few years have been above average, then the laws of averages suggest there's a strong possibility of below average returns for the next few.

So, history tells us that just repeating the strategies we used in the 1990s bull market, or indeed more recently, might not work in any new stock market era that's maybe neither bull nor bear market, but something in between the two.

We could of course go back to the fundamental tools and theories of earlier eras when more stable, range-bound markets were the norm. But wacky theories like Gann, Elliott Wave, or even astrology are probably not the real solution to the problem of coping with markets like this.

Table (i) – Barclays Capital's Equity-Gilt Study

Annual real returns

Period	Equities(%)	Gilts(%)	Cash(%)
1947-52	-4.0	-0.9	-4.8
1960-62	-2.4	3.5	1.2
1969-73	-4.1	-4.7	-1.6
1975-81	4.9	-0.4	-1.0
1987-90	2.8	-0.9	5.4
Last 3yrs	14.8	2.8	1.6
Last 10yrs	4.2	5.7	2.8
Last 20 yrs	6.7	6.2	3.9
Last 50 yrs	7.0	2.3	2.0
1900-2005	5.2	1.2	1.0

Source: Barclays Capital

Don't get me wrong. There's nothing bad with selecting investments on value investing criteria, or looking for cheap growth stocks among smaller companies, or indeed trying to time entry and exit points in the ups and downs of the markets using mainstream technical analysis.

But I also think it will pay to look more closely at some of the more straightforward tools that are available to help our most basic of investment decisions. We should not cut ourselves off from a host of new techniques and investment products that have been devised from the mid-1970s onwards, and some of them much more recently. They can help boost returns in what may be a particularly unrewarding period for 'normal' investment techniques.

What are the new techniques we need to survive?

These tools and techniques allow all investors to address what are likely to be some of the main features of the era that we find ourselves in right now. I've reduced these to some key bullet points illustrating investors' needs in the markets we may face for the next few years:

- We need to be nimble. Buy and hold investing on its own is not going to yield us decent returns, at least for the time being.

- We need, if we can, to have a means of getting money into and out of the index quickly at a low cost and with the minimum of fuss.

- If returns are persistently low, we need to keep transaction costs to an absolute minimum. The more charges we can avoid or minimise the better.

- We need to be able to make money if the market is falling as well as if it is rising For a few years yet the market will be switching between periods of elation and depression, and we need to be able to capitalise on those swings.

- Since markets are going to be volatile, we need ways of controlling our risk.

- Finally, we need to try and magnify our returns wherever possible. Since overall returns are likely to be low, this means using our judgement and some of the new tools available to produce bigger returns when the time is right.

These are the topics we are aiming to cover in this book. We'll look at all of the new everyday derivatives that private investors can and should be using: how they work, when and when *not* to use them, how to deal in them, who to deal with, where to get information about them, and why they make sense for managing our investments with real 21st century savvy.

So, turn to the next chapter to begin this journey to understanding the mysteries of everyday derivatives and how they can help you make money in the markets, and hang on to it.

1

Derivatives History

Introduction

I've already mentioned the fact that derivatives – that dreaded D-word again – are tools you can use in your everyday investing. Later in this book we'll explain how. But first let's have a brief look at how the ideas behind futures, options and similar products developed. Looking at the way the concepts evolved at the start is a good way of seeing how they can work for you.

Some of the gadgets in the toolbox are age-old, some of them thoroughly modern. It's certainly not true to say, for example, that options are new-fangled. They date back at least to the Middle Ages, and possibly to before that. What is newer is our understanding of how they work and the development of systems by which they can be freely traded.

In fact, trading in futures and options over commodities probably dates back a long way in history – perhaps as far back as the start of systematic agriculture. Certainly it goes back long before the establishment of joint stock companies and the notion of trading shares in them on exchanges.

Let's take just a few episodes in the history of derivatives to illustrate this point.

Early days

Wags in the derivatives market reckon that the first recorded futures transaction was in the Bible – when Esau sold his birthright for a mess of pottage. An alternative biblical analogy was Jacob entering into a contract to exchange his labour for the hand of Rachel.

Opinions differ about whether this was a *future* or an *option*. Jacob laboured for the right to marry Rachel, but maybe did not have the obligation to – a crucial distinction. Some view it as a *swap* – his labour in exchange for marrying his girlfriend.

In Ancient Greece, Thales – a shrewd merchant – forecast a bumper olive crop. Rather than speculate on a fall in the price of olives or olive oil, he came to the conclusion that olive presses would be in short supply. Since he had only limited capital, he decided to arrange to pay a deposit for the right to buy some presses.

When the harvest came in he could, if things worked out, pay the balance and buy the presses. Or if things didn't happen as planned, he would be able to walk away, losing only his deposit. History suggests he was right. He cleaned up when a bumper harvest occurred and the owners of olive groves clamoured to use the presses he controlled. This seems to be the first recorded instance of the use of what we now term a *call option*.

The next step in the story dates from the 12th century. In Southern Europe at that time, trade fairs had developed. They allowed the cities of Florence and Venice, as well as other northern Italian towns, to participate in trade with cities in France, Belgium and the Netherlands.

Whether it was for convenience, or more likely because they didn't trust each other, the trade fairs began to revolve around codes of conduct that developed into elementary *contracts*. The contracts were agreements to exchange goods in the future based around samples available to be inspected on the spot. These forward delivery agreements – known as *lettres de faire* – were originally just between one merchant and another, but eventually came to be traded more widely among the merchants. Eventually some merchants began trading just the contracts rather than the underlying commodities.

Table 1.1 – Ancient derivatives history timeline

Date	Event
BC 600	Thales exercises options to buy olive presses
AD 1150	Creation of primitive futures contracts for trading at trade fairs
AD 1350	Development of forward foreign exchange contracts
AD 1501	Trading in spice contracts for 'when arrived' delivery
AD 1505	Antwerp options bourse 'renovated'
AD 1600	Development of rice futures contracts in feudal Japan
AD 1634-7	Futures and options widely used in Dutch tulip bubble
AD 1730	Dojima rice futures market begins in Japan

Forward foreign exchange transactions were first recorded in the 14th century. London branches of Italian banking houses had contracts with the Papal Nuncio in England to remit papal taxes gathered in England. The rates for these exchange transactions, though not the precise amounts involved, were set a year in advance.

Some types of futures or forward contracts developed in their earliest serious form in the early 16th century. In 1501 the King of Portugal used Antwerp as the port in which to sell spices which his ships were bringing from the Indies. Merchants competed for the contracts. They paid in advance for spices to be delivered when the fleet arrived. The delay between setting the price and the delivery date meant the contracts were, like present-day futures, speculative and very volatile in price.

In 17th century Japan, serfs who leased their land from the local noblemen were allowed to pay rent in the form of a portion of the following year's harvest. Contracts were issued to the nobleman and secured against the collateral of the rice harvest. Eventually, a century or more later, the contracts themselves came to be standardised and traded through a rudimentary exchange – the *Dojima* market. The noblemen sold these rights to the crop in case bad weather or warfare reduced its value.

As an aside, one of the more arcane forms of technical analysis, known as *candlestick charting*, developed around the same time. Traders used it to attempt to predict prices from past history. It is still used today, as the chart below shows:

Figure 1.1 – Candlestick charting of Vodafone's share price

© Winstock Software

In the 16th and 17th century, options – at that time called *premium transactions* – were also being developed more systematically. One origin of the use of options was by sea captains venturing to the East Indies. They sold options on part of their expected cargo to merchants in Amsterdam and Antwerp in order to finance the voyages. The risk that the boats would not return fully laden, or might sink, was thus transferred in part to the buyers of the options.

Shakespeare seems to have had much the same in mind in the Merchant of Venice, whose plot turns on the fortune of Antonio's ships (argosies, or 'bottoms' in the jargon of the time). As a good venture capitalist, Antonio diversified his risk, sending several ships to different destinations As he said –

> *'My ventures are not in one bottom trusted, nor to one place; nor is my whole estate upon the fortune of this present year. Therefore my merchandise makes me not sad.'*

Rather than pay interest to Shylock when his ships were overdue, Antonio contracted to borrow three thousand ducats for three months. Instead of interest Shylock agreed to take an option over a pound of Antonio's flesh –

> *'If you repay me not on such a day and in such a place, such sum or sums as are expressed in the condition, let the forfeit be nominated for an equal pound of your fair flesh, to be cut and taken in what part of your body pleaseth me.'*

We can argue whether or not this is a bond with a particularly unpleasant conversion right, or some form of option. Either way it shows that forms of derivative were used to finance trade in Shakespeare's day. In the end Shylock went to court to enforce the contract, but Antonio's ships came home in the nick of time.

The most authoritative documentation of the use of options comes in the Dutch tulip bubble in the early 16th century. What began as a normal trade among growers, gardeners and collectors snowballed into a boom of epic proportions. As Peter Bernstein records in his book *Against the Gods* –

> *'Much of the famous Dutch tulip bubble involved trading in options on tulips rather than in the tulips themselves; trading that was in many ways as sophisticated as anything that goes on in our own times.'*

Bernstein says that new research shows that tales that options fuelled the boom are wide of the mark. They simply allowed more people to participate in a market that had hitherto been beyond their reach.

Figure 1.2 – The subject of 'tulipomania'

> *'The opprobrium that attached to options during the so-called bubble was in fact cultivated by vested interests who resented the intrusion of interlopers onto their turf.'*

However, Charles Mackay's classic book, *Extraordinary Popular Delusions and the Madness of Crowds,* suggests otherwise. As prices began to fall, he describes how the derivatives used by everyone by that time exacerbated the situation.

> *'A had agreed to purchase ten Semper Augustines from B at 4000 florins each, at six weeks after the signing of the contract. B was ready with the flowers at the appointed time; but the price had fallen to three or four hundred florins, and A refused either to pay the difference or receive the tulips.'*

Speculation of different forms was also rife. Dutch currency dealers entered into bets on exchange rates, based on percentage movements up or down, and settled their debts by transferring the margin between the loser's speculation and the actual rate. This looks like an early form of contract for difference (CFD).

Help for farmers

Fast forward to mid-19th century Chicago. In New York and elsewhere, stock exchanges had been founded and options traded, but Chicago's position close to the fertile farmland of the Midwest meant it was ideally placed to develop a market for trading in derivatives based on farm products like wheat, oats, chickens and beef.

One reason for the development was sharp price fluctuations caused by dislocations in supply and demand, and problems with transport and storage. To avoid these, farmers needed to have a way of getting a guaranteed price for their harvest when the time came. The result was the development of a *futures market*. Farmers could sell all of their anticipated crops ahead of time, and gain the security that their revenue was fixed for the forthcoming season.

Table 1.2 – Early futures timeline

Date	Event
1854	Buenos Aires Cereal Exchange founded
1858	CBOT established to trade 'on arrival' contracts in flour and hay
1859	Greasy and Fine Wool Exchange founded in Sydney (later SFE)
1865	CBOT introduces standardised tradable contracts
1868	Trade starts in wheat, pork bellies, and copper futures at CBOT
1870	Other US exchanges formed including NY Butter and Cheese Exchange
1870	New York Cotton Exchange founded
1898	Chicago Butter and Egg Board founded (later CME)

The Chicago Board of Trade set up shop to facilitate this in 1848. The first contracts were quoted on a *delivery on arrival* basis for products like flour and hay. Forward contracts in wheat developed soon after and became very popular. In 1865, after some defaults on forward contracts, the CBOT introduced *standardised*, *tradable* futures contracts. It also introduced *margin*, the performance bond required to make sure the contract is honoured. Standardised contracts and margin are the twin pillars on which all futures markets have since developed. The system is still used today in all forms of futures contracts and other similar products based around them.

By the 1870s, futures trading had really taken off. But business was no longer solely in the hands of farmers and commercial buyers of grain. Speculative trading had begun in earnest. Many other futures exchanges had also formed, trading all manner of agricultural commodities, including cotton, butter, eggs, coffee and cocoa. The present day Nymex, for example started life as the Butter and Cheese Exchange of New York.

From the earliest days futures markets relied on so-called *open outcry* trading, where competing dealers gather together in trading *pits* each identified by different coloured jackets and shout bids and offers at each other in a noisy and frenetic system. Though chaotic, it seems to work. The tradition in open outcry is that a bid or offer is good 'for as long as the breath is warm'. In other words, a few seconds and no more.

Dealers also developed an elaborate system of sign language to communicate bids and offers to each other and with colleagues when new orders were received or deals had been done. All of this was fixed in the public's mind – in the UK at least – as the quintessence of Thatcher-style capitalism. In fact, it had been around for a century or more before Thatcher came along. In the US, open outcry remains as an institution, although many orders are traded electronically. Many futures markets in the UK, Germany and elsewhere are now exclusively electronic.

Despite the speculative tag that futures trading has, a tag that's certainly not discouraged by the image of brightly dressed traders shouting at each other in the trading pits, there is an element in all this that is not quite what it seems.

As Peter Bernstein records in *Against the Gods* most financial transactions -

> *'are a bet in which the buyer hopes to be buying low and the seller hopes to be selling high. One side is always doomed to disappointment. Risk management products are different. They exist, not necessarily because someone is seeking a profit, but because there is a demand for instruments that transfer risk from a risk-averse party to someone willing to bear risk.'*

This essential quality applies to any derivative and any type of underlying commodity on which it might be based. Futures trading started out in commodities, first in the USA and then elsewhere. But it has found its full and most recent and exotic flowering in the area of financial futures. These are futures contracts based on financial products and financial concepts like bonds, interest rates, stock market indices and exchange rates, rather than on more tangible products like wheat, barley, potatoes or beef.

But before we look at the modern development of products like this, we need to take a look at how options markets developed.

The magic formula

In popular parlance, for anyone with half an eye to the way financial markets function, futures and options are always linked together. But the link is far from inextricable. As we have already seen, options were some of the earliest derivative products.

For example, in 17th century Holland, puts and calls were already being traded actively. But futures did not really get going in earnest until 19th century America. Before that their appearance had been far from widespread, and only in rather unusual markets like rice trading in feudal Japan.

So it is perhaps more surprising that, although options existed as a concept somewhat earlier than futures, and options contracts had been traded on a bilateral basis throughout history, their development into products that were traded on exchanges happened somewhat later than futures.

Table 1.3 – Options timeline

Date	Options event
1600	Active trading in options in Holland
1968	Fisher Black and Myron Scholes begin collaboration
1973	Black-Scholes formula for pricing options published
1973	Chicago Board Options Exchange founded
1979	London Traded Options Market launched
1982	London International Financial Futures Exchange founded
1992	LIFFE and LTOM merge
1997	Merton and Scholes awarded Nobel prize
1998	LTCM collapse
2001	French, Dutch and UK options markets united under LIFFE

For example, the stock options exchange in Chicago did not set up shop until 1973 and the one in London not until six years later. The basic reason for this is that options are inherently much more complicated products to value than futures.

The price of a future, as we shall see in a later chapter, is linked closely to the price of the underlying commodity or security on which it based. There is only a small price difference to allow for the benefit (in terms of use of capital) that futures buyers get from the fact that there may be some time to go until delivery, and because until then the full purchase price does not have to be paid.

With options, there are many more factors involved. These include not only the time to go until the contract expires, but also the current price of the underlying on which it is based, the exercise price of the option, whether or not it is an option to buy or to sell, whether or not it can be exercised only on its expiry date or at any time up till then, the level of interest rates, the volatility in the price of the underlying security on which it is based, and so on.

Without an accurate means of relating all of the these variables to each other, and assigning them an appropriate weighting, option traders would always be in the dark about precisely how much the option they were buying or selling was actually worth.

The logjam was broken in 1973 when two American academics – Fisher Black and Myron Scholes – published a seminal paper, *The Pricing of Options and Corporate Liabilities*. This provided a logical and transparent basis, mathematically derived, for arriving at the price of an option. In 1997, in what some reckoned was a belated recognition of this contribution, Robert Merton, another collaborator, and Myron Scholes received the Nobel Prize for Economics.

Other formulas for pricing options have since been developed, but the results they produce are much the same. In one of those quirks of fate that both amuse and humble us, having developed the formula for pricing options, Scholes had gone on – in the frenetic atmosphere of mid 1990s Wall Street – to join John Meriwether's ill-fated hedge fund, Long Term Capital Management.

The fund specialised in sophisticated – and supposedly risk-free – arbitrage strategies that made extensive use of derivatives. It collapsed amid much acrimony in 1998, nearly bringing the financial system down with it. Scholes lost a lot of money in the collapse, as did many Wall Street luminaries who you might have thought would have known better.

In his book *Inventing Money*, Nick Dunbar describes meeting a soft-spoken former academic (who could perhaps have been Scholes) after the crisis. He says:

> *'His eyes gave him away. They were the eyes of the Ancient Mariner; they had witnessed scenes of indescribable violence and suffering. Not real bloodshed, but rather the sight of some beautiful intricate construction being torn to pieces in front of its impotent creators.'*

The words sound melodramatic, but they are something of a warning to all those who dabble in derivatives. They are useful tools, but not to be treated lightly or used to excess.

Yet Scholes' place in the history of finance is assured. Because of his and others' work, options can now be priced accurately simply by entering a few figures into a simple computer model.

In Chicago, the CBOE began life in 1973 listing call options on 16 stocks. Put options followed four years later. CBOE now lists options in more than 1500 stocks as well as many major indices. It reckons to account for around half of all options trading in the US and more than 90% of index options trading. Index options were first introduced in 1983.

Figure 1.3 – The CBOE's home page

© Chicago Board Options Exchange

In the meantime in 1979, the London Traded Options Market had started life in a corner of the London Stock Exchange trading floor in much the same cautious way. LIFFE, London's financial futures exchange, began life in 1982 trading a limited range of financial futures across the street in the venerable Royal Exchange building.

Futures markets proliferate

During the 1980s and early 1990s futures exchanges opened in almost every major economy in Europe and further afield. Having a futures exchange became something of a prerequisite for any country with international aspirations – something akin to having a national airline.

Often these 'flag carriers' had little going for them. Futures trading needs liquidity and active trading to function efficiently, and even in the largest markets and major financial centres the liquidity has not been there in many products. The pattern has generally been that most markets can sustain futures trading in their own stock market index and in a futures contract based around the local short-term interest rate, but other trading tends to be patchy. Often the way trading has developed has been quirky.

For many years LIFFE's biggest product was the future of the Bund, a German government bond, which you might have thought would have had its natural home in Frankfurt. Then LIFFE slipped up. It did not respond quickly enough to the German futures exchange's initiative to move trading onto an electronic platform. Liquidity in the Bund quickly migrated to Frankfurt. LIFFE subsequently went electronic but never recouped all of the business it had lost.

> 'UK investors have been cautious when it comes to trading futures and options. In Sweden and Holland, private investors have been much more active.'

It did, however, successfully launch other products. As of late 2006 its largest single product in terms of contracts traded is the three-month EURIBOR future, a short term interest rate future related to European Central Bank interest rates.

In the early 1990s LIFFE absorbed the London Traded Options Market to become a one-stop derivatives shop offering financial futures and options. In 1996 it merged with the London Commodities Exchange, bringing in trading in futures and options in soft commodities. In 2000 it launched futures products on a range of individual stocks in the UK, US and Europe.

By the year 2000, across Europe futures and options exchanges had been merging. The German futures market merged with the Swiss derivatives exchange to form Eurex, and share and futures and options markets in Holland, Belgium and France merged to form Euronext, which subsequently also took over LIFFE in 2001.

In general UK investors have been cautious when it comes to trading futures and options. For example, LIFFE no longer offers single stock futures to private investors, partly because those who want to speculate in this way can do so through CFDs and spread betting. In Sweden and Holland, private investors have been much more active in exchange traded derivatives, notably options. This is partly because of the history of those financial markets and the ease with which they could be traded.

Options have had a long history in Holland, as our earlier history shows. In both Holland and Sweden, exchanges and banks have made it easy for investors to buy and sell options through their bank branches. In the UK, the old stock exchange account system made it easy for private investors to trade short term using little capital. Until this system was phased out, there was little need for investors to consider using options.

Table 1.4 – Futures exchange post-war timeline

Date	Event
1982	LIFFE created
1985	Sweden's OM market launched
1985	Futures market established in Brazil (BM&F)
1986	Creation of MATIF (French futures market)
1989	Futures market established in Spain (MEFF)
1989	Tokyo futures exchange (TIFFE) founded
1991	Moscow Currency Exchange set up
1992	Malaysia Financial Market founded
1995	Warsaw Currency Exchange set up
1997	Taiwan Futures Exchange founded
1997	Vienna SE merges with OTOB (Austrian futures market)
1998	Creation of Eurex from DTB and Soffex
2000	Launch of ICE (merged with IPE in 2001)
2001	LIFFE acquired by Euronext

In fact, the ending of the account system coincided with lurid tales of big losses made by some option traders during the 1987 stock market crash, which set back the popularity of options trading among private investors.

Over the years LIFFE has had varied views over how actively it wanted to promote options to private investors. And more recently new products have allowed investors to speculate easily without the administrative constraints that futures and options trading can entail.

New products take the limelight

One of the biggest of these revolutions in the UK in recent years has undoubtedly been the rise of spread betting and contracts for difference.

Spread betting

Spread betting began to take off in earnest among City professionals in the 1980s. Trading began with a limited range of instruments.

IG Index, one of the largest spread betting firms, was so called because the initials stood for Index Gold. In 1975, when it began life, its main service was to allow investors to speculate on the gold price. It, and other firms, also began offering spread betting in the major indices, and City insiders had a field day using this method to back their judgement.

In the bear market, spread betting firms were particularly active marketers. Spread betting became and has remained popular. One reason is the ease with which it enables investors to speculate on a fall in the price of a share or index. The number of investors with spread betting accounts has increased dramatically, perhaps without those taking them out realising that they are, to all intents and purposes, trading futures by another name.

Binary betting

Binary betting is an offshoot of spread betting. Akin to the ante-post system in horse racing, it really amounts to buying and selling continuously changing fixed odds on a particular stock market outcome. Is the index going to be higher or lower at the end of the trading day? Is it going to be more than 20 points up, or 20 points down? The product was first launched in 2003. IG Index claim to have invented it, after some of its employees began making prices among themselves in the likelihood of new recruits passing or failing their City exams. Whatever its origins, most firms that offer conventional spread betting now also offer binary betting as well.

Contracts for difference

Contracts for difference have grown up in much the same way as spread betting. They are aimed at the more serious and well-heeled punter. Both offer investors a one-stop shop with cheap dealing. They also offer the ability to have tightly controlled risk limits in the form of *guaranteed stop-losses* (a service for which few conventional brokers have any appetite) and, in the case of spread betting, tax free gains as well.

Exchange-traded funds

Exchange-traded funds have also become an established part of the stock market scene in recent years. The products date back to New York in the mid 1980s and have become a major force in the US stock market. The exchange-traded fund based around the NASDAQ 100 index is frequently one of the most actively traded stocks in the US market.

ETFs are shares that replicate exactly the movement of an index. They can be used for a variety of purposes, one being to put money into the market quickly with no fear that the investment will underperform.

The concept was introduced in the UK in 2000 and has been gaining steady acceptance. Instruments like this are derivatives in a technical sense, but do not have the gearing and volatility of, for example, futures and options.

In the last year or so there has been a sharp increase in the number of areas covered. ETFs now cover a range of UK and foreign stock market indices, as well as commodities like gold and oil.

Table 1.5 – New products timeline

Date	*New product introduction*
1974	Spread betting service initiated by IG Index
1979	London Traded Options Market launches
1982	LIFFE launches
1992	Effective start of exchange-traded funds market in USA
1995	IG Index launches spread bets on UK shares
2000	BGI launches first iShares ETFs in the UK
2000	LIFFE launches Universal Stock Futures
2002	LSE launches UK covered warrants market
2003	IG Index launches binary betting

Warrants

Last but not least, warrants. Warrants are rather like options, and have a long history in many markets. They have often been issued as an equity sweetener to accompany a staid bond-type investment, or as part of the payment that a company might make for an acquisition.

In Continental Europe, particularly Germany, so-called *covered warrants* have grown rapidly in popularity in recent years and late in 2002 were also launched by the London Stock Exchange. The LSE's conversion to derivatives markets is interesting since it had singularly failed to capitalise on the potential in traded options, and opted out of that market by selling it to LIFFE in the early 1990s.

Covered warrants, issued by investment banks, have all of the characteristics of options but are traded through a conventional stockbroker. They differ from options mainly in the sense that the issuing process is less formally structured than the LIFFE options market. Banks are freer to issue warrants in whatever form they choose. Expiry dates in particular tend to be somewhat longer than those available in the conventional options market. The product range on offer in the UK has expanded in the last few years to include *certificates*, warrants that function like index trackers (some with an added twist), although these have been in common use in Continental warrant markets for some time.

Will the market take off? Even four years on, it's still early days. Interest has been patchy, certainly among private investors. One problem has been the ambivalent attitude of market regulators. Despite the presence of plentiful opportunities for investors to gear up through spread betting and CFDs, regulators have insisted that private investors in covered warrants be made fully aware of the risks and that personnel are trained and qualified to deal with the product.

At the time of writing this has meant that some brokers who might otherwise have offered dealing in these products have not. Online dealing in covered warrants is now fairly widely available, but there are some gaps, and arguably the instruments are not widely promoted by brokers.

The new era – investing with a toolbox

So, this is where this short history of derivatives ends. There are plenty of derivative products on offer. You can have all these tools in your investing toolbox and use them as you see fit.

Spread betting, CFDs and ETFs offer easy ways to gain market exposure and 'hedge your bets'. They allow you to take on extra risk, or lay it off. Options and the covered warrants market, separate and big subjects in themselves, are equally useful for making controlled bets on the markets, for hedging or (in the case of equity options) for generating income. This has been their enduring appeal. Centuries of history have proved their worth. And now there is no reason why, with a little study, you can't learn to use them effectively too.

That's the purpose of this book. So please read on.

2

Basic Concepts

In Chapter 1 we looked at the history of derivatives. The ideas on which they are based have been around a long time. They are the risk-reducers and return-boosters we can all use to improve our investment performance. But before looking at each of them in more detail, we need to get to grips with some basic concepts.

Whether they're futures, options, warrants, spread betting, contracts for difference (CFDs) or exchange-traded funds (ETFs), all derivatives have certain things in common. Before we can understand how each of the products work, we need to master these basic building blocks. So let's start right off by listing them and looking at how they are relevant.

The table overleaf might look a formidable list, but I think derivatives are a lot easier to understand if you look at their component parts first. You can then work out a menu of the concepts you need to understand for each derivative you might want to trade.

> 'Derivatives are a lot easier to understand if you look at their component parts first.'

So let's have a look at each of these ideas in turn. When you reach the end of the chapter it might be worth re-reading it to make sure you've got these ideas firmly planted in your mind. And you may want to refer to it again when we come to look at each of the main products later in the book.

Table 2.1 – Basic components of derivatives

Building block	*Relevant to*
Contracts	All except ETFs
Cash settlement	All except ETFs
Expiry dates	All futures and options, warrants, spread betting
Fair value	Options, futures, and spread betting (indirectly)
Gearing	All except ETFs
Hedging	All options and warrants
Indexes	Index futures and options, ETFs
Margin	All futures, some option trades, CFDs, spread betting
Short selling	All futures, CFDs, spread betting, binary betting
Time value	All options and warrants
Volatility	All options and warrants
Underlying	All including ETFs

Underlying

We will be using the term *underlying* as a noun rather than an adjective quite a few times in the book, so let's start by defining exactly what it means. Quite simply, the *underlying* is the share, index, commodity or other instrument on which a futures, options or other derivative contract is based. The price of the derivative is *derived from* the price of the underlying. Just to confuse matters, the market price of the underlying is sometimes also referred to as the *cash* or *spot* price.

> **Key concept**
>
> - The price of the derivative is largely determined by the price of the underlying. Using the word *underlying* is a reference to the share, index, or commodity on which the derivative is based.

Contracts

The next concept to get your head round is the idea that you are buying and selling a *contract* rather than an *asset*. This is fundamental to almost all derivatives. When you buy a share you own an asset: a small piece of a listed company. If you buy a unit trust, you have a stake in the fund's portfolio.

Futures, options and warrants are different. Here, you are entering into an *agreement*, or a contract. It has certain rights and obligations attached. In other words, if you buy or sell a derivative you are in fact making an agreement that holds good until you *close* the trade. So you are trading a *promise* to do something, not dealing in the underlying item on which your promise is based.

That contract can take one of several forms. It can simply be a promise to buy (or sell) a fixed quantity of something at a specified time in the future, paying or receiving today's price for it. This is called a *future*.

But you might want to pay to have the *choice* of either buying (or selling) something *or not* at a fixed price in the future. In other words you want to have the *option* of buying (or selling) it. But if it isn't in your interest to do so, you don't want to be forced into making the purchase (or sale). This is called an *option*.

Most derivatives are based on one or other of these two principles: buying (or selling) something at the ruling price at some specific time in the future (a *future*); or paying a small amount extra now to give yourself the right to buy or sell something at a fixed price in the future, but not to have the obligation to do so (an *option*).

Table 2.2 – Key attributes of futures and options

Attribute	*Futures*	*Options*
Standardised contract	Yes	Yes
Commitment to buy (or sell)	Yes	No
Right to buy (or sell), but not obligation	No	Yes
Time limit (expiry date)	Yes	Yes
Gearing from margin	Yes	No
Gearing from premium	No	Yes
Trade can be closed before expiry for cash	Yes	Yes
Traded on exchanges	Yes	Yes
Traded via spread betting	Yes	Yes

We'll cover some more of these concepts later in the chapter, but meanwhile here's an example of how and why futures work.

How and Why Futures and Options Work

Farmer Giles in Norfolk expects to have at least 1,000 bushels of wheat to deliver in September. It's now March. If, in the jargon, he sells his crop forward he raises money at today's price of £10 a bushel. Alternatively he could sell a September wheat future. This has a slightly different effect. By doing this he fixes the price at which he can sell and deliver his wheat in September.

In both cases the risk is the same: that the price may move higher between now and September. If it does, he could have got a better deal if he'd waited.

The advantage of the *forward* sale to him is that he gets £10,000 in cash now, which can go in the bank and earn interest. And even selling a future, he knows now what price he will get for his crop, and can plan accordingly.

On the other side of the coin, the *buyer* of the future is fixing the price he pays now in the hope that it will rise between now (March) and September, and he will be able to sell the wheat at a profit when he takes delivery.

An alternative way for the farmer to get a guaranteed price for his crop would be to take out a contract that gives him the option to sell his 1,000 bushels at £10 in September. To do this he would have to pay the person granting him the option a small premium. He gets a guaranteed minimum price of £10 a bushel. If the wheat price is below £10 in September he simply exercises his option and gets the £10 price for his crop, less the cost of the option. If the price rises, he can write off the cost of the option and sell at the market price. In other words, the option becomes a form of insurance.

You might not think that this farming example is very relevant, but in fact this is exactly how futures started – as a means of giving farmers a way of fixing prices in advance for their future crops.

If we take this a stage further we can see even more clearly how futures (and options) work. The future (or option) is simply a contract that can be bought and sold. If the price of wheat goes up to, say, £12, the value of the futures contract to the buyer rises, because he will be able to get more money for the wheat he has contracted to buy for £10 when he takes delivery – assuming the price stays where it is until then.

If he wanted to *cash* in now, he could sell the contract to someone else based on the £12 price. So the price of the future will closely reflect the underlying price (usually termed the cash price – because it's what you pay in cash to get the wheat delivered today). The futures price isn't exactly the same value as the cash price, but it is derived from it – hence the word derivative.

Let's be clear. Whenever we talk about futures and use the term *cash price* or *cash market*, what we mean is the current market price of the underlying.

Futures and options markets grew not just because they offered a market place, but because they saw the merit in standardising the size of the contract and specifying the quality required, and because they took steps to ensure that all the participants adhered to the terms of the contracts. Because buyers and sellers know this, the contracts are interchangeable.

If the buyer of the futures contract for 1,000 bushels of wheat wants to sell at £12 rather than wait and take delivery of the physical wheat, he can sell the contract to someone else. He need not persuade the original farmer to buy the contract back. The buyer of the contract at £12 would be taking the view the price might rise further. He in turn could sell the contract to someone else, and so on.

Key concepts

- Futures prices are derived from and closely reflect the underlying *cash* price.

- Futures contracts are interchangeable, and can be bought from and sold to anyone in the market.

- Options can provide price *insurance*.

Cash settlement

The farming example we used earlier covered a situation where the seller (Farmer Giles) had something physical to deliver. But many derivatives are based on something less tangible. In the financial futures market, for example, there are contracts based around interest rates and around long-term government bond prices. There are futures and options based around stock market indices.

In these cases it is either impossible or impractical to have physical delivery of the underlying interest rate, bond or share index. Imagine, for example, in the case of a stock market index, having to assemble the 100 shares in the FTSE 100 in the exact proportions and at the exact price they were at the time the contract was settled. It just wouldn't work.

So an alternative has been devised. For many futures products it is possible simply to settle in cash for the difference between your buying and selling price. The exchange determines the settlement value of the contract, based on the prevailing market prices and certain other rules, when the time comes to settle. Those with contracts outstanding simply pay or receive the difference between the settlement price and the price they dealt at when they 'opened' their trade. Here's an example.

Example 2.1 – Cash settlement

The main FTSE 100 futures contract traded on LIFFE is settled on the basis of £10 per index point. Let's say you buy one contract at 6050 and subsequently sell at 6150.

You neither have to buy nor sell the 100 underlying shares. You simply pocket your cash profit. In this case it would be £10 x 100 points, or £1,000.

A similar principle works for any financial future and for index options. Only in the case of options on individual shares do you have to buy or sell the underlying shares if required.

Key concept

- Most *financial futures*, and *index* options, are settled by money changing hands, and not by delivering a physical commodity.

Expiry dates

Probably the biggest differences between derivatives and their underlyings is the fact that derivatives have limited lives. Shares and bonds can be bought and held for long periods: derivatives *expire*.

Both options and futures have time limits. Futures have delivery dates, normally at monthly intervals. This is when the buyer of a future can expect to take delivery of whatever the contract stipulated, whether it was a cargo of sugar, some frozen pork bellies, or 100 tonnes of copper wire. In the case of a financial future, the delivery date is when the settlement value is worked out and cash changes hands. When you buy a future, you have to choose which delivery month you require.

In fact, most futures transactions don't get as far as the delivery date. The futures trader sells before the delivery date, taking a profit or loss.

Table 2.3 – LIFFE futures and options expiry dates

Contract	Monthly/Quarterly?	When during month?
FTSE 100 futures	Q	3rd Friday
FTSE 100 options	M	3rd Friday
Individual equity options*	Q	3rd Friday

Source: LIFFE

All options (and warrants) have an expiry date. You need to make use of the option by exercising it, or else selling it, before it expires. Only if the price has moved so as to make the option not worth having would you let it expire and take no action. When you buy an option, you have to choose which expiry month you require.

Long-term 'buy and hold' not valid

With futures, options and warrants, and many spread bets and CFDs, what the time limits really mean is that buying and holding – as many investors do with their shares – simply isn't a decision that's open to you. You have to watch the positions closely. It's wise to sell the future before the delivery date. And by definition, an option has no value after its expiry date has come and gone.

Derivatives exchanges set expiry dates so that not all futures and options expire on the same day. There are usually several days each month when different futures and options expire, and a few times each year they coincide in what is usually known as a *double witching* or *triple witching*.

So remember that futures, options and warrants (and products that are based on futures, like spread betting) are subject to a time limit. When this is reached, your trade will be closed out automatically. Many options are worthless at expiry.

Key concepts

- Almost all derivatives (other than ETFs) involve a time limit. How close to or far away from the time limit they are affects their value.

- Remember, you *invest* in shares, but you always *trade* derivatives. Derivatives (other than ETFs) are not held for the long-term.

- Don't be too concerned about the exact details of expiry and settlement – the great majority of futures and options trades are closed out before expiry (simply by selling, or buying back, the contracts in the market).

Fair value

One of the advantages of derivatives is that they bear a precise mathematical relationship to the underlying they represent. For any underlying price it is therefore possible to calculate a *fair value* price for the future, option, or warrant.

In the case of most financial futures, the fair value reflects a range of factors including the interest saved because the future can be bought with a small down payment, less any income that might have been earned if the underlying had been bought in the cash market.

In a stock index future for example, the price of the future will be the cash price (i.e. the index value today) plus an amount to reflect the interest saving – because an investor only has to put up a small down payment rather than pay for the whole underlying value of the contract. But the futures price will also bear a deduction to offset the fact that some index stocks will pay dividends during the period of the contract, to which the holder of the future is not entitled.

Calculating the fair value of a futures contract

There are several definitions of how to calculate the fair value of a future. The conventional one for an index future is:

```
FV = Index Price [ 1 + Interest rate(days to expiry/365)]
- dividends paid
```

In other words, add to the value of the index the interest you would pay between now and expiry on money borrowed to acquire the full value of the contract, and subtract the value of any dividends received.

Since you can't easily work out what dividends on index stocks would be paid and when, in practice this formula becomes:

```
FV = Index price x 1 + [ (interest rate - dividend rate)
x (days to expiry/365)
```

Let's see how this works in practice. Say the FTSE 100 index is 6000, UK interest rates are 4.25% and the dividend yield on the index is 3.75%. It is now 21st March, and the June FTSE 100 future expires on 20th June.

Calculation of fair value would be:

```
FV = 6000 x 1 + [ 0.0425-0.0375) x (91/365)]
FV = 6000 x 1 + [ 0.005 x 0.25]
FV = 6000 x (1 + 0.00125)
FV = 6000 x 1.00125
FV = 6007.5
```

What this means is that the *fair value* price of the future will normally be slightly above or slightly below the actual *cash* price, depending on the interplay between these factors. If interest rates are higher than the yield on the index, as in this example, the fair value of the future will be higher than the index. But the future will always converge with the cash price as the delivery date approaches.

One issue that often puzzles investors new to futures is why the futures price and the cash always stay so close to each other. The answer is that if they diverged significantly traders would be able to profit from the difference by selling the more expensive of the two and buying the cheaper equivalent. This is called *arbitrage*.

The fair value of options is a much more complicated subject that we'll cover in detail later.

Key concepts

- Fair value in a future reflects the interest saved by holding the future rather than the underlying, because only a small initial margin payment is required on the future. But the calculation also reflects, on the minus side, the fact that dividends or other income that might be foregone as a result.

- The actual futures price will fluctuate closely about its fair value. Any big differences are removed by arbitrage.

- Fair value will converge to the actual underlying cash price when the futures contract expires.

Gearing

Most ways of dealing in derivatives involve gearing. The gearing is either inherent to the derivative itself (as with options) or, as is the case with futures, created because of the way they are traded.

Gearing is both an attraction and a disadvantage. The gearing element in a future is represented by the fact that futures exchanges allow you to trade their contracts by putting up a small down payment (called *margin*). If the price moves up, the effect of this feature is to gear up the return on your capital.

It's rather like buying a house on a mortgage. It's fine if the price goes up – your equity in the house multiplies. But if you get it wrong, you can end up with large negative equity.

When you are trading derivatives you need to take care. The gearing works both ways. You could double your money, or be wiped out, by a small move up or down in the underlying price.

Example 2.2 – Gearing in futures contracts

1. The index future of the Ruritanian stock market is quoted at 99-100. Initial margin (see below) is 15%.
    Action: Buy 1 contract at 100

    Contract value: £1000

    Margin: £150

2. Prices rises to 110-111
    Action: Sell 1 contract at 110

    Contract value: £1100

3. Profit = £100

The return on capital for this futures trade was 66.7% (100/150), even though the actual futures price only increased 10% (100 offered to 110 bid). The result of the *gearing* was that the trade yielded over six times more than the price movement.

Similarly with options, the price (or premium) you pay for an option rises and falls disproportionately with movements in the underlying price. But, though it's created in a slightly different way, the result of the gearing is the same as for futures. An option can become worth a lot, or become worthless, very quickly.

But don't worry. There are ways of trading that allow you to avoid, or limit, the risk that this gearing implies. The easiest way you can avoid it is to make sure, when you deal in futures or options, that you reduce the size of your stake accordingly. If you normally buy shares in £5000 lumps, make sure your option deals are, say, in £500 lots. The gearing in futures allows you to gain a larger amount of exposure than your capital would normally permit. But just because you can get that exposure doesn't mean you *have* to take it.

Key concepts

- Futures and options (and spread betting) give you geared up profits and losses.
- You can limit your exposure by simply staking less.

Hedging

Because they are contracts and don't involve buying and selling specific physical assets, futures and options allow you to speculate on price movements in either direction. There are options to sell shares as well as options to buy them. Futures contracts can be traded with ease in both directions.

But speculation isn't the only choice you have. You can use options, for example, to insure against (or hedge) the possibility of an adverse price movement in a share or group of shares you own. It's where the *risk reduction* aspect of derivatives comes in.

A hedge is a transaction that is constructed to produce a compensating profit if the value of a holding falls. This insurance aspect of options is one reason why an option's price is often called its *premium*.

There are also special techniques, again open to any investor, to use options as a way of generating more or less guaranteed returns.

Futures and options generally were devised to allow investors, and in the case of futures, producers of commodities and other physical products, to transfer and reduce risk. But index futures and options involve no physical delivery and allow stock market investors to adjust their risk level without selling their stocks and incurring potential tax liabilities.

I think that for this reason alone derivatives merit the attention of all serious investors.

Many investors see derivatives as inherently risky, but they don't have to be. Anyone with a capped rate mortgage, or who owns a capital protected bond or unit trust, has a product that only exists courtesy of the hedging possibilities offered by the derivatives markets.

Key concept

- Futures and options allow you to insure your investments against unexpected market events.

Indexes

Understanding how stock market indexes work is crucial to evaluating the derivatives that most investors deal in. These are index futures and options, and spread betting and CFDs based on them. Many investors also have index tracking funds. Exchange traded funds (ETFs) are a form of an index tracker, as are some certificates in the covered warrant market.

The indexes on which derivatives are based come in many shapes and sizes, but most commonly they involve *capitalisation-weighted averages* of their constituents (although the Dow Jones is an exception to this).

What this means is that the bigger the company in terms of its market capitalisation, the bigger the impact a 1% movement in its price will have on the index. Most broad market indices have recently introduced refinements to this system, specifically to deal with index constituents that have major shareholders. In this instance, the weighting is modified to reflect the fact that a portion of the issued shares is unlikely to be to freely tradable. By eliminating major stakes and cross-shareholdings, the weightings in the index more closely reflect the realities of trading in shares in the market. FTSE100, the S&P500, the CAC40 in France and DAX in Germany have all moved to this so-called 'free float adjusted' basis over the last few years.

Figure 2.1 – The FTSE 100 since inception in 1984

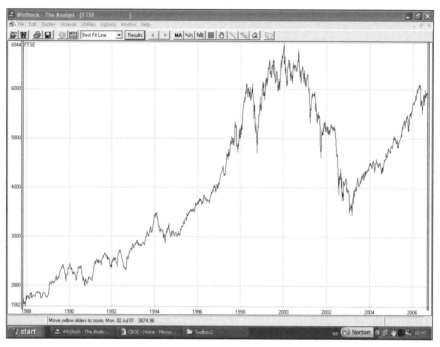

How do indexes like this work in practice?

Take the FTSE 100. It was launched with a value of 1000 in mid-1984. It was devised mainly for the benefit of futures traders. They need an index benchmark that is calculated in a consistent way and that can be used as a proxy for the UK equity market as a whole.

An independent committee acts as referee, and decides on the periodic changes that need to be made to the index's constituents. The committee meets quarterly, or more frequently if necessary.

Its work covers setting the rules for inclusion and exclusion of particular companies, and what happens in the event of takeovers, right issues, new issues, and suspensions.

As far as the procedure for inclusion in the list is concerned, the ideal is for the index to contain the largest 100 companies by market capitalisation at any one time. However, because this can change daily, the committee reviews the list quarterly and adopts a 90/110 rule. This means that any company whose market capitalisation has risen to the 90th position or above is automatically included. Any that has fallen below 110th place is ejected.

Table 2.4 – Key stock market indices on which futures and options are available

Index	Country	Constituents	Weighting by:	Free float adj.?
S&P 500	USA	500	Capitalisation	Yes
DJIA	USA	30	Price	No
NASDAQ 100	USA	100	Capitalisation	Yes
FTSE 100	UK	100	Capitalisation	Yes
DAX	Germany	30	Capitalisation	Yes
CAC40	France	40	Capitalisation	Yes
Nikkei	Japan	225	Price	No

Sources: Various

That's not all. Constituents that are between the 101st and 110th rank may be removed to make room for the stock or stocks that have a higher value. In addition there is a reserve list of stocks to take account of any necessary changes between reviews, usually because of takeovers or demergers.

The biggest, HSBC, has a market value around five times that of Aviva, the 20th largest and eight times that of Scottish & Southern Energy, the 30th largest. A 5% price change in HSBC's market capitalisation of £106bn has 44 times the impact of a similar change in the market value of Drax, the index's smallest constituent.

The 100 companies together, worth about £1.4 trillion in total, represent about four fifths of the overall value of the UK stock market. But the top 5 companies account for 33% of the index's total value, and the top 10 account for just less than half the total.

Other indices also have their quirks as well. The moral of the story is that before you deal in a derivative based around a stock market index, make sure you understand exactly the basis that it's drawn up on. This particularly applies to exchange-traded funds, which are available on many different indices.

Key concept

- There are many derivatives based around stock market indices. The way the indexes are compiled varies. You need to understand what makes them tick before dealing in the derivative.

Margin

The idea of margin is integral to many aspects of using derivatives. In the context of a futures trade, margin is an upfront payment that you make via your broker to guarantee to the exchange that you can meet the obligations of the contract. Usually you will be asked to deposit some margin when you buy or sell a futures contract ('initial' margin). This fixed amount will be a small percentage of the contract's underlying size. If the trade moves the wrong way you may be asked for more money to make up the difference ('variation' margin).

Here's an example.

Example 2.2 – Margin on a futures trade

Let's say, for the sake of argument, that you have bought a futures contract. The contract's underlying value is £50,000 and the initial margin required is £5,000. Assume the contract's value drops from £50,000 to £48,000 as the futures price falls.

In round figures, you will be asked by your broker for a further £2,000 of variation margin to make up the difference. If you can't meet the margin call, the contract will be sold on your behalf without further ado.

Table 2.5 – Initial margin requirements for various futures contracts

Contract	Amount	% of contract value
FTSE 100	£2900	4.9
Short sterling	£290	0.3
Long gilt	£1,650	1.5
Bund	€ 1,900	1.6

Source: ODL Securities

The level of initial margin required is governed by the extent to which the price of the underlying asset swings around in price. If it's fairly stable, the percentage deposit will be a small proportion. If it's prone to wild swings, the margin percentage required will be bigger.

The fact that futures contracts operate on margin is what gives them their gearing element. You can buy a big exposure for a small amount of money. This offers the potential for big gains, but big losses too.

As we'll see later, margin is also required on some options trades. Spread betting and CFDs – as futures by proxy – also involve margin, although it may be called by another name.

Key concepts

- Initial margin is the upfront deposit you make when you buy or sell a futures contract.

- Additional 'variation' margin will be required if your trade goes the wrong way.

- Margin is why futures have gearing.

Short selling

Short selling is a curiosity. It is selling something you don't own in the hope that the price will fall, at which point you buy it back and pocket the difference. It's a concept that many share investors find difficult to grasp. In the share market, the mechanics of short selling are: borrow the stock from a long-term investor; sell it; buy it back (hopefully at a lower price); and then return it to the lender.

For the most part, this has always been a professionals' market. Although brokers can borrow stock, they will normally only facilitate short selling for very large clients. While it's controversial, it can be argued that it contributes to the smooth running of the market by providing extra liquidity.

But now you don't need to master the complex mechanics of short selling. Futures, spread betting and CFDs allow you to bet on a fall in either an individual stock or the market as a whole. **In other words you can short sell, but without any of the hassle of borrowing stock.**

This is because, as we discovered earlier, derivatives are *contracts*. They do not involve the direct buying or selling of the underlying stock or commodity. Therefore you don't have to worry about borrowing or returning stock. There is nothing to stop you selling a futures contract without having first bought it. You are simply taking a view that the market in question will fall in the future.

Stock futures, spread betting and CFDs allow ordinary investors to short sell a wide range of stocks if they wish. Since their introduction to the investment mainstream a few years ago, private investors have had access to the same tools that the professionals have been using for decades. And it's important right now. That's because they offer the astute investor a way of increasing their returns in markets that are fluctuating but which have no strong trend, or in those which are falling.

Key concept

- Futures, spread betting (including binary betting) and CFDs allow you, if you wish, a hassle-free way to bet on a fall in price instead of a rise.

Time value

This is a concept that relates primarily to *options* and *warrants*. We've already established that in buying an option you buy the right, but not the obligation, to buy or sell a stock at a fixed price for a limited period of time.

Provided they have a while to run, even options that look pretty unlikely ever to be exercised at a profit will still fetch a price in the market. This is because, however unlikely that eventuality might be, there is always the possibility that a sharp move in the price of the underlying will occur. If so, this would allow the option holder to cash in the option at a profit. Investors will pay for that possibility.

The longer the period until the option expires, the greater is this so-called *time value*. Time value will, of course, be zero just before the option expires, and it will decrease very sharply in the last few weeks of an option's life. We'll look at this in more detail later. The same time value concept also applies to warrants.

> Key concept
>
> - Time value reflects the chance that, if an option or warrant has time remaining before expiry, there is always a chance it can be cashed in at a profit.

Volatility

Volatility is one of the most important concepts when it comes to trading options. In this case the volatility refers to the degree to which the price of a share or index swings around. It can be measured statistically. It differs from share to share and index to index, and it changes hour-by-hour, day-by-day and week-by-week. You can see this in the way a stock market index or a share goes through periods of stability and then moves erratically for a spell.

The bigger the swings in price, the greater the volatility.

Volatility is a key component of the price of an option or warrant. The bigger the volatility, the greater is the chance that the holder of an option will be able to sell it at a profit, simply because big swings in price could be sufficient for option holders to be in-the-money. So sellers and option market makers will adjust the price to reflect the extra risk that options buyers will make money at their expense.

And it also follows from this that an option or warrant's price will, other things being equal, imply a particular level of volatility. Don't worry too much if this seems Double Dutch at this stage. I promise that you will get the idea fairly quickly when we come to look at options and warrants in more detail in later chapters.

Remember though that volatility is a statistical concept and can be precisely measured from a history of price changes. In the US volatility has a special index of its known, known as the VIX, which measures the short term volatility of the S&P500 index, the broad US market benchmark.

Figure 2.2 – The VIX – a US index of market volatility

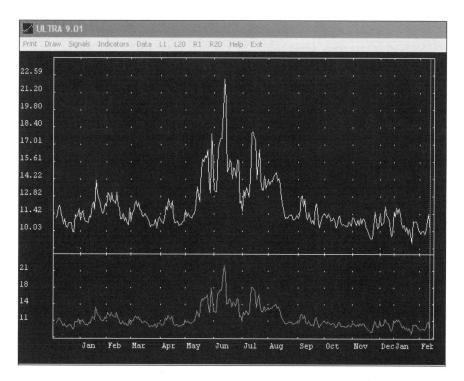

> **Key concept**
>
> - Volatility measures how much the price of an underlying swings about. It means greater risk for an option seller or market maker. When volatility increases, so do option prices.

The next chapter takes some of the building blocks we've explored earlier in this chapter – contracts, expiry dates, fair value, and margin – and shows how they come together in trading.

3

Futures

Many investors imagine that futures are complex and risky, and therefore not for them. But if you've lost money in technology shares, as many investors have in the last few years, or simply held a share in a company that issued a profit warning, you know that shares can be risky too. Futures are, in fact, quite simple. It is only the jargon that makes them complicated.

Basic futures

Although futures do involve gearing, you can also look at them as a way of investing using modest amounts of capital. The important point is to have good trading discipline and an efficient way of limiting your losses.

Rather than get ahead of ourselves, let's recap what we already know.

In Chapter 2, we discovered that derivatives are *contracts*. This means they are legally enforceable agreements. The derivative part comes because their price is based on (derived from) the movement of an underlying variable like a share or a stock market index.

A future is a binding agreement to buy or sell a specific quantity of a commodity (or share, or index, or some other instrument) at the market price prevailing at some predetermined point in the future. There is no fixed price element in the contract, other than the price at the time delivery is scheduled to take place.

But the point about a future is that it isn't an agreement with anyone in particular. It is not a bilateral agreement with another person or company. You buy a futures contract from anyone and sell it to anyone, via an exchange. You never know, or need to know, who that other buyer or seller might be.

Futures contacts are standardised

Futures contracts are tradable because they are standardised. This standardisation is to eliminate any other possible factor – other than the underlying price – that might affect the value of the contract, and to allow traders to trade a standardised product with similar terms – without having to check all the terms of the contract.

Here's an example from real life. Say I negotiate a futures contract to buy a sought-after sports car from my local dealer in six months time. Later I change my mind about buying it. I decide to sell this contract to another sports car enthusiast, allowing him to buy the car in my place. He will only buy at a price that reflects the fair value of the contract if he can be sure precisely what the contract stipulates.

Unless the contract guarantees that the vehicle is of a specified type, make and registration year, any buyer, however enthusiastic, will be harder to convince that it's what he wants. It's the same with a commodity or financial futures contract. The contract stipulates, in the case of a commodity, a specific quantity and a specific grade of say coffee, cocoa, or copper wire. In the case of a future on an index it is a specific number of those shares. In the case of a bond future it is a selection of bonds of specific coupon and maturity date. And so on.

> 'Because futures contracts are tightly defined they can be easily traded without first having to check their specific terms. To use futures market jargon, they are fungible.'

The point is that because futures contracts are tightly defined they can be easily traded without first having to check their specific terms. To use futures market jargon, they are *fungible*.

If I sell a wheat futures contract and then change my mind and decide to buy it back, I don't necessarily have to seek out the same person who bought it in the market at the same time as I sold, and persuade him to sell it back to me. I simply buy the same standardised package from another trader, because all the contracts are identical and interchangeable.

Flexibility of futures markets

The reason futures contracts are interesting for investors is precisely because of the ease with which they can be bought and sold and because there are a number of natural buyers and sellers in the market.

This is particularly true in agricultural commodity futures where food manufacturers are the natural buyers, and farmers are the natural sellers. Private investors do not want the actual commodity, whether it is 1000 bushels of wheat or a tonne of copper wire, but the futures market allows them to take a view on the price without having to take delivery of the physical product.

Margin

What makes everything a whole lot easier for investors is that futures are traded on *margin*. Buyers and sellers have only to put up a small proportion of the underlying value of the contract to be able to trade in it. It is the movement in the value of the contract that determines their profit or loss, but the capital tied up is much less. As we say in Chapter 2, margin comes in two parts:

1.   **Initial margin** is what you pay at the outset.

2.   **Variation margin** is an extra payment that you might have to make from time to time if the price goes against you.

The margin amount required differs from future to future. The size of the initial margin deposit will vary according to how much the underlying price swings around. This is called *volatility*, and it's all about risk. The more volatile the underlying price, the greater the risk that the futures price might move quickly against a trader's position, and therefore the higher the amount of margin required to make sure the contract is honoured. For example, the percentage margin on bond futures, where price moves are small, is less than the percentage margin on commodities or on a share like Vodafone, where prices can swing round alarmingly.

Because of the margin system, futures are *highly geared investments* – in both directions. So you need to be realistic about how much exposure you can really afford. Don't invest in a futures contract in the same way you might in a share. You need to keep in mind the underlying value of the contract, not the amount you have to stump up in margin.

Be careful to limit your exposure.

For the sake of argument, let's say you would normally invest £5,000 in a share. Take the futures contract in Vodafone and assume the price is 125p. One Vodafone futures contract represents 1,000 shares, or £1,250. The initial margin is 20%, or £250. You only need to buy four contracts to get your £5,000 of exposure, and four contracts will only cost you £1,000.

Don't make the mistake of buying 20 contracts at margin of £250, investing £5000, because by doing that you will have much more exposure – and more risk – than you might normally take on.

Have a look at the example below to see how gearing works.

Example 3.1 – Gearing inherent in a futures contract in Vodafone

Vodafone June futures price 124-125; margin 20%

Action: Buy 1 Vodafone June

Contract value: £1250

Margin: £250

1. Things go well: price rises to 150-51 (+20.8%)

Action: Sell 1 Vodafone June

Contract value: £1,500

Profit: £250 (giving you a return of +100%)

2. Things go badly: price falls to 100-101 (-19.2%)

Action: Sell 1 Vodafone June

Contract value: £1,000

Loss: £250 (giving you a return of –100%)

Let's recap for a moment

- A futures contract has **standard terms**. It has a specified delivery date and dictates the amount and type of the underlying product being traded.

- The contract can be **bought or sold**. If you buy you are said to be 'long' of the contract. If you sell you are said to be 'short'. A subsequent sale of a contract you have bought (or a purchase of a contract you have previously sold) is known as 'closing a trade'.

- You don't put up the full price of the futures contract at the outset. What is required if you buy or sell a futures contract is simply a good faith deposit, called **initial margin**, a small percentage of the total value.

- If you buy or sell a contract, however, you are subject to **variation margin**. This is an additional part payment – recalculated as the price changes – that ensures you will be able to honour your obligations under the contract.

- Only if you end up taking **delivery of the underlying commodity** will the full amount of its value change hands. But in reality fewer than 3% of futures contracts are actually held to expiry – requiring delivery. The rest are closed out before this becomes necessary.

- Futures contracts are **geared-up investments**. Make sure that you pay close attention to the underlying exposure you are taking on, not just the amount you have to pay in terms of initial margin.

I am cheating using Vodafone as an example here, because individual stock futures are no longer available to private investors in the UK having in effect been superseded by CFDs and spread betting. However, the principle is roughly the same in these cases too, since spread bets and CFD trades are also done on margin.

Futures prices

Futures prices are inextricably linked with the price of the underlying commodity – whether it's wheat, gold, or a stock market index. The underlying price is known as the *cash* or *spot* price.

But there isn't one single futures price for each underlying. Futures contracts come in a spectrum of delivery months usually based on monthly or quarterly intervals. Each of these futures contracts trades simultaneously in the market and the price of futures expiring in different months will all differ slightly.

The link between the spot price and the futures price is close – but not exact. The futures price of the delivery month closest to the present will bear the closest resemblance to the actual price, and follow the movements in the cash price most faithfully. This contract is usually the most actively traded and is normally known as the *front month* contract.

For contracts with delivery times six or nine months away, futures prices will reflect the views of traders about a variety of other factors that might by then have influenced the price. Conversely, traders might feel that factors that are affecting the price now may not be as important in a few months.

So the price of the future will rarely be precisely the same as the cash price, for a number of reasons. But on any given day there is a 'correct' price for the future for any given level of the cash price. Often it is a small premium. The size of the premium is affected by how far away the delivery date for the contract happens to be. This is known as the *fair value* price.

You can derive the fair value price mathematically (see page 38 in the previous chapter), because it represents the difference between buying the underlying commodity now and tying up capital and maybe incurring storage costs, or buying the future now, earning interest on the cash you free up and taking delivery of the product on the delivery date.

The further away from the delivery date, the more buying the physical product would cost in terms of storage and interest costs, the greater the premium of the fair value price of the future over the cash price. This is true for commodities that generate no income, but not for index futures, for example, or for the single stock futures that are available in some markets.

Where there is dividend income involved the calculation of the fair value is slightly different. Here, interest saving in a futures position is offset (sometimes more than offset) by dividend income foregone, so that the fair value of the future can be less than the cash market price.

Arbitrage keeps prices in line

Futures prices generally stay close to fair value because of the impact of arbitrage. If the prices get too far out of line it will be profitable for traders to exploit the difference.

It's easiest to see how arbitrage works using an example.

Figure 3.1 – The theory of how futures prices converge with cash price

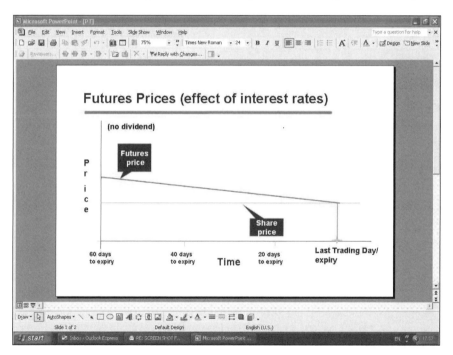

Source and © LIFFE

Imagine someone trading a commodity like wheat. The trader notices the futures price is too high relative to the cash price. Delivery for the future is, say, one month away. There may be a profit to be locked in.

A trader could buy the equivalent amount of wheat now and sell the future, delivering his 'physical' wheat to satisfy the contract in a month's time and profit from the difference in value.

The futures price must be a sufficient amount over the cost of the physical wheat plus any interest costs, storage cost and dealing charges. If it is, the trader can then simply wait for the delivery day and then deliver the cheap wheat against the futures contract and pocket the difference. If enough traders do this, the prices will converge (by bidding up the wheat price, and depressing the futures price) to iron out the discrepancy.

So, to recap, the fair value for the futures contract will usually be different from the cash price, reflecting storage costs (in the case of a commodity) and interest costs for whatever period of time remains until delivery. Futures in physical products tend always to trade at a premium to the cash price, because the underlying commodity generates no income. In the case of financial products like index futures, the incidence of dividend payments means that the futures price can be either at a discount to the cash price or at a premium.

Either way, it follows that the fair value price for the future and the cash price of the underlying commodity converge as the delivery date approaches until, just before delivery is due, they are virtually identical.

The position of the actual futures price relative to its fair value may give you a short-term clue about where the market is headed. If the future is trading below fair value it suggests traders expect the market to fall. If the futures price is trading above fair value, it suggests the market as a whole is feeling bullish.

What you can trade

If you have enough cash at your disposal, there is virtually no limit to the futures markets you can trade in. But you need to be aware that it isn't as easy as it looks. Large professional sellers and buyers dominate all futures markets.

That isn't to say you can't make money, but it's certainly true that these professionals are likely to have much better information and faster reaction times than you do. You have to recognise that you start with a handicap.

For this reason, it is, I think, important to trade something close to home and in a market you know. For most of us, this means our local stock market index and perhaps the movements in interest rates and gilt prices.

LIFFE – a local market

In the UK, this means dealing through a futures broker at LIFFE, London's Financial Futures Exchange, now part of the Euronext pan-European market.

Conveniently, in view of what I've just suggested, LIFFE has futures contracts in a wide range of financial products, including short-term sterling interest rates, long-term government bonds, commodities, and the FTSE 100 stock market index. It also offers futures contracts based on the share prices of a range of leading international companies, although these are no longer available to private investors.

The table over the page shows a summary of the more prominent futures and options contracts traded on LIFFE and how actively they trade. Don't worry too much about the precise numbers here. The statistics themselves are in thousands of contracts.

Before jumping to conclusions, however, remember that these contracts have different underlying values. The value of an individual options contract can be as little as £1,000, the FTSE 100 index futures contract has a value around £60,000 and the short sterling contract value is around £500,000.

Table 3.1 – LIFFE Futures and Options: Volume in 2005

Contract	Average daily volume (000s)
FTSE 100 Future	83
FTSE 100 Options	66
Individual equity options	32
Three month Euribor	653
Short sterling	268
Long gilt	67
All other products	487
Total	**1656**

Source: LIFFE

We'll cover the mechanics of futures dealing in a later chapter. But one point needs stressing. There are big variations in *contract size* and, as we saw from the section on margin in the previous chapter, big variations in *margin requirements*.

Index futures

Let's take index futures first. You might think that the futures contract based on the FTSE 100 at £10 per index point, is a little rich for your investing style. With the FTSE at, say, 6,000, every time you buy one contract, your exposure is the same as investing £60,000 in the underlying equities. Speculating in a contract with an underlying value of around £60,000 may not be quite what you had in mind.

At one time LIFFE had followed some of the US futures exchanges in attempting to make its contracts more private investor-friendly and launched a *mini contract* based around the FTSE 100 index, which allowed private investors to trade the FTSE future with relatively less exposure.

The *Mini-FTSE 100 Index Futures* had a value of just £2 per index point. In money terms this meant its overall value was double the value of the index (about £12,000 with the FTSE at 6,000). This was a fifth of the size of the regular contract. Initial margin on the contract was a relatively modest £1200.

LIFFE has, however, recently de-listed this product, so if you want to trade mini futures contracts and have access to a broker that will let you trade US futures, you might like to know that the S&P500 Index future is also available from the CME in a mini version. With the index at its current level (1444 at the time of writing), this has an approximate underlying value of $72,000 and initial margin somewhere in the region of $5,000 (about £2600 at current exchange rates) per contract. These and some other contracts offered in this form are shown in the table below.

Table 3.1a – Comparison of Mini Futures Contracts

Index	Index value (Aug 06)	Exchange	Multiplier (per point)	Value per contract	Initial mgn £/$	Initial margin %
S&P500	1444	CME	50	72000	5000	6.1
Nasdaq100	1822	CME	20	36500	4375	12.0
Russell2000	813	CME	100	81300	4000	4.9

Source: CME

Because there is less trading in the minis, their bid-offer spreads may be wider than in the full-size contract but on the other hand you aren't risking as much money either in terms of underlying value or upfront margin.

Single stock futures

LIFFE has been one of the pioneers of *single stock futures*. Here each futures contract is based around the individual share price of one of a range of well over 100 large, well-known international companies based in the UK, USA and Europe. Hence, there are futures available on shares in Vodafone, and on shares in Deutsche Telekom, on Carrefour and Wal-Mart, and so on. However, these are now only available to institutional investors, so we have not included detailed trading information on them in this edition of the book.

Table 3.2 – LIFFE Universal Stock Futures: Non-UK Companies

USA	Belgium	Denmark	Finland	France	Germany
Amgen	Dexia	Danske Bank	Nokia	Accor	Allianz
AOL	Inbev	Novo-Nordisk	Stora Enso	Air Liquide	BASF
Cisco	KBC		UPM-Kymmene	Alcatel	Bayer
Citigroup	Solvay			AGF	BMW
Exxon Mobil				Axa	Commerzbank
GEC				BNP Paribas	DaimlerChrysler
IBM				Bouygues	Deutsche Bank
Intel				Carrefour	Deutsche Post
Johnson & Johnson				Saint Gobain	Deutsche Telekom
Merck				Credit Agricole	E.ON
Microsoft				EADS	Hypo Real Estate
Pfizer				France Telecom	HVB
SBC				Groupe Danone	Metro
Verizon				Lafarge	Munich Re
Wal-Mart				Lagardere	Porsche
				L'Oreal	RWE
				LVMH	SAP
				Mittal Sreel	Schering
				Pernod Ricard	Siemens
				Peugeot	ThyssenKrupp
				Pinault-Printemps	Volkswagen
				Renault	
				Sanofi-Aventis	
				Schneider Electric	
				Societe Generale	
				Sodexho Alliance	
				Suez	
				TFI	
				Total	
				Vivendi	

Italy	*Netherlands*	*Norway*	*Spain*	*Sweden*	*Switzerland*
Autostrada	ABN Amro	Norsk Hydro	Abertis	Ericsson	Credit Suisse
Banca Intesa	Aegon	Statoil	Altadis	Hennes & Mauritz	Nestle
BPV	Ahold		Banco de Sabadell	Nordea	Novartis
Capitalia	ASML		Banco Popular Espanol	Svenska Handelsbanken	Richemont
Enel	Azco		BBV	TeliaSonera	Roche
Eni	DSM		CEPSA		Swiss Re
Fiat	Fortis		Endesa		Swisscom
Generali	Heineken		Gas Natural		UBS
MediaSet	ING		Iberdrola		Zurich
Mediobanca	KPN		Inditex		
San Paolo-IMI	Phillips Electronics		Repsol		
SNAM Rete Gas	Reed Elsevier		SCH		
ST Microelectronics	Rodamco		Telefonica Moviles		
TIR	Royal Dutch		Telefonica Moviles		
Telecom Italia	TNT		Union Fenosa		
UniCredito	Unilever				
	VNU				
	Wolters Kluwer				

Source: LIFFE

Figure 3.2 – LIFFE's dedicated private investor site

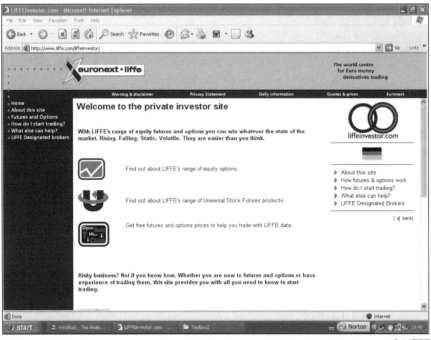

© LIFFE

It may be that the demise of single stock futures for UK private investors is no bad thing. It followed on from a lack of interest in them among private investors anyway, one reason perhaps being the exposure that they give to the volatility of an individual share. Trading an index future, by contrast, leaves you exposed only to the general movements in the market, not to the vagaries of an individual stock. There isn't much evidence that this is a lot safer, but at least with an index you aren't exposed to the risk of profit warnings, dodgy accounting, fraud and general venality at an individual company.

Interest rate futures

Interest rate futures allow you to take a view on the movement of short-term interest rates or longer-term bond prices. But these are heavy-duty contracts. The underlying value of one short sterling futures contract – essentially a bet on three-month interest rates – is around £500,000. On the plus side, margin on this contract is fairly modest, because its movements are general fairly small.

The contract trades on the basis of a discount to 100. If the market expects short-term interest rates to be around 4.25% when delivery comes around, the contract trades at 95.75 (i.e. 100.00 – 4.25). If views change and the market suddenly expects short-term rates to fall to 4%, the contract price would move up to 96.00 (i.e.100.00 - 4.00). This quarter of a percentage point movement in price equates to a movement of £1250 in the underlying value of the contract. That's the reason why margin requirements for this contract are not huge, especially when interest rates are seen as being fairly stable for the time being.

Because it works on this '100 minus expected interest rate' basis, the short sterling futures is a good guide to what the market expects movements in interest rates to be in the immediate future. The views of traders will reflect the odds on a change in rates by the Bank of England. Currently, for example (February 07) the three-month contract stands at 94.30, an implied rate of 5.7% compared to the official rate of 5.25%. This suggests the market has strong expectations of a further rate rise in the short term.

LIFFE's *long gilt* future is based around a notional government bond of specified maturity and coupon. Here the futures price is a reflection of the likely price of such a bond, and not a subtraction of the expected return from 100. The result is that, for the moment at least, it stands above par. Here the contract size is smaller – around £100,000 – and movements in it tend to be somewhat larger. But government bond prices are inherently much less volatile than shares and so margin requirements are less. Typical initial margin on the long gilt future will be in the region of £1650 per contract, just over 1% of its underlying value.

Influences over the price of bond futures – and most futures markets have them – are longer-term in nature:

• movements in the general level of interest rates

• economic news (a slowing economy is good for bonds)

• predictions about inflation (rising inflation is bad for bonds)

The short sterling and long gilt markets are largely the preserve of professional traders, so if you are dealing in this market you need to keep your wits about you. You certainly need to keep well aware of the timing of announcements of key economic statistics and interest rate decisions at home and abroad. Bond markets can also be affected by geopolitical uncertainties. Money tends to gravitate to safe havens like bond markets in times of crisis, and leave when the panic subsides.

Smaller commitment with spread betting

As we shall see in Chapter 5, financial spread betting is largely based around the futures market. This means it is possible to deal in many of these futures contracts and some more besides, through the medium of spread betting. This is often a good place to start, because your financial commitment doesn't have to be at the same level as a futures contract, but can be scaled back to a more modest level. Spreads are wider, but the financial commitment needn't be as great.

However, you do need to think about why you want to deal in instruments like this. Most investors have no need, for example, to either speculate on or hedge against movements in interest rates or bond prices. If you hold shares, there are good reasons why you might want to use futures, options, warrants or spread betting to hedge your portfolio. The strategies you can adopt for that purpose are covered in later chapters.

You might think it's a neat idea to speculate on the future movement in interest rates – but bear in mind it probably will be precisely that, a speculation with all the risk that that entails.

In short, and as we've noted before, it pays to stick to what you know. It's true of all investment decisions, but it applies in a big way in the futures markets where the risks are bigger.

Beware the professionals

Professional traders dominate the futures market. This is one reason why you need to treat the market with care. The professionals know more than you do.

You have to be realistic. It is inevitable that most of the rest of the market will be better informed than you are and have more capital than you have. This does not, however, mean that you can't trade successfully. It just means you need to be vigilant.

The cast of characters differs from market to market. Professional traders in the sugar market will differ from those in the metals market. These will be different again from those that trade interest rate futures or those in stock and stock index futures markets.

In the commodity markets, there will be professionals working for investment banks, various specialised investment funds, and *locals*. Locals exist in all futures markets. They are independent professional traders using their own capital to make money from short -term day-to-day price movements.

In commodity markets too there will be big companies that use the commodity – Tate & Lyle in the sugar market, Cadbury in the cocoa market and so on. In the metals market the big players will be the big international mining groups. These companies use the market to secure regular deliveries of the underlying commodity for their production requirements or to insure themselves against adverse price movements. Unless you have specialist knowledge of these markets, you may be taking big risks. The professionals may know when Tate & Lyle is likely to come into the market to buy its annual requirements of sugar, or Cadbury its cocoa. It's hard for you to match that knowledge. So the best thing to do is stay away.

Equally there will be suppliers of the commodity involved in the market: farmers, farmers' cooperatives, smaller mines, and so on. Some commodities have central organisations that attempt to smooth out price fluctuations by selling into price rises and buying when the price falls back.

In financial futures markets, there will be:

- professional traders, working for investment banks and hedge funds, seeking to exploit small price anomalies, the effect being to keep prices in line with fair value

- individual traders doing the same thing on their own account

- big corporate users – the banks and the treasury departments of big companies and commercial banks – who are counterparts to the Tate & Lyles and Cadburys in the commodity market. They will use financial futures markets not just to speculate in, but also to minimise their own borrowing costs or reduce the fluctuations in them. Companies also use currency futures markets to try and reduce their exposure to adverse exchange rate movements.

You may think – as a clued-up investor – that your view on the course of the stock market, interest rates and currency movements is as good as the next man's.

It could be, or that could just be overconfidence on your part. But it's probably fair to say that *financial* futures markets are more actively traded. This means they are less likely to be distorted by one large buyer or seller in the way that commodity futures markets might be. And they are less likely to be subject to the vagaries of unknown and essentially unpredictable variables, such as the weather. This gives you a better chance that your judgement will be proved correct.

> **Futures do's and don'ts**
>
> - Pick a market you know
>
> - Keep well informed
>
> - Don't use gearing just because it's there
>
> - Make sure you can meet margin calls
>
> - Use stop-losses to get out of losing trades quickly.
>
> - Remember the pros may know more than you

Figure 3.3 – The FTSE 100 'trigger page' on Yahoo! Finance

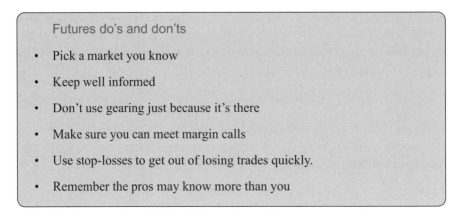

© Yahoo! Finance

The real secret is to pick a market that you are close to geographically and about which you can stay well informed. That intangible *feel* for a market is important. There is plenty of information and commentary on the US stock market available for the avid investor, so it's perfectly natural for you to feel competent and informed enough to trade S&P 500 futures as well as the FTSE.

But keep it simple. If you're in the UK, why not trade contracts based around UK interest rates, bond prices and the stock market, or perhaps a US market index? Better this than get involved in trading something more esoteric like Japanese Yen currency futures or the price of frozen pork bellies in Chicago.

That covers this introduction to futures. We'll talk more about trading strategies and the mechanics of dealing in futures in later chapters.

4

Contracts for Difference

When I was first putting this book together, I puzzled for quite a long time over which order to put the chapters on futures, spread betting and contracts for difference. In the end I settled on looking at futures first, then at contracts for difference (CFDs), and then at spread betting. But I could have rearranged the order. The truth is that in many senses they all work in basically the same way.

The similarities come in the fundamental things they do for you as an investor.

1. They are all *paper contracts*.

2. They all give you a direct link to the price of an underlying investment.

3. They all allow you to *gear up*, because you only have to put up a small percentage of the underlying value of the investment.

4. And finally, while you can use them as you would normally invest, buying in the hope of a rise in price, they also allow you, if you wish, to go *short*.

So in the last chapter we looked at futures and the basics of how they work. In this chapter we look at CFDs, and in the next one we look at spread betting.

Why have three separate chapters on products that are essentially similar?

The answer is that *the devil is in the detail*.

Although they are similar in terms of the effects they can have on your wallet, the risks they entail, and the fundamental ways you can use them as return-boosters or risk-reducers, each of the three works in slightly different ways. The numbers involved are different, the tax treatment is different, and there are a number of little idiosyncrasies that mark each one out from the other.

CFD Basics

The simplest way of looking at a CFD is to think of it as a way of buying shares using a short-term loan.

You stump up your initial deposit, you get a loan to buy the shares, and you pay interest on a daily basis. When you sell, you use the proceeds to pay off the loan and pocket (or pay) the difference. Because you are borrowing most of the cost of the shares, your return, if the shares go up, is magnified. Of course if they go down, your percentage loss is magnified as well.

The table below shows how this works. Assume you buy the Vodafone CFD when its share price is 100, and its price then moves up to 120p or down to 80p. The table shows the result:

Example 4.1 – CFD in 10,000 Vodafone (share price currently 100p)*

Vodafone at:	100p	120p	80p
Deposit	£2,000	£2,000	£2,000
Underlying value	£10,000	£12,000	£8,000
Gain/loss	£0	£2,000	-£2,000
Capital after closing trade*	£2,000	£4,000	£0
Return on capital	0%	100%	- 100%

*dealing costs have been ignored

In other words a 20% move in either direction means the difference between making 100% on your money and wiping out your starting capital of £2,000.

Gearing works both ways

It's also worth noting here that you can easily lose more than you put up at the outset. If your initial deposit in the example above had been 10% rather than 20%, for example, the profits and losses would be the same, but the return on the gain would be 200% and the loss would be double the initial margin deposit. That's what I mean by gearing!

In short, the smaller the percentage you put up as your initial deposit, the bigger the gearing you have to movements in the underlying share in either direction, and the bigger the potential percentage gains *and losses*.

Strict definition of CFDs

There are some problems with the simple definition I used earlier. In the first place, as we've said before, you can use a CFD not just to buy shares but also to go short. And secondly, you never technically own the underlying shares on which a CFD is based.

The more complicated but accurate definition is that a CFD is:

> **'A contract between a buyer and seller to pay, in cash, when the contract is terminated, the difference between the opening and closing value of the shares (or index) on which the contract is based.'**

In fact the absolutely correct definition is that a CFD is 'a total return equity swap, designed to replicate the economic performance and cash flows of a conventional share investment.'

Differences with futures and spread betting

The mention of cash flows does however hint at some of the differences between CFDs on the one hand, and futures and spread betting on the other.

One fundamental difference is that the contract is *open-ended*. There is no expiry date as there is with a future or a futures-based spread bet.

The second difference is that the *cost of the financing* inherent in the contract is actually separate from the price, not included in it. In a future, the price you pay includes an element that reflects the interest saving you get by buying the future on margin rather than the underlying. This difference narrows as the future approaches the delivery date.

In a CFD, the price you pay is at or very close to the price in the cash market, but the interest on the margin loan is debited or credited to your account on a daily basis depending on whether you are going long or short. Interest is calculated on the terms specified by your CFD provider, but normally debited at a premium to the overnight rate and credited at a discount to the overnight rate.

Although you don't technically own the underlying shares, the contract (and the outside world) assumes you do. If you are long and the share goes ex-dividend during the time your CFD is open, your account is credited with the net dividend. By the same token if you are short and the same thing happens, your account is debited with the gross dividend.

This contrasts with spread betting and futures, where there is no right to any dividends on the shares that might be the subject of a bet or a futures trade, although ex-dividend effects tend to be built into futures prices automatically by the market.

This de facto ownership property of CFDs is not without controversy. Predators have built stakes in companies through the CFD market, a factor which the targets of their attentions do not view particularly kindly, as the activity is harder to trace.

Commissions and tax

Finally, CFD brokers in the main do charge commission, usually on the underlying value of the contract. Commission is paid on both the opening and closing sides of a deal, and can be a significant factor in the cost of a trade. CFDs are exempt from the stamp duty that share transactions attract. They do, however, fall under the CGT regime.

Once again this is slightly different from spread betting and futures. Futures get caught by the CGT net, but spread betting doesn't. Spread betting firms (see next chapter) don't charge commission, but the cost is built into the spread. There is no stamp duty to pay for futures, spread bets, or CFDs, because they are paper contracts rather than physical transactions.

Figure 4.1 – CMC Markets CFD Homepage

© CMC Markets

Below is a summary of these basic characteristics.

> ### Basic CFD characteristics
>
> - You can go long (or short)
> - Daily interest is charged (or credited) to your account
> - Dividends are credited (or charged) to your account
> - Cash flows on trades are calculated each day
> - You deal at the cash market price
> - Commission is payable on underlying value
> - You are liable to CGT, but not to stamp duty

Because CFDs are rather different to other types of investment, and a bit more complicated than either futures or spread betting, I want to look in more detail at precisely how they work on a day-to-day basis using a worked example. I then want to go on to look at some of the advantages and pitfalls involved in trading CFDs and the rules of the road when it comes to trading them.

CFD mathematics

Accounting for a CFD trade is a little bit more complicated than it is for buying and selling shares.

With shares, the costs are stamp duty at 0.5% of the consideration, and commission, which might be just, say, a flat £14.99 for the buying and selling side. You receive any dividends net.

With CFDs there are more things to consider. Commission is normally charged as 0.25% *of the underlying value*, and interest is charged or credited. The dividend is received net or debited gross.

For both shares and CFDs there is the bid-offer spread to consider.

Let's have a look at how it works on the ground.

Example 4.2 – Comparison of shares and CFDs when going LONG

First of all we need to make some assumptions.

- Commission is £14.99 per trade for shares; 0.25% for CFD
- Interest is charged at 5.475% (or £1.50 per day)

Your objective is to get exposure to £10,000-worth of Vodafone shares.

- The price of Vodafone is now 100p; your CFD margin deposit is 20%
- After three months Vodafone is 110p
- A dividend of 1p is paid just before you close the trade

The table opposite shows how the P&L account stacks up between shares and the CFD.

Table 4.1 – Using CFDs or shares to go long

	Shares	*CFD*
Investment at 100p	£10,000	£2,000
Underlying holding	10,000	10,000
Starting value	£10,000	£10,000
Commission	-£14.99	-£25.00
Stamp	-£50.00	Nil
Dividend	£100.00	£100.00
Interest (90 days)	Nil	-£135.00
Sale proceeds at 110p	£11,000	£11,000
Sale commission	-£14.99	-£27.50
Profit incl. dividend	£1,100	£1,100
Net costs	-£79.98	-£187.50
Net profit	£1,020.02	£912.50
Return on capital	10.20%	45.63%

We need to analyse this a bit more closely. For the same percentage movement in the underlying share price, we have achieved a broadly similar money return, but a much bigger percentage return on capital we have invested. In the CFD we have had the same level of exposure to the underlying shares, but only tied up a fifth of the capital. We have paid interest for the privilege, but we might also have earned interest on the capital we had saved. I haven't counted this in the example.

The net dividend of 1p a share is credited to the CFD as having been received when the shares go ex-dividend (not when the payment to shareholders is made, by the way). Commission rates are higher on the CFD than they would be for an execution-only share broker. Total costs – commission and interest – are substantially higher than the commission and stamp paid on the share transaction.

Now let's look at the same calculation if you are going short.

Example 4.3 – Comparison of shares and CFDs when going SHORT

This time I'm going to assume that:

- the shareholder already has £10,000-worth of Vodafone shares,

- the CFD trader shorts them at 100p,

- Vodafone shares then go down to 90p, and

- dividend payments, interest, commission and the like are all the same as in the previous example.

There is a slight wrinkle as far as the dividend payment is concerned. When you short a share using a CFD the gross amount of any dividend that occurs during the period is charged to your trade as a cost. This contrasts with the long example previously, where the net dividend only is credited. As I've already mentioned, in both cases the credit or charge happens when the shares go ex-dividend, not when the dividend is actually paid.

The profit and loss calculation on the short CFD trade is shown in the table overleaf, and compared with the costs of selling an existing holding of the shares, and then buying them back at the lower price.

Table 4.2 – Using CFDs to go short

	Shares	*CFD*
Capital involved	£10,000	£2,000
Underlying holding	10,000	10,000
Sale value	£10,000	£10,000
Sale Commission	-£14.99	-£25.00
Stamp (on buyback)	-£45.00	Nil
Dividend	0	-£111.00
Interest (90 days)	Nil	+£135.00
Buyback cost	£9,000	£9,000
Commission on buyback	-£14.99	-£22.50
Loss avoided or profit made	£1,000	£1,000
Net costs	-£74.98	-£23.50
Net profit	£925.02	£976.50
Return on capital	9.25%	48.83%

Here you can see how to some degree the trade mirrors what happened in the earlier example.

Interest is credited to the CFD rather than debited, but the grossed up dividend (100 x 0.9) is debited from the CFD account rather than credited. The shareholder does not receive the dividend because (until he buys back the holding) he does not own the shares.

In this instance, the costs of the CFD trade are slightly less than the sale and subsequent buyback of the shares. In fact, though, you do need to factor in the fact that the share seller could also earn interest on the £10,000 released by the sale, provided it is placed automatically in a broker money market account.

The return on the capital involved is again much higher in the case of the CFD. In fact the numbers could be even greater than this. Some brokers require only 10% initial margin at present on a Vodafone CFD, although this could change if the shares suddenly become more volatile. Lower margin magnifies the return if you get the trade right, but also magnifies the risk to your capital if you get it wrong.

CFD Rules of the Road

There is a temptation to see CFDs as spread betting on steroids. Or maybe spread betting is like CFDs on valium! I'll leave you to read the next chapter and then judge.

Either way, the point is that CFDs generally dictate a much bigger financial commitment and therefore bigger risk for you. You really do need to be comfortable that the money you have committed to CFD trading is money you can afford to lose.

This brings us to the number one rule when it comes to trading in CFDs.

Rule #1

It sounds obvious, but *you have to be able to afford it*. CFD firms will only open an account for you if they are satisfied that you are an experienced and reasonably affluent investor. This is as much for the protection of their good name as for any interest in your financial well-being. You need to demonstrate that you have been actively trading shares or futures for a long time, or have experience in the investment business, or have substantial surplus net assets in a readily liquid form.

The way CFD firms deal with this in practical terms is by setting fairly high minimum amounts that you will be required to deposit in your account before you can begin trading. We'll go into this in more detail in our chapter on dealing, but you will need anything from £5,000 to £25,000 as a minimum amount to deposit.

Rule #2

Remember that *margin requirements differ from stock to stock*. It varies to some degree with the underlying volatility of the share in question. But unless the stock concerned is particularly illiquid, a good rule of thumb is that you can usually borrow between 5 and 10 times the amount of underlying cash deposited. Or to put it more accurately if you want to deal in a stock to the tune of an underlying value of £10,000, you probably need to have at least £2,000 in your account, and a bit more to be on the safe side.

The table overleaf shows examples of the upfront deposit (or margin) that you need to put up for different types of shares.

As with both futures and spread betting, extra margin will be debited from your account or called from you if the trade goes the wrong way.

Table 4.3 – Typical initial margin requirements in CFDs

Instrument	*Deposit required (% of underlying value)*
Stock indices	5% or 10%
UK top 350 (SETS) shares	10% or 20%
UK top 350 (non-SETS) shares	15% or 25%
Other UK shares	25% plus
European shares	10% plus
US shares	10% plus
Options	100% of option premium

Source: CFD brokers

Rule #3

You probably won't have quite the same choice of instruments as you do with futures and spread betting. Although CFDs can in theory be used for trading any stock or commodity with a liquid underlying price, they are primarily used for trading shares and stock market indexes and sometimes for trading options. They are to some degree a half-way house between futures and spread betting, bearing in mind the technical differences that we have already mentioned.

With futures you can only trade a limited range of international shares, but you can trade many other instruments and commodities too, including interest rate and bond futures. With CFDs, many brokers confine themselves to trading UK shares and options, leading foreign shares, and foreign exchange. Spread betting tends to combine the two. You can trade a wider range of shares than are available in the futures market, but also the other futures based instruments that aren't widely available in CFDs.

Rule #4

If you want to trade CFDs, make sure that it forms an *integrated part of your overall investing activity*. Reputable firms that offer CFDs and spread betting – and many do both – want their clients to make dealing in them only a part of their overall trading. It should be complementary to rather than competitive to your conventional share buying and selling.

One reason for this is that CFD buyers will rarely make money through doing single speculative transactions one after the other. The cannier traders tend to use CFDs in conjunction with an underlying holding or portfolio, in other words as a hedge, or else use combinations of CFDs simultaneously that spread and even neutralise some of the risk that they are running.

We'll cover this later in the chapter on strategies, but a good example might be what is known as *pairs trading*. You might think Vodafone is cheap relative to BT. By shorting a CFD of BT and going long a similar underlying amount in a CFD of Vodafone, you are giving effect to this view. At the same time, you reduce the risk that you will be burnt by a general downturn in the market as a whole or the telecoms sector in particular.

Figure 4.2 – GNI's home page

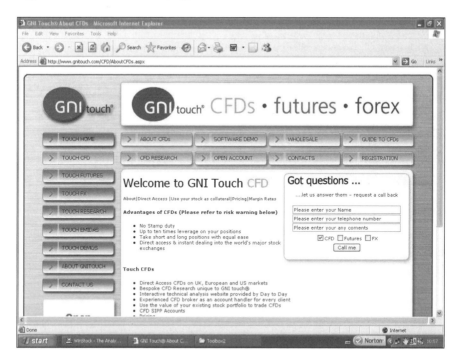

Rule #5

Keep an eye on your gearing and monitor your trades very closely.

Trading in CFDs can give you huge amounts of gearing and a commensurate amount of risk. Many large shares can be traded with as little as 10% down. This means you magnify the effect of a change in the price of the shares tenfold in terms of its effect on your wallet. Put another way, your capital will be hit very badly indeed if the price moves in a way you don't expect.

CFDs need strong nerves, constant monitoring, iron risk control, and a lot of money even before you start playing. Risk control is a separate subject in itself.

Because of the gearing you have at your disposal in a CFD, if you want to limit your risk you may be able to do so via controlled risk protection, sometimes known as a *guaranteed stop-loss*. One point that it's vital to remember here is that stop-losses may not be available on *all* CFD transactions, so you need to check before you deal. Brokers are not stupid, and they will not want to have guaranteed stops in either very volatile or very illiquid shares. Stop-losses are also not available in CFDs on options, whereas you may be able to have them when you deal in options through a conventional options broker.

Figure 4.3 – Sucden's home page for CFD traders

© Sucden

In some senses, because there is no time limit on a CFD trade in a normal share, you might feel that having a stop-loss is less important than it would be in a futures trade or spread bet. This is true, but the speed with which an individual share can move the wrong way and blow a hole in your account sometimes startles newcomers to the market. Unless there is a natural hedge for your CFD – like a holding of the underlying shares or a countervailing position in another CFD (as in the pairs trade example above), **you should seriously consider only trading where you *can* have a guaranteed stop-loss.**

Rule #6

Keep track of costs.

As the example on pages 78-81 shows, once the different costs are taken into account, a similar capital commitment to a stock – long or short – made via a CFD rather than an underlying share purchase, will, as a rough rule of thumb, produce a little under five times the return on capital if the investment moves in the right direction. This is on the assumption that you have to put up 20% of the underlying value as an initial margin deposit. If the deposit percentage is lower, say 10%, the gearing will be commensurately higher, around nine times.

Commission charges are typically higher on a CFD than on an underlying share transaction if you buy and sell shares using an execution only broker and deal in reasonable size. This is because CFD commission is based on the total underlying value of the shares you are trading, not the amount you put down in initial margin. A CFD broker like Deal4Free, as its name implies, offers commission-free trading, but here the cost of the commission charge is either built into the spread or, more likely, into the interest charge on the margin loan. There is no such thing as a free lunch.

It also follows that in deciding when and what shares to go short or long of, you should monitor ex-dividend dates and the amount of the dividend paid on that particular date very closely indeed, since these will be debited or credited to your account.

In the case of some actively traded stocks, LIFFE's Universal Stock Futures product was competing directly with CFDs. But CFDs have tended to win out in this battle and, as we have said already, USFs are no longer available for private investors to trade.

> ### General Rules for CFD Trading
>
> - Make sure you can afford it
> - Remember that margin requirements vary from stock to stock
> - Use CFDs mainly in shares and stock indexes
> - Integrate CFD trading with the rest of your investing
> - Monitor your trades closely, especially gearing
> - Remember that stop-losses not available in all cases
> - Keep track of commission and interest costs
> - Monitor ex-dividend dates

A final word on gearing and risk

Gearing is a double edged tool. It's obvious that it works both ways – *for* you if things go right, and *against* you if they don't.

Control your gearing

But it pays to look at gearing another way. If you are accustomed to dealing in shares in, let's say, £10,000 lumps, then if you substitute a CFD trade for a share trade, all it means is that you tie up less capital. You can get £10,000 of exposure for £2,000 and use the remaining £8000 to earn interest or invest elsewhere. You should not feel at all compelled to trade in amounts that are five or ten times the level you would normally deal in, simply because CFDs allow you to do so.

Greater diversification

Having said that, one use of gearing is that CFDs would allow you to get exposure to five different shares worth £50,000 in total, for the same £10,000 you might commit to one share via a share purchase. Provided the shares are not correlated, this route could be a better and more diverse and less risky way of proceeding than simply putting £10,000 into buying one share that may promptly suffer a profit warning.

Minimum account and trade sizes

Above all, make sure the broker fits in with what you want to do, not the other way round. What you do need to bear in mind, for example, is that not only do CFD brokers have minimum deposit levels for opening an account, but they also stipulate minimum trade sizes. You may not be able to open a CFD trade unless, for instance, you are prepared to deal in a contract with an underlying value of at least £10,000.

When you are choosing a broker with which to deal, pay particular attention not only to minimum *balance size* but also to minimum *trade sizes* too. If you can't find a broker that will allow you to open an account and deal in sizes that are comfortable to you, then it's best to look elsewhere.

The financial commitment required for spread betting accounts is generally somewhat less and you may therefore find this medium more suitable for you. Spread betting is the subject of the next chapter.

5

Spread and Binary Betting

The previous two chapters looked at futures and CFDs as tools you can use to either boost your returns or lay off risk. The higher returns you get come with risks attached. If you take advantage of the gearing that futures and CFDs offer, you have open-ended risk if the view you are taking is incorrect. In short, as we've seen, you can lose a lot of money very quickly. Traders get round this by using guaranteed stop-loss orders, and so should you. See below for more detail on this.

Spread betting is very similar to trading futures, but with some important differences. Binary betting, which we include for the first time in this edition, is a slightly different way of trading. There is a separate section on binary betting later in the chapter.

Like futures trading, spread betting is a way of dealing – both long and short – in shares, stock market indices, and other investment types without putting up the full amount of capital involved. Instead of dealing in fixed-size contracts, you dictate the amount you want to invest by nominating what size of stake you want (this is explained further below).

In conventional stock market trading you have to put up the full value of an investment when you buy a share or bond. You receive capital back when the investment is sold. The capital you get back will depend on the change in the price over the period you have the investment. The difference between what you put in and what you get back is your profit and loss on the transaction.

Like CFDs and futures, spread betting allows you to profit from or suffer this difference by just putting up an initial deposit when you place an order, and lets you receive the profit or pay the loss that arises when you close the trade. You close the trade by placing a similar order in the opposite direction.

- If you buy hoping to profit from a rise in price, and subsequently sell, this means you are going long.

- If you sell first and buy back later, this means you are going short. You expect to profit from a fall in price.

The *betting* part of the term spread betting sometimes gives rise to confusion. Most people associate betting with fixed odds 'first-past-the-post' betting on racehorses. Binary betting on stock markets is a form of fixed odds betting (see later section for more detail). But for the moment let's concentrate on the spreads aspect.

In fact, trading spreads on sporting events has been a long-established part of the betting industry.

Punters might, for example, buy or sell on a quoted spread to gamble on the total number of points scored in a rugby match, or the total number of goals in a football tournament. Financial spread betting takes this principle and applies it to shares, commodities and other financial products.

Some spread betting firms prefer to give financial spread betting the slightly different name of *spread trading*, to avoid just this confusion.

Advantages of spread betting

How does spread betting work, and why is it worth considering? The technique has a number of distinct advantages. But let's look first in simple terms at how it works. It's basically quite easy.

When you trade using spread betting, you simply make *up bets* and *down bets* instead of buying and selling. In fact as we'll find out later in the chapter on dealing, this really goes by the board when you are placing a spread bet. You simply ask for the two-way price and indicate whether you want to buy or sell and the size of your stake. You would say, for example –

> *'buy Vodafone in £2 a point'*

rather than say....

> *'I want to place an up-bet in Vodafone with a stake of £2 a point'*

although this is, in precise terms, what you mean.

How easy is it?

- The spread-betting firm quotes you a two-way price.

- You indicate whether you want to buy or sell.

- You tell them the size of the deal, in £ per point

That's it.

If you do an up bet in Vodafone at £10 a point, and Vodafone rises 20p and you subsequently close the trade, your gain is 20 times the £10 stake on which the bet is based, or £200. It's that simple.

Actually, it's not quite that simple, because as with a conventional share trade, you do have to factor out the cost of the spread. In the example above, Vodafone might be quoted with a 1p spread between the up bet and down bet. So in the case of this example your actual profit would be 19 times £10, or £190.

This is illustrated in the example below.

Example 5.1 – Placing an up bet on Vodafone

1. *Quote*: The spread bet company quotes Vodafone at: 99-100
   Action: You place an up bet on Vodafone at 100 for £10 a point

2. Market: Vodafone shares rise.

3. *Quote*: The spread bet company now quotes Vodafone at: 119-120
   Action: You close out the position by selling at 119

   Result: You make 19 points at £10 a point = £190

This example hints at some of the big advantages of spread betting.

The first is that it's basically WYSIWYG. *What you see is what you get.* You have a buying and selling price. You nominate the size of the deal. There is no commission, stamp duty, stock exchange levies or any other costs. Any costs that the spread betting firm has to bear (betting duty, for example) are built into the spread rather than charged to you separately.

This does mean that in some stocks the spread quoted by the spread betting firm will be wider than a broker would quote for dealing in the underlying shares. But it almost certainly won't be any wider, and will probably be less, once you factor out the effect of stamp duty and broker commission.

Here's an example from my own personal dealing. Back in 2003 I bought £5,000 worth of Capita Group shares when the share quote was 225-226p. By the time stamp duty and commission had been taken into account, I worked out that the cost of the purchase was 228.2p. But the spread quoted at Cantor Index for the same share at the time was 2p. Including costs, the spread on the share was 3.2p. No contest! Except that at that time I didn't have a spread betting account.

Figure 5.1 – Page displaying live prices of popular spread bets at Cantor

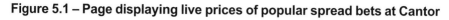

© Cantor Index

The second plus point is that there is, under present tax rules, *no capital gains tax to pay* on spread betting. This is because the gains technically arise from bets. The spread-betting firm pays any betting tax due.

There are other advantages too. One big one is that financial bookmakers who offer spread betting generally offer more than just spread betting in UK shares or stock market indices. Some offer spread bets in:

• index options

• commodities like gold and crude oil

• interest rates and government bond futures, and

• overseas shares and stock market indices

Normally to deal in many of these markets you would need to have several different broking accounts: one with a futures and options broker, another with a US stockbroker and so on. **Spread betting firms are a 'one-stop shop' for a very wide range of markets.**

The other point is that the financial commitment you need to make to trade some of these instruments is much greater than you would need to put up when spread betting.

Here's a simple example:

Buying an index option on the FTSE at, say, 150 involves you committing £1,500. Spread betting the same option at £2 a point involves you committing £300. If you are, for example, buying an index put option to hedge your portfolio against a market fall (see chapter 11 for this strategy in more detail), you have much more flexibility using spread betting as the medium, because you can vary the stake size to tailor the option to the size of your portfolio.

Most investors use spread betting as a substitute for buying, but you can just as easily go short of a share or index you feel is overvalued. This is a choice not normally open to private investors in shares and is similar to the advantages also offered by futures trading and CFDs.

> ### Advantages of spread betting
>
> - No hidden charges or commission
> - No CGT or betting duty to pay
> - One stop shop for most types of investment
> - Lower financial commitment
> - Ability to go short or long
> - Can pay to have guaranteed stop-losses

Finally, keep in mind that you can have a spread betting account that allows you to use guaranteed stop-losses. A stop-loss is an automatically triggered order that gets you out of a trade if the price hits a predetermined level. Traders use stop-losses to get out of a trade that's going the wrong way.

Most conventional stockbrokers won't offer a stop-loss facility to ordinary private investors and in any case they cannot offer a guarantee that the stop-loss will be executed at the price specified – only at a dealing price immediately after the order has been triggered. With markets as volatile as they have been, a stock can easily go down through a stop-loss very sharply and have fallen a substantial percentage before your broker gets round to executing the order.

With spread betting, because you are entering into a contract with the spread betting firm rather than dealing on an exchange, the stop-loss *will* be executed at the price you specify. That guarantee comes at a price, of course, in the form of a small extra cost built into the spread. But the price is worth it in terms of the benefits the system gives you in terms of controlling your risk.

Margin

We'll look in more detail at precisely how spread betting works from a dealing standpoint in a later chapter. But there is one aspect of it that it's worth covering upfront.

This is the issue of margin.

As we've already said, spread betting is similar to futures trading. Spread betting firms use the futures market to lay off the liability that their clients' activities generate, and their spreads track futures prices closely.

The similarity with futures extends to the question of margin. Spread betting firms usually call it something other than margin, but the principle is the same.

When you open an account with a spread betting firm you have to deposit cash before you can begin trading. For each deal you undertake, a margin figure is calculated based on the size of your stake multiplied by a *bet factor*, which differs from instrument to instrument.

The result is called the *notional trading requirement* (or NTR). This is margin by another name. You must have at least this amount on deposit in your account before you trade. If the trade goes wrong, you will be asked to top up your account to the tune of any losses.

Table 5.1 – Bet size factors / NTR for typical spread bets

Instrument	Bet size factor	Tick size
FTSE future	250	1pt
Wall Street future	500	1pt
DAX Future	250	1pt
CAC40 future	250	1pt
S&P500 future	500	0.1pt
Nasdaq 100 future	150	1pt
Nikkei 225 future	500	1pt
Gilt future	100	1 tick
Bund future	100	1 tick
Brent Crude	100	1 tick
Gold	150	$0.1

Instrument	Bet size factor Tick size
UK shares	NTR = 10% of contract value
Dow/S&P shares	NTR = 10% of contract value
Nasdaq shares	NTR = 15% of contract value
Options	NTR = 100% of option premium

Note. Daily index bets have a bet size factor half that for the corresponding future.

Source: Cantor Index

The NTR acts as a cash cushion. In theory it should prevent you from getting in too deep. Let's look at an example.

Example 5.2 – Spread betting and NTR

- You place a down bet in a share that has a bet size factor of 200.

- You bet £4 a point.

- The notional trading requirement is therefore £800.

- You have £1,000 deposited in your spread betting account. (The point about the NTR is that your bet earmarks £800 of the £1,000 in your account.)

Now let's say the share rises in price by 50p.

- Because you placed a down bet, your trade is now losing money to the tune of £4 times 50, or £200.

- Added to the NTR of £800 this bet has now absorbed the entire £1000 deposited in your account.

The NTR combined with the loss you've made (even though it's unrealised) equate to exactly the funds in your account. If the bet continues to go against you, you will be expected either to close the bet and take the loss, or provide extra cash to boost the funds in your account. This is known as a margin call. If you ignore a margin call, the bet will be closed without further notice.

Let's say you close the trade. It's worth stressing that you haven't lost your entire £1,000, but only the £200 that took you up to the limit. The NTR is there to give you pause for thought and stop you losing more than you can afford.

The bet size factor varies according to the volatility of the underlying product. The more volatile the index or share, the bigger the factor and the more notional headroom you'll be expected to have in your account.

> ### NTR Summarised
>
> - Multiply bet size factor by your stake to get NTR.
>
> - Bet size factor varies with underlying volatility.
>
> - NTR is notional. You don't lose NTR if the trade goes wrong.
>
> - NTR sometimes calculated as a percentage of exposure.
>
> - NTR sometimes equates to 100% of your bet (e.g. in options).
>
> - NTR is often higher percentage than futures margin.

You need to be aware of the bet size factor before you place a bet. Don't place a bet that could result in your being asked for further cash if only a small movement occurs in the underlying price.

There are a couple of other aspects to NTRs and margin when you are spread betting. One is that some spread betting firms will calculate the NTR on some bets as a simple percentage of the underlying exposure.

Here's an example:

Let's say the spread betting firm calculates NTR on a stock as 10% of underlying exposure. The price of the shares is 150p and you are betting £5 a point. The NTR would simply be 10% of £5 times 150. That's to say 10% of £750, or £75. In the case of options, however, the NTR will often be equivalent to 100% of your initial exposure – that's to say the option price multiplied by your stake. This is because an option's price can be very volatile indeed.

The effective level of margin required is also sometimes bigger than it would be if you were trading the equivalent future. And because the system encourages you to keep your account fully funded, you will often have more cash sitting in your account than actually needs to be there, giving the bookmaker the benefit of earning interest on it. Some bookmakers offer interest on credit balances, but you need to check on this before you open an account.

Types of bet

Those who have never indulged in spread betting are probably inclined to see the spread betting industry as rather homogeneous, offering a single basic product. This is not the case.

While there is a common thread and a number of common bets that run through the product offerings of all the different firms involved in spread betting, there are differences between the firms. Some of them are big ones. Firms diverge in the range of instruments on which they will accept bets. Many spread betting firms don't offer bets in index options, for example. They also diverge in the type of bets they offer.

The broad types of conventional spreads bets offered are probably a good place to start.

Spread bets fall into two broad categories:

1.   Those that are good for a **single day**; generally called 'cash bets'; and

2.   Those that can potentially last **until a specified date** in the future.

Some firms offer a hybrid bet that combines aspects of the two.

Figure 5.2 – IG Index spread betting home page

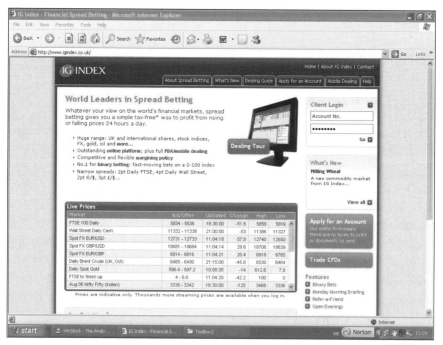

© IG Index

Cash bets

Bets that are good for a single day only, or *cash bets*, are frequently traded on a very short-term basis over periods from as long as a few hours to as short as a few minutes.

Spreads are usually significantly narrower on bets that will simply be open for a day or less. Cantor's spread on the daily FTSE 100 index bet is six points. On futures-based bets that can be kept open for longer, the spread ranges from 8-12 points.

Daily spread bets that are not closed during that particular day will be closed out automatically by the spread betting firm at the closing price. There are some risks in allowing this to happen, so avoid it if at all possible. We'll look at this later in the book when we cover trading strategies.

Table 5.2 – Key features of types of spread bet

Type of bet	Spread	Typical user	Offered by	Feature
Daily Cash	Tight	Professional	All	Close in day
Rolling cash	Tight	Pro/Am	Some	Financing +/-
Futures	Looser	Amateur	All	Expiry date
GSL	Looser	All	Most	Stop-loss
Options	Looser	Some	Some	Mimics option

Should you use daily bets?

Those in the know often advise people new to the market – even if they are experienced private investors – to **avoid daily bets in the indices,** simply because it is impossible for private traders to beat the professionals at their own game.

Every second you have a daily bet open, you would arguably need to be sat in front of a professional's trading screen with direct access to the market to be able to play the game properly against the pros. For obvious reasons a lot of people either don't want to do this or can't afford the cost of the equipment that would be needed to do it properly.

There's another reason why you might not want to use daily cash bets. The aim of this book is to show you how to use futures, options, spread betting and the like as a way of boosting your returns and limiting your risk. If you are ordinarily a medium to long-term investor, it follows that you aren't really tuned in to trading on a day-to-day basis. This means you should avoid daily bets.

Longer-term bets

Bets other than daily ones are usually based around futures contracts. This means that there will normally be a series of expiry months each with slightly different spreads and prices. For example the spread on the front month future may be 10 ticks and that on the next expiry month might be 12 ticks.

As we explained in an earlier chapter, futures prices differ from the cash market price (the actual index value or share price) partly because they reflect expectations, but mainly because using a future to buy exposure to a product allows the buyer an interest saving. This is because the futures product can be traded on margin. The futures price is therefore generally at a small premium or discount to the cash price, which decreases as the delivery date approaches.

In other words, fair value for a future will not be the same as the underlying cash product, and the disparity will be bigger the further in the future the expiry date is.

It's probably fair to say therefore, for most investors using these products for return-boosting and hedging purposes, that futures based bets are the logical choice. You don't have the time pressure that a cash bet entails. Provided you have a bit of nerve and enough leeway in your account, you can stand a short-term loss if you are convinced your judgement is correct.

Rolling cash bets

However, there is another choice that may be suitable for our purposes. This type of bet, originated by the spread-betting firm CMC Markets, is called a *rolling cash bet*. This is a cash bet, on a tight spread, that is carried over from one day to the next for as long as the punter wants.

This allows you to have a bet open for as long as you wish, subject only to paying the financing costs associated with it. In effect it is replicating a CFD. The interest is calculated on the total amount of the exposure that underlies the bet. A bet at £10 a point on a share priced at 160p has an underlying exposure of £1,600. Interest is typically charged at an official overnight rate plus a small premium for an up bet or credited at the overnight rate less a small discount for a down bet. The interest charged on a bet of this size might, for example, be in the region of 20p a day for an up bet, or a credit of 5p a day for a down bet.

I reckon that this is quite a good wheeze, since one of the ways you can use spread bets is to hedge an individual stock you already hold, or a portfolio. This means that you will typically use a down bet and get an interest credit each day.

Another wrinkle worth bearing in mind with a rolling cash bet is that if you are using it as a proxy for owning the underlying share by having an up bet, the spread will mirror very closely the underlying spread in the underlying share on the stock exchange, while you will also, if the share goes ex-dividend, get a credit equivalent to the amount of the dividend.

Figure 5.3 – CMC's explanation of its innovative 'rolling cash' bet

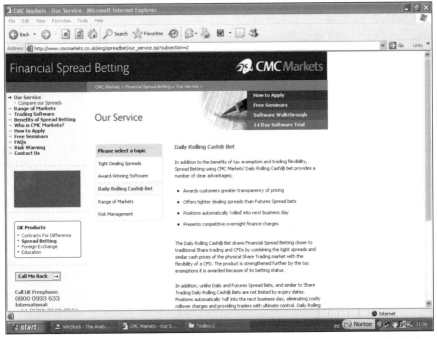

Controlled risk bets

Controlled risk bets, sometimes called guaranteed stop-loss bets, allow you, at the time you deal, simultaneously to place a stop-loss order, in order to limit your risk if the trade starts to go wrong. Generally, spread betting firms require you to have a separate account for controlled risk bets. Spreads are slightly wider to reflect the cost of offering the service. While a normal spread bet may be able to be transacted online with the minimum of fuss, you may need to talk to a dealer to place a controlled risk bet. Brokers' online systems are designed for the broad mass of users, which actually means punters who do not use a guaranteed stop-loss service.

It's also worth remembering that you can spread bet on option prices. These bets are also not normally available online. However, spread bets on options mimic the underlying price of the option. On individual equity options, a small initial premium to the prevailing option price (not usually more than four points) is payable when the trade is opened.

Spreads on index options are generally also a few points wider than the underlying option premium, but there are no dealing costs or capital gains considerations to take into account. Not all firms offer spread betting on LIFFE options. The firms that do offer spread betting on index options also offer them on major international indices as well as those available on the FTSE 100.

Binary Betting

Binary betting is a form of spread betting that was introduced a few years ago. This section is a brief introduction to it. It may or may not be your cup of tea. It is a more volatile and short term market than mainstream spread betting.

What is binary betting?

Binary betting is the City's equivalent of the ante post betting market in horse racing. It is based on whether or not an individual event occurs. Will the FTSE100 close up or down? Will it close up or down by more than 20 points? The odds change constantly right up to the last moment. If the expected event doesn't occur, the 'make-up price', at which the bets are settled, is zero. If it does occur, the 'make up' price is 100.

The price at which you buy determines the fixed odds of the bet at the time you make it. If you buy at 50, you are betting on the basis of even-money odds, because you stand to win or lose the same amount (of 50, because the bet will 'make-up' at either 100 or 0). If you buy at 25, the odds of winning are 3/1 against. You stand to win three times what you will lose.

The crucial difference between this and conventional fixed odds betting is that you can close your bet at any time in the course of the day, to either pocket your winnings or cut your losses.

A simple example

Let's take as an example a simple bet that the FTSE100 will be up at the close of trading today. At the outset the binary spread may be 45-50 (equally likely to be up or down at the end of the day). If you think the FTSE100 will be up at the close, you would buy at 50, and make 50 points if you're right (as the market would settle at 100) If you think the FTSE100 will not end up, then you would sell at 45, and make 45 points if you're right (as the market would settle at 0).

Let's say you buy at 50 because you think the index will be up on the day.

Later that morning the index trades around 10 points.

It is now more likely that it will close up for the day, so the binary spread may have moved up to 66-67. You could sell now and take a 16 point profit on the bet, or wait in the hope that the trend will persist until the close and the make–up price of 100 pays out.

In fixed odds terms, the bet has moved from 'even money' to '2 to 1 on'

But let's say that Wall Street opens lower and the 'footsie' suddenly slips to being five points down. The likelihood has now shifted in favour of the bet being a loser, with a make-up price of zero. The binary spread in this instance could switch around completely at trade down from 66-67 to 24-26. This means the odds have switched from '2 to 1 on' to '3 to 1 against'.

As with normal spread betting you can vary the size of the bet in money terms by choosing the appropriate size of stake. In the example in the preceding paragraph, at £5 a point bet at 50, you are in effect making an even money bet of £250 (£5 x 50).

In simple terms it's possible to see that this makes binary betting, while a simple proposition, very volatile and very short term in nature, and therefore not appropriate for everyone.

It's possible to argue that there are some ways in which you can use binary betting as a hedging tool, but in reality – and for most of those who play in this market – it is pure speculation.

Types of binary betting

As with mainstream spread betting, products offered in binary betting differ slightly from firm to firm.

Most firms, however, offer binary betting in the FTSE100, Dow Jones, S&P500, NASDAQ100, DAX, CAC40 and in a range of other indices. Some also offer currencies.

For some or all of these the offering might be based on hourly, half-daily, daily or weekly movements. Some bets are even offers on index moves as short as five minutes. Some are offered for an index movement outside or within a particular threshold, some on the daily range of the market.

In all cases they share the common theme that if the event does take place the bet settles at 100, if it doesn't the bet settles at zero. Some firms also offer binary or decimal trading. Binary is analogous to the spread betting scenario described above. Decimal allows you to back or lay off a fixed amount at fixed odds. The two systems are, of course, mathematically equivalent.

Table 5.2 – Binary to fixed odds conversion

Sell binary at:	Fixed odds equivalent	Buy binary at:
99.0	99/1	1.0
98.7	75/1	1.3
98.5	66/1	1.5
98.0	50/1	2.0
97.1	33/1	2.9
96.2	25/1	3.8
95.2	20/1	4.8
94.1	16/1	5.9
92.3	12/1	7.7
90.9	10/1	9.1
90.0	9/1	10.0
88.9	8/1	11.1
87.5	7/1	12.5
85.7	6/1	14.3
83.3	5/1	16.7
81.8	9/2	18.2
80.0	4/1	20.0
75.0	3/1	25.0
66.7	2/1	33.3
60.0	6/4	40.0
55.6	5/4	44.4
50.0	evens	50.0
44.4	4/5	55.6
40.0	4/6	60.0

......and so on.

Can you win?

Ultimately it depends on how good a trader you are and on rigorous money management. Begin by reflecting that it is rare to see a poor bookmaker, of whatever type. The presence of the spread means that the odds are skewed against you.

You might get lucky, but you need to be prepared for a string of losing bets.

This makes it imperative not to bet too big and not to be too greedy. Treat each bet as a 'trade'. For each trade only bet a small percentage (perhaps a twentieth or less) of the capital you have committed to this activity at the outset. If you see a decent profit on any trade, take it. Cut losses quickly.

A final word

What's the best way of using spread betting? The answer is that it depends on your temperament.

I work from home. I occasionally like to spread bet on the US indices in a modest way. As I normally work in the evenings I can take out a spread bet on the S&P500, tune in to Bloomberg, my favourite financial TV station, and get live US indices until the close at around 9pm UK time. This means I can check on the progress of my 'trade' while I finish off my day's work.

It's really another way of saying that close monitoring of all your trades is really necessary, even if you use conventional spread betting and not the binary variety. You need to have your wits about you. A spread bet or CFD can lose you money – as I know from bitter experience – in the time it takes to walk into the kitchen to get a glass of water.

Check list when picking a spread betting firm

Does your would-be spread betting firm . . .

1. Have the **tightest spreads**? ☐

2. Have the best **administration**? ☐

3. Offer the **types of bets** you want to place? ☐

4. Have bets in a **full range** of instruments? ☐

5. Offer betting on **options**, especially index options? ☐

6. Offer **interest** on your unused account balance? ☐

Where I think spread betting scores goes back to the reason behind this book. It allows you to speculate and particularly to hedge, with the minimum of fuss in a range of markets, from the same account.

One point I think needs stressing above all of the others. Not all spread betting firms are the same. I'll deal with opening an account in Chapter 9. But you do need to check that the firm you choose offers all of the types of spread bets that you are likely to want to use, and that its spreads are competitive.

A tight spread means it is easier for you to make a profit on the trade. You also need to check the minimum bet sizes to see if they are compatible with the amount of cash you have at your disposal and the purposes that you want to use your account for.

Many serious investors open spread betting accounts with more than one firm, simply to have the ability to shop around for the best spread, or because a particular firm offers products that none of the others do, or has longer dealing hours, or is known for its ultra-efficient administration, or offers interest on account balances. Bear in mind too that some of the newer firms don't have the broad range of bets that the larger, more established players have. Check carefully first.

We'll cover all of these aspects of spread betting more closely in the section on dealing and account opening and in the appendix on sources of information.

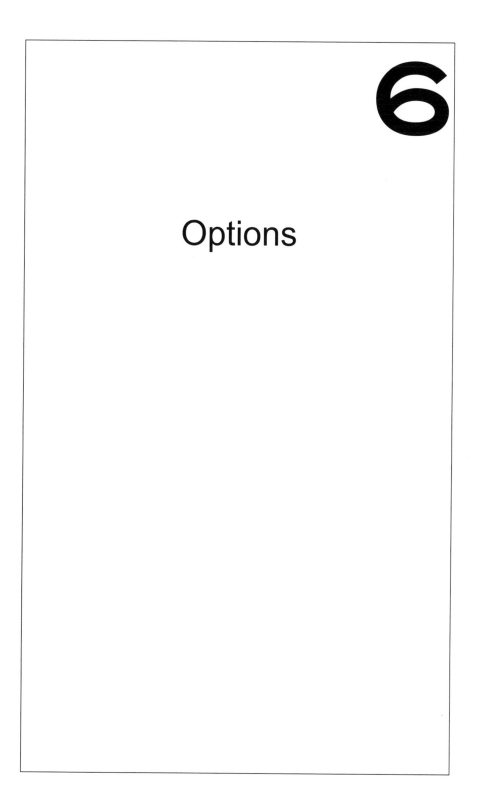

6

Options

The last three chapters have looked at how futures work and at how CFDs and spread betting function in roughly the same way. This chapter and the next one look at the other main branch of derivatives – options. Chapter 7 looks at warrants, and especially at covered warrants. This is a new market but one that is very similar to options. This chapter looks at the basics of options.

Before we start on options, let's recap on some of the main concepts we covered in Chapter 2, or at least those relevant to the options market.

We need to remember the idea that options, like futures, are *financial contracts*. They have expiry dates, they can be bought and sold in the market for cash, and they have gearing to the price movements of the underlying.

Have a look at the table overleaf. The right-hand column shows the characteristics of options. You can see at a glance how they differ from futures.

Look at the two attributes at the bottom of the table. They are ones that apply specifically to options.

One is the relationship of the price to the time left before the expiry of the option. The other is that the price of an option is heavily influenced by the volatility of the underlying share or other security on which it is based.

We'll come to these later. Before we get ahead of ourselves, let's just look at some basic facts about options and how they work.

What is an option?

Options are simply about choice. The classic definition of an option is that it is a contract that confers on the holder the right, *but not the obligation*, to buy (or sell) a predetermined quantity of shares at a fixed price for a known period of time.

Table 6.1 – Key attributes of futures and options

Attribute	*Futures*	*Options*
Standardised contract	Yes	Yes
Commitment to buy (or sell)	Yes	No
Right to buy (or sell), but not obligation	No	Yes
Time limit (expiry date)	Yes	Yes
Gearing from margin	Yes	No
Gearing from premium	No	Yes
Can be sold before expiry for cash	Yes	Yes
Traded on exchanges	Yes	Yes
Traded via spread betting	Yes	Yes
Price related to time value	No	Yes
Price related to volatility	No	Yes

Let's break this down into its component parts. First, "An option holder has the right, but not the obligation, to buy (or sell) . . ."

In other words you have the right to choose to exercise your option if the terms look attractive. But because you have no obligation to use the option, you can choose to forfeit the small upfront premium you paid for it if exercising is not worth your while. Simply let the option lapse: end of story.

But there is another element to this choice. You can also choose to sell your option in the market at a profit rather than undergo the process of exercising it. Or you can sell it some time before expiry even if you can't exercise it at a profit. You may be able to recoup a part of the upfront cost of the option even if you have to sell it at a loss.

One thing is certain: if the option can't be exercised at a profit, when it expires it will have no value.

Calls and Puts

The next question is why, in the definition I used above, did I use the phrase *option to buy (or sell)*? The answer is simple. Options come in two flavours – call options and put options:

- A **call option** is an option to *buy* at a fixed price for a known period of time.
- A **put option** is an option to *sell* at a fixed price for a known period of time.

The fixed price at which you can buy (or sell, in the case of a put) the shares during the life of the option is known as the exercise price, or strike price.

There are a couple of things that follow from this. One is that if the price of the underlying on which the option is based moves in the right direction, the value of the option will rise.

Let's say you have an option to *buy* 1,000 Vodafone shares at 100p for the next six months. If Vodafone shares rise from 100p to 120p, it follows that your call option at 100p would become more valuable. In theory you could exercise the option, take delivery of the shares at a price of 100p and then sell them immediately for 120p. This is how a call option works.

Similarly if you had an option to *sell* 1000 Vodafone shares at 100p for the next six months, and Vodafone fell in price from 100p to 80p, the option would become more valuable. You could exercise your right to sell your Vodafone shares at 100p and buy them back at 80p immediately. This is how a put option works.

- **Call option** prices move in the *same direction* as the price of the underlying security because the right to buy at a fixed price automatically becomes more valuable if the underlying price goes up, and becomes less valuable if the price falls.

- **Put option** prices move in the *opposite direction* to the price of the underlying because the right to sell becomes more valuable if the price of the underlying falls, and less valuable if it rises.

Let's summarise this in a table.

Table 6.2 – How option prices move

Underlying price	Call option price	Put option price
Up	Up	Down
Down	Down	Up

There is a proviso here. And it is a big one. It is that **the passage of time also affects the price of an option.**

When you buy an option, you are buying a contract that has a time limit. That time limit is the expiry date of the option.

In other words to make money buying an option you have to make forecasts. Not only do you have to predict the movement in the underlying price correctly, but it also has to happen before the option expires. The option is what an accountant would term a 'wasting' asset. On top of anything that might happen to the price of the option as a result of the movement in the price of the underlying is the fact that time is passing. We'll return to this shortly.

In and out-of-the-money

The concept of *in-the-money*, *at-the-money* and *out-of-the-money* is crucial to the way options work. So let's have a look at this next.

It's intuitively easier to understand in the case of call options. With call options, *in-the-money* options are those where the price of the underlying shares stands above the exercise price of the option.

Imagine we have a Vodafone call option with an exercise price of 100. The shares stand at 115p. So this option is in-the-money to the tune of 15p. We could exercise the option to buy the shares at 100, sell them at 115 and make an immediate 15p profit. With the shares at 100p and a strike price of the option of 100 the option is *at-the-money*. If the shares were, let's say, 90p, the option would be *out-of-the-money*. It could not currently be exercised at a profit.

For put options it works in reverse. A put option is in-the-money if the underlying price is below the exercise price and out-of-the-money if the price is above the exercise price. This is because the option to sell has more value the further the price falls below the exercise price, and no inherent value if it is above the exercise price.

Once again, let's summarise this in a table.

Table 6.3 – Terms describing relationship of underlying to strike price

	In-the-money	*At-the-money*	*Out-of-the-money*
Call	above	same as . .	below
Put	below	same as . .	above

There is another way of looking at this. It is that an option that is in-the-money has some *intrinsic value*: it could be exercised immediately and the resulting shares sold (or bought back) for a profit.

If you are buying an in-the-money option, it means that you have to pay more to cover the inbuilt profit that's already there.

But even out-of-the-money options have some value. This is because they still have time to go before they expire. This means there is a chance that a movement in the underlying shares could happen between now and expiry that would mean they could be exercised or sold at a profit.

Some investors will pay good money for that chance. Because of this, most out-of-the-money options will cost something to buy. The price of an option that is out-of-the-money solely reflects this so-called time value.

In-the-money options have two components to their price. They too have *time value*. But they also have the intrinsic value on top.

Let's take an example from real life to show how this works

Example 6.1 – Marks & Spencer option prices

At the time of writing, M&S shares are at **580p**. Some of its option prices are as follows:

October 2006 Call Option (underlying shares at 580p)

Strike	Option Price	Intrinsic Value	Tme value
550	47.75	30.0 (580-550)	17.75 (47.75 – 30.0)
600	19.25	0.00	19.25 (19.25 - 0.00)

October 2006 Put Option (underlying shares at 580p)

Strike	Option Price	Intrinsic Value	Time value
550	11.25	0.00	11.25 (11.25 - 0.00)
600	33.00	20.00(600-580)	13.00 (33.0 – 20.0)

Source: FT (for option prices)

As you can see, you can work out the time value of an option by subtracting its intrinsic value from the price of the option. The intrinsic value is the amount by which, in the case of a call option, the underlying price is above the strike price of the option. If the underlying price is below the strike price, the intrinsic is value is zero.

In the case of a put option, the intrinsic value is the amount by which the underlying price is below the strike price of the option. If the underlying price is above the strike price, the intrinsic value is zero.

Intrinsic value cannot be negative. It is either a positive number or zero.

So to work out time value, first work out intrinsic value, then subtract it from the price of the option to get time value. If the option is out-of-the-money, the price of the option and the option's time value are one and the same, because the intrinsic value is zero.

Figure 6.1 – Sucden's options traders' home page

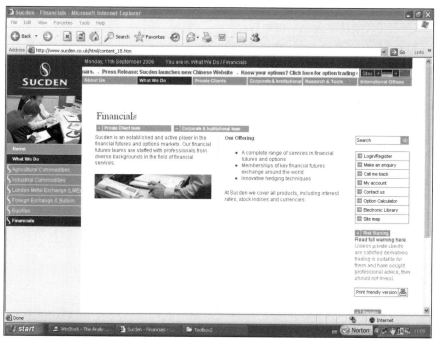

© Sucden

As you can also see from Example 6.1, time value can vary from option to option, even if they have the same expiry date. If there are variations like this, they reflect the market's view about the imminent future direction of the share price. In Example 6.1, both the call and the put with the strike price closest to the current price of the shares have similar time values.

Volatility

I mentioned earlier that one of the other factors that affects the price of an option is the volatility of the underlying price of the share (or index, or other security or commodity) on which the option is based.

In fact this understates the importance of volatility. It is probably the single most important (and most often ignored or misunderstood) component of an option's price.

Understanding how volatility works is the key to making money trading options.

The easiest way to think of *volatility* is that it's a measure of a share's or a market's mood swings. The market can be either calm, with prices varying little from day to day, or very erratic, with big swings from hour to hour and day to day.

And just as different people have different characters and different moods, so do different shares. It's called volatility.

Historic volatility

The difference between shares and individuals is that a share's level of volatility can be measured precisely. The volatility that's already happened up to now – called *historic volatility* – can be worked out through a statistical analysis of the share price. It equates to what statisticians term the *standard deviation* of the share price history.

In practical terms, it is a statistical fact that one standard deviation either side of the share price trend represents a band inside which the share price would be expected to remain two-thirds of the time.

A share with volatility of 20% standing at 100p would therefore expect to see its share price fluctuate between 80p and 120p – with only a one-in-three chance of moving outside these bands.

But historic volatility is only a snapshot. And volatility isn't a fixed quantity.

Volatility is different for each share. Even with the same share it can change hour-by-hour, day-by-day and month-by-month.

Some shares move around more violently than others. Equally there are times when an individual share goes through a quiet period, when little movement occurs in its price, and then subsequently explodes into life.

Volatility measures these mood swings. The mood can swing from extreme pessimism to optimism and back again. The direction of the swing doesn't matter. But if a big mood swing happens, volatility goes up. If everything calms down, volatility falls.

Figure 6.2 – Fluctuations in the volatility of Vodafone's shares

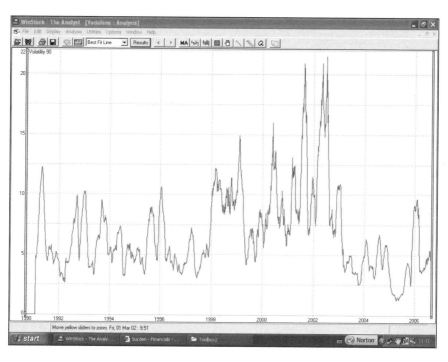

© Winstock Software

What matters for option prices is not really what historic volatility is or has been, but where it might go from here. It's a variation on the familiar theme that past share price performance, and therefore historic volatility, whilst important, may not be a reliable guide for the future.

Implied volatility

Analysing past share price movements is one thing. But we might also want to know what the market thinks volatility is now.

Using simple option pricing software, an option's *fair price* can be worked out for any given level of volatility (other things being equal). Reversing the calculation, the volatility implied by the current market price of the options can also be calculated. This is called *implied volatility* and it can be (and usually is) different from the historic volatility figure. It tells you what level of volatility is implied by the option prices that the market has set at any one time.

Future volatility

The third type of volatility is *future volatility*. This is the big unknown. But we probably do know both the 'normal' and extreme levels that historic volatility has reached in the past (many chart software packages, for example, have the ability to graph volatility over time) and under what circumstances it has reached these extremes.

Why is volatility so important?

Quite simply, this is because option prices are very sensitive to changes in volatility. The reason is that the more the price swings around, the more chance holders of options are likely to get to exercise or sell their options at a profit. And if there's a bigger chance of exercising or selling the option at a profit, the option itself becomes more valuable, even if nothing else changes.

Understanding this is the key to options trading. When you buy an option you are taking as much a view on the likely future trend in volatility as you are in the expectation that the underlying price will rise (if you hold a call) or fall (if you hold a put).

Changes in volatility either reinforce or dampen down changes in option prices occurring as a result of the other factors.

Let's summarise this in a table:

Table 6.4 – Types of volatility

Name	Ascertained from	Calculated using
Historic volatility	Price history of underlying	Standard deviation
Implied volatility	Market price of option	Simple software
Future volatility	Past trends in volatility	Charts of volatility

In summary, what we are interested in when we buy an option is

1. the realistic size of a **price movement** in the underlying,
2. the **time period** in which it occurs, and
3. what might happen to **volatility** over that period.

We can determine none of these things with precision, but we can project different combinations of events and work out what might happen to the price of the option as a result.

Options prices and how they are calculated

Who determines the premium, or price, of an option?

It's trite to say that the price will reflect the balance of buyers and sellers in the market. This is true, but it isn't the whole story. Option prices always reflect and are calculated according to certain mathematical formulas and rules. All market players know what these rules dictate, and make their bids and offers accordingly.

So what are these variables that, when combined, go to form an option's price?

1. **Time** – how close the option is to its expiry date
2. **Price** – of the underlying relative to strike price of the option
3. **Volatility** – of the price of the 'underlying'
4. **Interest rates** – now and in the period until the option expires
5. **Dividend yield** – on the 'underlying'

We've met some of these before. Let's just recap on why they are important.

Time

One big factor behind the price of an option is simply how long it has to run to expiry. As a rule, the longer the life of the option, the more valuable it will be. If you think about it, this is obvious. It's because there is a bigger chance that you will be able to exercise the option at a profit before it expires.

Intrinsic value or not?

Another factor is where the price of the underlying stands relative to the exercise price of the option. If the price of the underlying is already above the exercise price of a call option (or below the exercise price of a put option), there's a built-in profit there already. The option has intrinsic value. But this inbuilt profit is directly reflected in the price of the option.

Volatility

As we've seen earlier, the more the underlying price swings around, the greater the chance the option can be exercised or sold at a profit, and therefore the more valuable it will be.

Interest rates

Buying an option is a cheap way of gaining exposure to a parcel of shares with a much larger money value. You might be able to buy an at-the-money call option for say 10% of the value of the underlying shares it represents. This means that you are saving 90% of the cost of the purchase price of shares and earning notional interest on the capital you haven't committed. This is reflected in the price of the option. And it follows that any change in interest rate will have an impact on the price of the option.

Dividends

Although they give you exposure to shares, or an index, you don't actually own the underlying shares if you hold an option. Therefore you don't qualify for dividend payments. So option prices also reflect the impact of dividends foregone.

The practicalities of calculating options prices

In reality you don't have to worry too much about the precise mechanics of how option pricing works. There is simple software available that does the job for you (see Chapter 11 for more information).

Typical software allows you to input the option's characteristics (put or call, days to expiry, strike price, underlying price, interest rates, dividend rate) and work out the fair value of the option for a given level of volatility.

Alternatively you can put in all of the above plus the option's market price and work out implied volatility.

Simple tools like this also allow you to put in hypothetical prices for volatility and the price of the underlying, and work out easily what might happen to the price of the option if your assumptions prove correct. Over the page is an an example of how it might work.

Example 6.1 – Assessing an options trade

Problem:

- Universal Widgets has a share price of 100p; its recent trading range is 95p to 130p.

- Historic volatility has ranged from 25% to 45% and is currently 30%. It does not pay a dividend. Interest rates are currently 3.75%.

- There is an at-the-money call option in Universal Widgets with 70 days to go to expiry. Its price is 4.5p.

- The company's results are due in ten days and you think they may be the catalyst for a re-rating on the shares. What sort of return could you get from buying the option?

Solution:

- Assume the shares trade at 125p in ten days time. They now have 60 days to go to expiry.

- Assume volatility rises to 45% as a result. Inputting the results into a simple option price calculator suggests the price in that eventuality would be 26.6p.

This is shown in the screen shot opposite.

In other words, if the shares rise by 25% to close at the top of their recent trading range and volatility increases to its historic high as a result, we can work out the impact on the option price and whether or not the trade is worth doing.

Equally, we can see what happens if there are less extreme movements, or if the movements are extreme but take longer to materialise. We simply input different parameters into the software and press the calculate button to find the probable option price.

The software I used in this case is called Optimum. It is free to download from www.warp9.org/nwsoft.

You'll probably have noticed that, at the bottom of the screen shot, there is a row of numbers under the heading 'Sensitivities'. These are 'The Greeks'.

Figure 6.3 – Pricing an option using Optimum

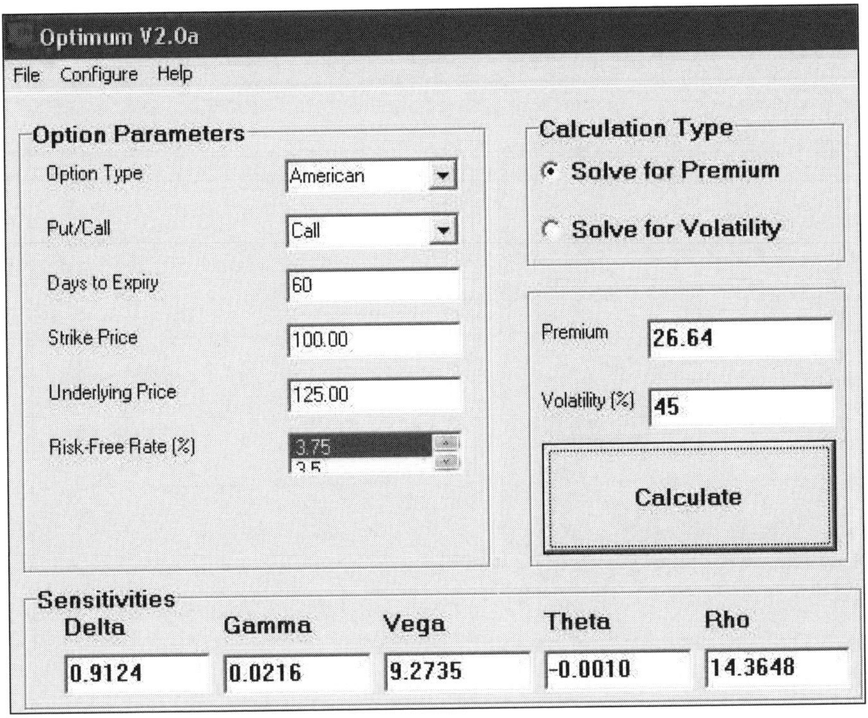

Optimum V2.0a

File Configure Help

Option Parameters

Option Type	American
Put/Call	Call
Days to Expiry	60
Strike Price	100.00
Underlying Price	125.00
Risk-Free Rate (%)	3.75 / 3.5

Calculation Type

⦿ Solve for Premium
○ Solve for Volatility

Premium **26.64**

Volatility (%) **45**

Calculate

Sensitivities

Delta	Gamma	Vega	Theta	Rho
0.9124	0.0216	9.2735	-0.0010	14.3648

© Nigel Webb Software

The Greeks

A by-product of calculating an option's price is that we can also get the software program to work out what separate impact a change in each of the key parameters of the price might have.

The parameters are always identified by Greek letters, but don't let that put you off. We can explain them in simple terms as follows-

Table 6.5 – Summary of the Greeks

Term	Means the change in option price for a given move in . .
Delta	underlying price
Gamma	delta
Theta	reduction in days to expiry
Vega	volatility
Rho	interest rates

There are just a couple of things to note here.

1. Delta will be *positive for a call option and negative for a put option*, indicating that the prices move in opposite direction.

2. By the same token, *theta (which relates to time) is always negative*, since reduction in days to expiry always results in a fall in the option's value. Theta – the daily loss in time value – gets progressively large the nearer the option gets to expiry.

For now, let's just note these terms and what they mean. We can apply them to trading strategies, but you can trade options perfectly well using the method I described in Example 6.1, provided you find the right type of stock and exercise good judgement.

You should, however, never buy an option without knowing what the underlying volatility is now, and where you expect it to go. When you buy an option you are buying volatility. You need to try and buy at low volatility and sell at a higher level of volatility since an increase in volatility usually results in an increase in the option's value.

Equally, when you buy an option you need to know all the key announcement dates that will impact on the share (and hence option) price. This doesn't rule out something appearing out of the blue, of course.

There are a couple of final things to remember about option pricing.

One is that there are two different ways in which options can normally be exercised, and the exercise method affects their price. The two different styles are

American style exercise and *European style* exercise. This is nothing whatsoever to do with where the options are listed or what companies they apply to. They are simply the name of different conventions.

- **American style** means you can exercise the option at *any time* up to expiry.

- **European style** means you can only exercise the option on *the day of expiry.*

In the UK all equity options are American style expiry. Some index options are European style expiry. European style options carry no risk of early exercise and are therefore normally cheaper than the American style equivalent, other things being equal.

The second important point is that option pricing is applicable to any option in any market for any commodity, stock market index, or share. The language of options is universal. You need only know the strike price, underlying price, time to expiry and volatility to get an approximation of any option price anywhere in the world.

Where to find options

Most stock exchanges or derivatives exchanges in Europe have options available on their leading shares and their benchmark stock market index.

Options that investors like you and me normally trade are those based on individual shares and stock market indices.

Not every share has an option, but most of the leading shares do. It's obviously impractical for every company to have an option available – dealers would find it hard to keep track of them all. So the exchanges regulate which shares have options.

They keep the list down to the biggest companies, or at least those whose shares are most actively traded. In London for example, just under 90 shares have options available. The table opposite shows you which ones they are.

In London, there are also options available on the FTSE 100 index. Index options are settled for cash at expiry on the basis of £10 per index point. Index option prices are quoted in index points too, so you need to multiply by £10 to get the cost of a single contract. An index option price at 150, for example, would cost £1,500 per contract to buy.

Equity options are (with very few exceptions) based on 1,000 shares per contract, so you need to multiply the option price in pennies by 1,000 to get the cost of the contract. An equity option priced at 50p will cost £500 per contract to buy (50p x 1,000).

Table 6.6 – List of LIFFE UK equity options stocks

3i	EMAP	P&O
Alliance & Leicester	EMI	Reckitt Benckiser
Amvescap	Gallaher	Reed Elsevier
Anglo American	GSK	Rentokil Initial
ARM	Hanson	Reuters
Astra Zeneca	HBOS	Rio Tinto
Aviva	Home Retail Group	Rolls-Royce
BAA	HSBC	Royal & Sun Alliance
BAE	ICI	Royal Bank of Scotland
Barclays	Imperial Tobacco	SAB Miller
BAT	Intercontinental Hotels	Sage
BG	International Power	Sainsbury (J)
BHP Billiton	Invensys	Scottish Power
BOC	ITV	Scottish & Newcastle
Boots	Kingfisher	Scottish & Southern Energy
BP	Ladbrokes	Royal Dutch Shell
British Airways	Land Securities	Shire Pharmaceuticals
British Energy	Legal & General	Smith & Nephew
BSKyB	Lloyds TSB	Standard Chartered
BT	LogicaCMG	Standard Life
Cable & Wireless	LSE	Tesco
Cadbury Schweppes	Man	Tomkins
Capita	Marks & Spencer	Unilever
Carnival	Mitchells & Butlers	United Utilities
Centrica	Morrison (Wm.)	Vodafone
Colt Telecom	National Grid	Whitbread
Compass	Next	William Hill
Corus	Northern Rock	WPP
Diageo	PartyGaming	Wolseley
DSG International	Pearson	Xstrata

Source: EuronextLIFFE

Option trading as speculation

Options can work for you in whatever way you want them to. You can use them to speculate or you can use them as insurance. Options are good for speculating because they allow you to get the full benefit of a movement in the price of an underlying for a small outlay.

Although this process can work in reverse if the price of the underlying share falls, you have a strict limit on your losses. **If you buy an option you can't lose more than it cost you.** Contrast this with the unlimited potential losses inherent in futures, CFDs and spread betting.

Provided you simply buy and sell options (in that order) and only invest in the option an amount you are prepared to lose, you have:

1. Gearing to a movement in the underlying price in the right direction during the life of the option, and

2. A known and unvarying risk.

Figure 6.4 – The prices page for a September 2006 index option on LIFFE

Euronext.liffe Equity Prices Service - Prices Page - Microsoft Internet Explorer

Address: http://www.liffe-data.com/PricesPageAll.aspx?t=OESX/O.LI

15Sep06

Calls										Strike	Puts									
Settle[1]	OI[2]	Total Daily Vol[3]	Vol[4]	Last Trade at	Last Trade	Bid	Offer	AQ Bid	AQ Offer	Strike	AQ Bid	AQ Offer	Bid	Offer	Last Trade at	Last Trade	Vol[4]	Total Daily Vol[3]	OI[2]	Settle[1]
656.5	3085	3	3	09:44:10	607	-	-	607	619	5225	0	1.5	-	-	-	-	-	0	23796	-
606.5	10	0	-	-	-	-	-	557	569	5275	0	1.5	-	-	-	-	-	0	4514	-
556.5	2887	0	-	-	-	-	-	507.5	519.5	5325	0	1.5	-	3.5	-	-	-	0	23689	0.5
507	176	0	-	-	-	-	-	457.5	469.5	5375	0	1.5	-	5	-	-	-	0	2775	0.5
457	5152	0	-	-	-	-	-	407.5	419.5	5425	0	2	-	-	-	-	-	0	16801	0.5
407.5	20	0	-	-	-	-	-	358	370	5475	0	2	-	1	-	-	-	0	4926	0.5
357.5	7626	0	-	-	-	-	-	308	320	5525	0	2.5	0.5	-	10:10:42	1.5	1	1	20943	1
308	537	0	-	-	-	-	-	259	271	5575	0	3	1.5	2	10:42:00	2	20	20	11110	1.5
259	14425	2	2	09:28:18	214	-	-	210	222	5625	1.5	4.5	3	3.5	10:33:35	3	75	220	32828	2
210	2879	22	2	10:13:54	169	165.5	170	162.5	174.5	5675	3.5	6.5	5	6	09:54:23	6	75	76	14859	3.5
162.5	17936	453	40	10:21:09	124	120.5	124.5	117	129	5725	7.5	11.5	9.5	11	10:36:22	10	5	1021	25345	5.5
117.5	2954	150	25	09:58:35	71	80.5	83	76.5	86.5	5775	16	20	18	19.5	10:33:44	18	5	2975	16109	10.5
76.5	22644	417	10	10:36:14	50	46.5	48.5	41.5	51.5	5825	30	36	34	36	10:28:43	35	1	2543	22703	20
43.5	5946	812	85	09:58:57	18	22.5	24.5	19.5	25.5	5875	54	64	59.5	61.5	09:56:58	67	1	75	3458	37
20.5	19171	154	10	10:36:16	10	8.5	10	6.5	10.5	5925	89	101	95.5	98	09:40:09	100.5	98	91	20120	63.5
7.5	3122	59	15	10:24:50	3.5	2.5	3	1	4	5975	133	145	138.5	142.5	10:47:11	139.5	2	36	907	100.5
2.5	18688	25	1	10:37:39	1	0.5	1.5	0	2	6025	181	193	186	191	10:04:12	193.5	24	44	11357	145.5
0.5	5027	0	-	-	-	-	1	0	1.5	6075	230.5	242.5	-	-	-	-	-	0	32	193.5
-	14056	0	-	-	-	-	0.5	0	1.5	6125	280.5	292.5	-	-	-	-	-	0	100	243
-	5741	0	-	-	-	-	-	0	1.5	6175	330.5	342.5	-	-	-	-	-	0	15	292.5
-	22380	0	-	-	-	-	-	0	1.5	6225	380.5	392.5	-	-	-	-	-	0	4535	342.5
-	483	0	-	-	-	-	-	0	1.5	6275	430.5	442.5	-	-	-	-	-	0	-	392.5
-	9160	0	-	-	-	-	10	0	1.5	6325	480	492	-	-	-	-	-	0	1	442.5
-	1720	0	-	-	-	-	0.5	0	1.5	6375	530	542	-	-	-	-	-	0	-	492.5
-	8149	0	-	-	-	-	0.5	0	1.5	6425	580	592	-	-	-	-	-	0	20	542.5

Autoquote, developed by Euronext.liffe in conjunction with market participants, is the exchange's theoretical pricing model for options. All Autoquote prices are shown in green. All LIFFE CONNECT® or traded prices appear in black and bold. Where a trade has taken place, the price on screen is the last traded price.

© LIFFE

If you typically invest, say, £5,000 in an individual share, it makes sense, if you want to use an option, to invest much less than this – say £750 – in an equivalent option. You would be unlucky in the extreme to lose all of the £5,000 in the shares, but it is easy to lose most or all of the £750 in the option if the underlying price goes the wrong way or if the move you expect doesn't happen until after the option expires.

So the big thing to remember if you're using options to speculate – as most option investors do – is that your judgement about the magnitude and direction of a change in price of the underlying has to be right. But that's not all. It has to be right *within the timescale of the option*. It's no good being wrong at any time. But it's also no good being right about the price of a share if the move you expect happens after the option you've bought has expired.

Even so, it's perfectly possible to speculate successfully using options, partly because options give you big gearing to underlying price movements. One big success can make up for lots of small losses.

Let's go back to our earlier Example 6.1 and see how the scenario we described there works out in terms of gearing.

Example 6.2 – Gearing in options

The facts

- Universal Widgets has a share price of 100p; its recent trading range is 95p to 130p.

- Historic volatility has ranged from 25% to 45% and is currently 30%. It does not pay a dividend. Interest rates are currently 3.75%

- There is an at-the-money call option in Universal Widgets with 70 days to go to expiry. Its price is 4.5p.

- The company's results are due in ten days and you think they may be the catalyst for a re-rating on the shares. What sort of gearing could you get from buying the option?

The gearing

Assume the shares trade at 125p in ten days time. They now have 60 days to go to expiry. Assume volatility rises to 45% as a result. Inputting the results into a simple option price calculator suggests the price in that eventuality would be 26.6p.

Look at the gearing this has given you.

* *Underlying price* up from 100p to 125p – a gain of **25%**
* *Option price* up from 4.5p to 26.6p – a gain of **491%**.

As we mentioned before, gearing works both ways. Gearing in both directions is lower if the option has some intrinsic value when you buy it. But the option itself will cost you more in this eventuality. The risk will be less, but you will need to commit more capital, and the prospective return if all goes well will be lower.

There are other wrinkles to bear in mind when dealing in low-priced options, which we'll cover in the chapter on dealing. Suffice to say, if you are buying a low-priced option, the bid-offer spread will be wide in percentage terms, and you will need to make up the flat rate dealing charges before you make a profit.

Option trading as insurance

Options, especially index options, are also good for hedging your bets. Options can be used in the same way and for the same reason you buy insurance. It's one reason that the price of an option is sometimes called its *premium*. You buy insurance to protect yourself from a specific risk. The less likely the event, the cheaper will be the insurance. Either way, you are paying a premium, which you are happy to write off, for the sake of peace of mind.

Options work particularly well as insurance if you've got a broadly spread portfolio of shares that you don't want to sell, maybe because you'd have a big capital gains tax bill. Let's look at a simple example.

Example 6.3 – Hedging with options, FTSE 100

Say you are nervous about the market and want to protect yourself in some way in case there's a sharp drop in the index. You can do this by buying an at-the-money put option on the index.

However, we saw earlier that at-the-money index options can entail a big outlay. At the time of revising this chapter for the second edition, the FTSE stood at 5838. An at-the-money put with a 5825 strike price for expiry three months hence cost 150. This meant you paid £1500 to *insure* a broad portfolio of index stocks worth roughly £58,250. The premium was 2.6% of the portfolio's value. Whether or not you were comfortable with paying this premium would depend on how worried you were about the situation.

Let's say, for the sake of argument, you had £120,000 invested in a broad range of eight or ten UK shares. You could buy two contracts of the three-month FTSE 5825 put for an outlay of £3,000.

Then let's say that over the course of a month the FTSE 100 drops from 5838 to 5000. With no change in volatility but the loss of a month's time value, the price of the option would have risen to approximately 650, or £13,000, a profit on your two contracts of £10,000.

If your portfolio of £120000 had fallen in line with the index, it would now be worth £102,775, but you have made a gain of £10,000 on the option trade, reducing your net loss to just over £7,000, ignoring the cost of the option. If you hadn't insured in this way, your loss would have been £17,000. That's not ideal, but it's better than doing nothing at all. And if you'd sold your shares, you might have had capital gains tax to pay.

Let's just summarise the maths.

Table 6.6 – The impact of using index options to hedge against a falling market

Item	Initially	A month later
Index value	5838	5000
Portfolio value	£120,000	£102,775
Price of index option	150	650
Value of 2 contracts	-£3,000	£13,000
Profit on contracts	0	£10,000
Net value of portfolio	£117,000	£112,775

The net value of the portfolio is cut by £3,000 to £117,000 if the market remains unchanged for the month. If the market falls as indicated, the hedge reduces the potential total loss in value from £17,225 to £7,225 – or just £4,225 if you adjust the original portfolio value for the cost of the option.

This technique is known as *hedging*, and options are ideal for it, because of their known downside risk and gearing to movement in the underlying.

The only problem for investors is the 'lumpiness' of index option contracts. Don't worry too much about this because it is possible to buy index options through the medium of spread betting. In this case you can simply vary the size of your stake to reflect the cover you need for your particular portfolio.

A standard index option contract is £10 a point and protection conferred by it is therefore £10 times the index value, currently about £58,000. If your portfolio is, for example, £25,000, you could stake roughly £4 a point (divide your portfolio's current value by the index to get the right number) to get the correct size of 'cover'.

Insurance is always cheaper if you're prepared to pay an excess. Options are no different. You can pay an excess in this case by the degree to which the put option you choose is out-of-the-money. If you are prepared to bear the first 200 points of the index's fall, for example, the insurance premium will be cheaper. An index option with a 5625 strike was, at the time of writing, 85 compared to the 150 you would pay for the at-the-money 5825 strike price.

Finally, you can also insure individual stocks if you feel there is specific risk out there that you want to cover. Remember that options normally relate to parcels of 1,000 underlying shares, so to get your hedge you need to buy one put option contract for every 1,000 shares you hold.

We'll go into the mechanics of this a bit more in our chapter on strategies, but to all intents and purposes, it really is that simple.

Postscript – writing options

For each buyer of an option there must be someone who is prepared to take the opposite tack. While an option buyer acquires the right but not the obligation to take a particular course of action, the person on the other side of the transaction assumes the obligation but not the right. This person is called an option *writer*.

The liability that the writer takes on is the obligation to make (or take, in the case of a put) delivery of the underlying stock at the exercise price if the holder exercises the option. So just as the buyer of the option thinks that the underlying share price will move sufficiently to more than offset the cost of the option, the writer expects that it will not.

In fact, in practical terms, an option writer is simply an option trader whose initial transaction is on the selling side rather than the buying side. Writing options actually makes money more often than not, but it's a risky strategy for you to undertake if you don't have the cash or shares to meet your obligations if the price of the underlying move against you.

If you write an option, you take on obligations, but you also get a reward. You receive the option premium, that is to say, the price paid by the buyer of the option. It's yours to keep. If the option expires unexercised and worthless, it's money for nothing.

Many brokers will not allow clients to write options because they feel it exposes them to too much risk. They may need evidence that you hold the underlying shares before allowing you to do this. If you can do it, however, it opens up a range of interesting trading strategies. Writing options is one of the building blocks of the strategies we'll look at in Chapter 11.

Having had this comprehensive examination of what makes the options market tick, the next chapter looks at a newer options-like market – *covered warrants*. It is slightly shorter because we will be referring back quite a bit to the concepts introduced in this chapter.

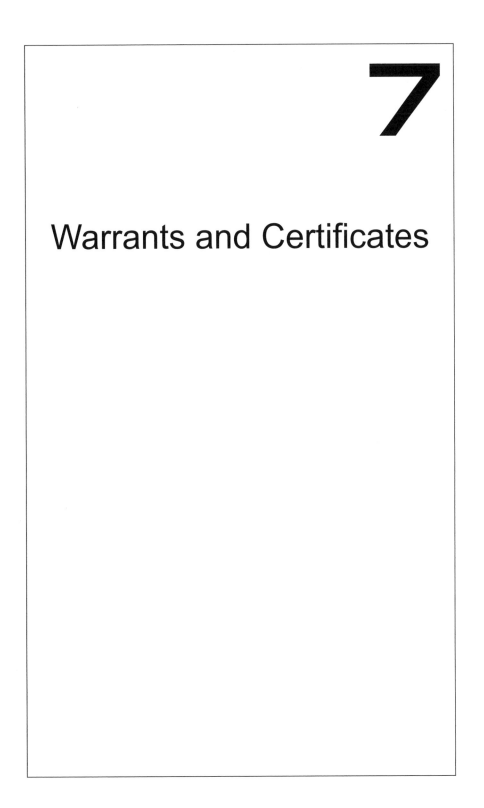

7

Warrants and Certificates

The last chapter looked at options, and we mentioned there that warrants worked in a similar way. So a lot of the material in Chapter 6 will be relevant here. This is particularly true when we come to ideas about how warrants are valued and how you can trade them.

So to some degree what we're going to concentrate on in this chapter is how warrants *differ* from options. What complicates matters is that there are two different types of warrants you can invest in, *traditional warrants* and *covered warrants*.

Few private investors use traditional warrants, so we're only going to mention them in passing, and I think it's probably a good thing to get this out of the way at the outset. we'll also cover the market in certificates, a specialised type of warrant that works like an index tracker, in brief at the end of the chapter.

Traditional warrants

A traditional warrant is a transferable, quoted option certificate issued by a company. It entitles the holder to buy a specific number of shares in the company at a specific price during a specified period of time in the future.

This looks suspiciously like a call option. But there are some differences between a call option and a traditional warrant.

The main one is that you may only be able to exercise it some time in the future. Traditional warrants are often issued as equity *kickers* to enhance the terms of an acquisition or a bond issue. In this case, the company won't want the extra shares coming on stream until it has had a chance to make the acquisition work and get the profits up, or pay back some of the bond.

So the warrant might start to become exercisable two or three years after the event. The other point is that the company will want to see some uplift in its share price before the new shares that will result from the warrant come into the calculation.

Table 7.1 – Traditional warrants versus LIFFE options

Feature	Traditional Warrant	LIFFE Option
Issuer	*Company*	*Exchange*
Type of underlying	Small companies; Inv. Trusts	Big companies.; indices
Exercise period	In the future*	From now to expiry
Exercise price	Out-of-the-money*	In/at/out-of-the-money
New strikes created	No	Yes
Expiry	Some years ahead*	Maximum 9 months
Where dealt	LSE	LIFFE
Calls/puts	Calls only	Calls and puts

*at time of issue

In other words the exercise price of the warrant will probably be substantially higher than the prevailing share price at the time the warrant is issued. To use option terminology, the warrant will be deeply out-of-the-money at the time it is issued. There is a single exercise price throughout the warrant's life. This contrasts with LIFFE equity options where new exercise (or 'strike') prices are automatically created as the underlying prices move up and down.

It follows from its other characteristics that a warrant like this will also have time to expiry that is substantially longer than a normal option. LIFFE equity options typically run for no more than nine months ahead, while a traditional warrant could have a life of five years or more.

The other point about traditional warrants is they trade alongside the company's shares on the stock exchange, not through LIFFE. They are also almost all calls, that's to say they give the holder the right to buy the shares.

Finally whereas normal options are usually available in the shares of companies that are household names, warrants are generally issued by less well-known entities.

Warrants issued by investment trusts account for about a quarter of the 85 traditional warrants in issue. This is largely because many investment trust warrants issued during the early 1990s have now expired. Most of the current traditional warrant issuers are AIM-listed companies.

Valuing traditional warrants

I don't want to spend too much time on traditional warrants, as the chances are that you won't be dealing in them. But it is worth noting a couple of other ways in which they differ from the way options are valued.

Traditional warrants are effectively long-expiry call options that are often deeply out-of-the-money. At a basic level you can value them in much the same way you would an option and the same things influence their price: the volatility of the underlying share; the position of the share price relative to the exercise price; and the length of time to expiry.

In the warrant market, however, the terms used differ slightly from those for options, even though they mean much the same. The exercise price is called the *conversion price*. Instead of an expiry date there is a *conversion period*. This is the period, which often lies some time in the future, during which the holder has the option to convert the warrant into the underlying shares.

LIFFE equity options usually represent a bundle of 1,000 shares, but warrants are different. In most cases traditional warrants are convertible into the underlying shares in a 1:1 ratio. You need to check the conversion terms before investing to make sure you are clear on this particular point, however, because this determines how many warrants you actually want to deal in. As we'll see later in the chapter, this concept of a conversion ratio applies to covered warrants too.

Figure 7.1 – Tipsheets.co.uk – advice about warrants from McHattie

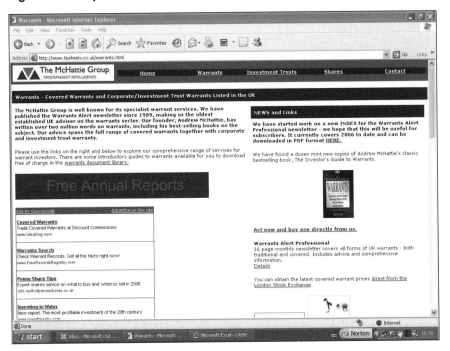

© McHattie Group

Most of the terminology used in connection with warrants is interchangeable with options, but there are some extra terms to master. These arise from the fact that traditional warrants are issued out-of-the-money.

Hurdle rate

Because a traditional warrant may have a lifespan in years and a conversion term that only begins some time in the future, you can work out what annual growth in the share price would be needed to leave the warrant at-the-money (that's to say the share price would equal the conversion price) at the time the conversion period starts. This is known as the *hurdle rate*.

Capital fulcrum point

Traditional warrants can also be assessed on what is called the *capital fulcrum point (CFP)*. The fulcrum point is the percentage per annum rate of growth in the underlying shares that means you could do equally well in percentage terms investing in either the equity or the warrant.

Ideally, investors in warrants are looking for a low premium (i.e. the warrant is not too far out-of-the-money), a low fulcrum point, rising volatility, a long period to go until the conversion rights expire, and relatively high gearing to the underlying movement in the share price. Few warrants possess all of these characteristics.

There are pluses and minuses to dealing in warrants compared to LIFFE options. One is that they are listed on the normal stock exchange and can be dealt in through your usual stockbroker. This applies to covered warrants too. But traditional warrants are one-way only. You can only use them to bet on a rise in price, not on a fall.

On the other hand a traditional warrant generally has a longer period to expiry, which means that the pressure to predict the share price movement correctly within a short period of time isn't as great. On the minus side, their terms are not standardised, unlike traded options.

The big disadvantage of traditional warrants, however, is that they aren't often available in household name companies. Often, only obscure smaller companies and investment trusts issue them. Covered warrants, by contrast – and for that matter equity options – are available in puts as well as calls, in a range of large companies and in stock market indices and leading commodities.

Key Factors when valuing traditional warrants

- Volatility
- Expiry date
- Price of underlying
- Hurdle rate
- Fulcrum point

Covered warrants

I'm going to devote the rest of this chapter to covered warrants. Covered warrants are a new market to London but have been very popular in markets on Continental Europe for a number of years. The London Stock Exchange launched the covered warrants market in late 2002.

But what are covered warrants, how do they work, and how easy is it to deal in them?

Like traditional warrants, covered warrants are close cousins of traded options. Like options, covered warrants come in two main varieties: call warrants and put warrants. Like options, these give the holder the right but not the obligation respectively to buy or to sell shares at a specific price before a known expiry date.

Just like options, there are different ways to exercise covered warrants. As is the case with options -

- *American-style* warrants are those that can be exercised at any time prior to expiry.
- *European-style* ones can be exercised only on the expiry date.

The type of exercise style says nothing about where the company concerned originates, by the way. There are European style warrants on American companies, and vice versa. Remember too that, as with options, most investors will use them to buy and sell, rather than to hold to expiry or exercise.

One of the biggest differences, though, is in the way they are issued. In the case of options, the LIFFE market governs which companies have options available and how different options are issued. In the case of covered warrants, a range of issuers, normally leading investment banks, issues the products as they see fit. The banks compete with each to issue products that will appeal to investors, but there is no formal structure that governs precisely how and under what circumstances new warrants will appear.

Another key point for investors is that like traditional warrants, covered warrants are dealt in through the London Stock Exchange, have conventional EPIC codes and are settled in CREST. Not all private client stockbrokers currently deal in covered warrants, but clients of those that do can deal in shares and covered warrants without finding a new broker. This contrasts with options, where most investors need to have one broker for their share dealing and another for options trading.

The warrants are called *covered* warrants, because the obligation on the issuing bank to supply stock at a specific price if the holder converts must be covered by stock that the bank holds on its own account or has contracted to buy in the market in the event of conversion.

Table 7.2 – Traditional warrants versus covered warrants

Feature	*Traditional*	*Covered*
Issuers	Companies	Banks
Type of underlying	Small cos./Inv. Trusts	Large companies
Calls and puts	Calls only	Calls and puts
Equity/index	Equities only	Equities and indices
UK/foreign cos.	UK only	UK and foreign
Sectors	No	Yes
Commodities	No	Some
Strikes	Out-of-the-money*	In and out-of-the-money
Expiries	Long dated*	Up to 18 months out
Dealt through	LSE	LSE
Spreads	Unregulated	Capped

* at time of issue

Similarities/differences between covered warrants and options

As the market has developed since its launch, however, there are some features common to covered warrants and traded options, as well as some differences too.

Both call and puts issued

First is that issuers have been prepared to issue both call warrants and put warrants, although unlike in the LIFFE options market, in the covered warrant markets there are at present roughly double the number of call warrants as there are put warrants.

Warrants issued on leading companies, stock indices and more

Second is that issuers have issued warrants on both leading companies and stock market indices. The range of companies on which warrants have been issued is not yet as broad as those for which options are available. Index warrants do, however, include some on foreign stock market indices. Warrants have also been issued on sector groups and on some select commodities. These include, at the time of writing, gold bullion and oil.

Figure 7.2 – One of the LSE's covered warrants web pages

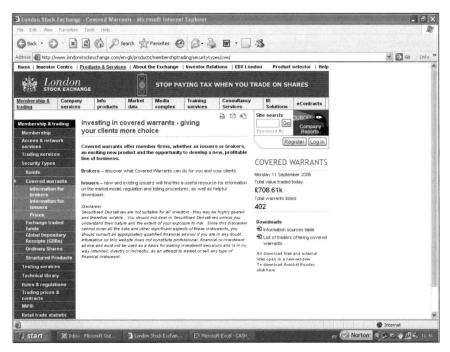

© London Stock Exchange

There are also some warrants on the shares of leading US companies, and there are likely to be more in the future. LIFFE equity options are strictly just on European (UK, Dutch and French) companies.

Expiry dates

Thirdly, expiry dates on covered warrants are generally somewhat longer than for LIFFE options, although not on the whole as long as would be available on some traditional warrants. For the most part warrants have expiries that range up to just over a year ahead. Some certificates (see below) have much longer expiry dates. Expiries in general may, however, lengthen further as the market develops.

Bid-offer spreads

Fourth, bid-offer spreads are tighter in covered warrants than they currently are in many parts of the options market. The LSE has instituted a rule on maximum spreads on covered warrant prices. In the options market spreads are dictated by market makers and have tended to be very wide in percentage terms on low-priced options.

Exotic warrant types

Fifthly, although initially the market only included call and put warrants in shares and indices, as the market has developed a wider range of products has been constructed. These include index tracking certificates, protected trackers, accelerated trackers, inverse trackers and so one. The range of products that could be made available is limited only by the ingenuity of investment banks. We'll look later in the chapter at the certificates market, the main part of the covered warrant arena where these developments have occurred.

Finally, one crucial difference between covered warrants and options is that with covered warrants, the investment bank issuing it is the writer of the option. With LIFFE options, as we explained in the previous chapter, there is nothing in theory to stop a private investor from acting as an option writer. Covered writing of options to generate income is a popular strategy in the options market.

Other strategies that we will cover later in the book also depend on being able to write options. To the extent that private individuals cannot write covered warrants, they are more limited in terms of the role they can play in complex trading strategies.

Table 7.3 – Covered Warrants versus LIFFE Options

Feature	Warrants	Options
Equity and index	Yes	Yes
Calls and puts	Yes	Yes
American/European exercise	Potentially	In index options
Similar no. of calls and puts	No, more calls	Yes
Range of leading shares	Yes	Yes
Foreign shares/indices	Yes	No
Sectors	Yes	No
Commodities	Yes	No
Zero strike products	Yes	No
Exotics	A few	No
Ability to 'write'	No	Yes
Traded through	LSE	LIFFE
Spreads	Capped	Uncapped

Let's round off this quick tour of the covered warrant market by looking at who are the main issuers.

Table 7.4 – Some UK covered warrant issuers

Company	Web address
Goldman Sachs	www.gs-warrants.co.uk
JP Morgan	www.jpmorganinvestor.com
SG	www.warrants.com
DrKW	www.warrants.dresdner.com

Source: London Stock Exchange; FT

You can see from this table that there are some big names here, so although when you buy a warrant you are dealing (via your broker) with a bank (rather than an exchange's clearing house) as the other party involved, you aren't really running much extra risk as a result.

Valuing covered warrants

Earlier in the chapter we found that there were some important practical differences between LIFFE options and covered warrants. It is worth stressing though, that when it comes to valuing warrants, you can employ the same concepts that you use to value options. We covered this at some length in the last chapter, so let's just recap it briefly here.

First things first, though. As with an option, do remember that warrants are much more volatile than the shares or indexes that underly them. So they need handling with care.

You have one advantage with a warrant. If you buy a warrant, your exposure is confined to the amount you pay out for the security. You can't lose more than you invest. You can lose all of it, or some of it, quite easily. The flip side, of course, is that the gearing to a movement in the underlying share, sector or index is quite high too. There's big money to be made if your judgement proves correct.

The concepts of underlying price versus exercise price, time to expiry, volatility and the like are all used to value warrants, in much the same way as they are used to value options. The only difference is that you may need to apply an adjustment factor if the warrant isn't convertible into the underlying share on a 1:1 basis. It's common sense really. You can use an option valuation tool to value a warrant. But if, for example, it takes 10 warrants to convert into one share, you will need to divide the

> ## Factors affecting a covered warrant price
>
> - Time to expiry
> - Price of underlying
> - Exercise price
> - Volatility of underlying price
> - Interest rates
> - Dividends on underlying
> - Cover ratio of warrant

resulting price calculation by 10 to get to the correct warrant price. The factor you need to apply to get from the 1:1 relationship to the one that's correct for the warrant is known as the *cover ratio*, or *parity*.

For example in the case of an index warrant on the FTSE 100 we might have a price of 30p and parity of 1,000. Multiplied together this means that the price of the warrant equates to 300 index points (1000 x 0.3), similar to the typical price you might have on a LIFFE index option.

Figure 7.3 – The covered warrants home page on SG's web site

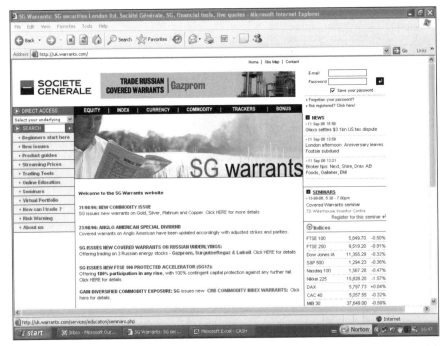

Many issuers have warrant calculators on their web sites, which in effect incorporate an option valuation model but add in the necessary bits and pieces that are specific to warrants, such as the cover ratio.

Other than this, the familiar option-related ideas of intrinsic value, time value, in-the-money, at-the-money, out-of-the-money, delta, gamma and so on, all apply to warrants in exactly the same way as they do to options. You can consult the previous chapter to review these as you wish.

As with options, you can use valuation software to calculate the right price for the warrant (or option) given various assumptions about where the underlying shares might go, and the level and direction of expected volatility. By using a series of *what if* scenarios, you can see where the price of the warrants might end up in response to a specific move in the price of a share or index.

Which warrant (or option) to buy for speculation?

- You must have a **strong directional view** on the underlying
- Expected **timing** of the move governs the length of expiry you choose
- Expected **size** of the move governs whether warrant is in or out-of-the-money
- If several similar warrants are available, choose the one with **lowest volatility**

This is very similar to the technique you might use for an option, first looking at the potential move in the underlying share or index, based perhaps on its price chart and the position of key support and resistance levels, and then looking at trends in volatility and working out how that might change. Plug the two together and you can work out how profitable a particular trade might be on both a realistic and best-case scenario.

Basic Strategies

As with options, remember that warrants aren't just for speculation. There are two other basic ways you can use them.

Cash extraction

One is to use a warrant as a substitute for a holding in the underlying equity, but using less capital. Let's say you have a holding of 1,000 shares in Vodafone. The current price is 100p. Your time horizon is 18 months. There is an at-the-money call warrant with 18 months to go to expiry that costs 25p. You could sell the shares and buy the warrant. By doing this you free up £750 of capital but still have exposure to the upside in the price above 125p. Your maximum loss is 25p (£250 in total). You can earn interest in the meantime on the £750. This is known as a *cash extraction* trade.

There are drawbacks to this:

1. You don't participate in all of the rise in the price, if there is one.

2. The value of the warrant will decay over time, so if the price you expect doesn't materialise, you are stuck with a wasting asset.

3. On the other hand, your downside risk is limited to 25p, not the 100p that's theoretically at risk if you hold the underlying share.

Hedging

Apart from their role in helping you economise on capital invested, another key role for warrants is that they can be used as a form of insurance.

You might, for example, have a broad portfolio of shares you don't wish to sell. But if you're nervous about the short-term direction of the market you can hedge (or insure) your portfolio by buying an index put warrant. The price of the warrant is your insurance premium. If the market falls, the value of the warrant will rise, and offset the drop in value of your underlying holding.

You can also do this with individual shares, but it's important to match the hedge with the size of your underlying holding so you don't buy too much or too little insurance. Of course if the market rises you have to write off the insurance premium, but you'll probably feel wealthier anyway.

Hedging requires you to make use of one of the numbers that pops out of the valuation model, namely the *delta*. As we found out in the chapter on options, the delta is a measure of how much the option (or warrant) price changes for a 1p move in the price of the underlying. The delta allows you to calculate exactly how many put warrants you need to buy to hedge an existing shareholding or portfolio against a fall in price.

Let's look at an example.

Example 7.1 – Hedging with covered warrants

Let's say you hold 1,000 Vodafone shares and the delta on the put warrant is – 0.5. This means that if the price of Vodafone goes down 1p the price of the warrant goes up 0.5p, and vice versa.

It follows that to match a fall in the price of Vodafone by a gain in the price of the warrant – the reason for hedging – you need to take account of the delta. Take the number of shares you hold and divide it by the delta. In this case 1,000/0.5 = 2000. So you need to buy 2,000 warrants (assuming a 1:1 conversion ratio) to get your insurance cover.

If Vodafone fell by 10p, your 1,000 shares would be worth £100 less. But the delta on the warrant means that it would rise by 0.5p for every 1p fall. The warrant price would rise by 5p, increasing the value of the warrant holding by 5p x 2000 = £100, which would offset the loss on the shares.

Figure 7.4 – Covered warrants statistics on Goldman Sachs's web site

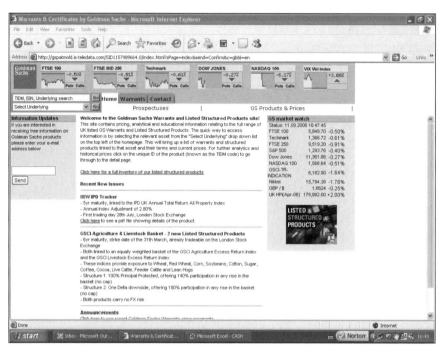

© Goldman Sachs

This is known as *delta neutral hedging*. In fact it isn't quite as simple as it sounds, because the delta changes as the warrant price changes. The more in-the-money a warrant gets the closer to 1.0 will be the delta. The more out-of-the-money the warrant is, the closer the delta will be to zero.

Remember too that delta is not the be all and end all. Volatility is a particularly important factor in determining the way a warrant price moves, and changes in it can easily produce a different price movement to the one that might have been expected from the delta. The delta simply tells you the expected price change for a given movement in the underlying, if all other variables remain unchanged.

It's also worth making the point that for private investors it is much easier to use warrants for accurate hedging than it is options. This is because warrants typically have a 1:1 relationship with the underlying shares, whereas option contracts come in lumpy amounts. If you own 1,500 shares in an option stock, for example, the chances of having a delta on the option that would enable you to buy whole numbers of contracts to get your delta neutral hedge is remote, whereas in the warrant market it is easy.

Hedging and speculation (through simply buying a call warrant if you expect the underlying price to rise, or a put warrant if you expect it to fall) are the most basic strategies you can use with warrants.

How the warrant market may develop from here

Trading in the covered warrants market in the UK started off slowly. In part this was because regulators were somewhat cautious about the participation of private investors. There were also some initial technical hitches experienced by some brokers. One was an initial confusion about whether or not covered warrants trades would bear stamp duty (they don't).

Another factor was the limited number of brokers who are approved to offer private client dealing in covered warrants. This is now improving, with many online brokers now offering a dealing service in covered warrants. There are, however, still a number of brokers who don't. Check the list in table x.x to see who does and doesn't.

We have, however, to assume that these are temporary (albeit rather protracted) teething troubles, and that the market will ultimately grow to rival those on the Continent both in size and in the diversity of products on offer

Volumes remain quite modest. The main changes since the first edition of this book was published have been the launching of warrants based on commodities (gold, silver, platinum and oil), and other underlyings like house prices, and the development of a market in certificates.

Certificates at their basic are covered warrants with a strike price of zero. This means that they track an underlying on a 1:1 basis rather than having substantial gearing to the price of the underlying and its volatility. Having said that, certificates have also been launched that offer a precisely geared return versus an index, that increase if an index falls, that have a protection feature that offers a minimum return that ratchets up as an underlying price rises, or that offer geared upside to an index movement versus normal 1:1 downside.

The range of products here is now so broad that readers interested in this aspect of the market should check the web sites of the main warrant providers (chiefly SG and Goldman Sachs) to find out what new products have been issued.

The following table gives some examples of recently issued products like this in the certificates market.

Table 7.5 – Some interesting products in the certificates market

Type	Characteristic	Expiry	Ticker	Issuer
FTSE100 Reverse Tracker	Price basis 10000 - FTSE100 index level	None	S599	SG
FTSE100 Tracker	Zero exercise price open ended call	None	S591	SG
FTSE100 Protected Accelerator	180% of any index gain if index stays above 4480	Mar-09	SG12	SG
FTSE100 Accelerated Tracker	200% of any gain up to 30%; 160% of any gain above 30%	Mar-09	SG07	SG
FTSE 100 Bonus Tracker	Greater of 6322 or bonus of 40%, if index stays above 3387	Feb-09	G998	Goldman
Stoxx50 PPP Certificate	Pays 100% + 118% of average rise in index in yr to Sept 2008	Sep-08	GA90	Goldman
UK IPD Tracker	1:1 tracking of IPD UK Annual Index	Mar-11	GB04	Goldman

Important Note: Check issuer web sites for detailed terms before dealing

What sort of other products might tempt investors?

There are two aspects here. One is widening the range of markets and instruments for which warrants are available. At the moment we have call and put warrants on a range of UK and international shares and on several UK and US stock market indices.

It is likely eventually that this will be extended to include:

• warrants on **sector baskets** at home and abroad

• warrants on **bonds and interest rates**

• **barrier, knock-out**, and **corridor** warrants

- **Barrier warrants** are puts and calls where the return is capped at a particular price level. If the price hits the barrier a predetermined return is paid out and the warrant expires immediately.

- **Knock-out warrants** expire worthless automatically if the price hits a certain level. Knock-in warrants are worthless *until* the price hits a specific level when the terms kick in and the warrant becomes more valuable the further beyond the barrier the price moves. Corridor warrants pay out a fixed amount for each day the underlying price stays within a predetermined maximum and minimum level.

The normal rationale for products like this is that the restrictions mean that they can be offered more cheaply. Effectively this means more risk for you, the buyer.

Personally, I think there will be very limited demand from private investors for products like these. With the so-called plain vanilla call and put warrants and certificates it is much easier for private investors to conduct gearing and hedging strategies, and relatively easy to value them.

Private investors have been cautious enough using products like options in the past. They may gravitate to using warrants as well, but keeping it simple will be the key to success for issuers, and will also help to keep the regulators happy.

Exchange-Traded Funds

Most investors are familiar with the idea of index-tracking investments. Investing through index-trackers is sometimes known as passive investing. You may even have bought index-tracking unit trusts yourself.

If so, you are in good company. Given that at any one time around three quarters of active investment managers do worse than the index, passive index-tracking investing has become increasingly popular among professional and private investors alike.

But there are some drawbacks to investing in index-trackers through unit trusts.

- All index-tracking funds have **management charges**. The charges are modest compared to actively managed funds, but significant nonetheless. They represent an obstacle to achieving a performance identical to the index.

- Many investors are also a bit wary of the **bureaucracy** associated with buying and selling unit trusts, and the inevitable time delays that sometimes occur. Admittedly the advent of fund supermarkets – which allow you to deal quickly and easily in funds over the phone or on the web – has allayed these fears to some extent. But the processes are more time-consuming than buying and selling a share, especially when you deal online.

This is where exchange-traded funds, or ETFs, come in. They are like index-tracking unit trusts, but you can buy and sell them through a broker, just like any other share.

They've been described as *unit trusts in drag*.

In fact they are a hybrid of a share and a tracker – a share that any investor can buy, but one that moves exactly in step with the index it is designed to replicate. Because of the way they are created, which we'll go into a bit later, they can I think be seen as akin to a derivative. But they don't have the gearing (or the same level of risk) that other derivative products have. If you own an ETF, you can more or less be assured that your holding will perform exactly in line with the index.

History of ETFs

ETFs started off in the early 1990s in the USA. First introduced by the American Stock Exchange, they proved exceptionally popular. The most successful ETF in the USA has been one that replicates the NASDAQ 100 Index. With a ticker symbol QQQ (popularly known as the *cubes*), it is commonly the most actively traded of any stock in the USA.

Figure 8.1 – An ETFs page on the NASDAQ web site

© NASDAQ

So successful have ETFs been in the US that they now have an overall market value of over $340bn.Around 275 ETFs are currently listed on US exchanges (mainly on NASDAQ), including trackers for major market indices, sectors, and investment styles. They also include several that track country indices outside America.

Assets under management within ETFs in the US has grown more than a hundredfold since 1996 and the products continue to attract new devotees. There are around 600 ETFs now listed around the world with assets under management of close to $500bn. ETFs are now listed on 36 exchanges worldwide. There are around 220 ETFs listed in Europe, with funds under management of around $70bn.

When comparing statistics about ETFs, we do need to bear in mind that the changes in the dollar amounts invested reflect not only investor acceptance of the concept, but also the movements in the underlying market as a whole, since this too affects the value of the funds' assets under management. These movements in the Dow Jones, the S&P 500 and the NASDAQ index probably overstated the popularity of ETFs prior to the market peak, but equally have understated the growth in their use since then.

The popularity differs considerably from market to market. In the UK, for example, they have been slower to gain acceptance, whereas in parts of Asia they have taken the market by storm. There are probably some historical and cultural reasons for this. Many British investors are conservative, and may already have made index-tracking investments through the unit trust market.

But they are here to stay and switched-on investors can make good use of them along with all the other return boosting and risk reducing tools described in this book.

How do ETFs work?

Like most derivative products, the underlying theory behind ETFs can be a bit complicated. But really all that you as an investor need to know is that they work in a predictable way and their characteristics.

The table below summarises what you can expect from an investment in an ETF.

Characteristics of ETFs

- You buy and sell them like a share (own ticker symbol).
- You pay a normal broking commission and bid-offer spread.
- They pay a dividend.
- There is a management charge (deducted from dividend income).
- They replicate a stock market index (or a sector).
- They are currently free of transaction taxes (i.e. no stamp duty in the UK).

The method by which ETFs are created is similar in most markets. It goes something like this.

An ETF is pretty much like any other open-ended investment company, like a unit trust. But there is a crucial difference. It is that investors can't subscribe or redeem units for cash. One reason for this is to minimise administration costs. It is also to avoid the fund bearing capital gains tax each time it changes its portfolio to make sure it mimics the index. The big difference between an ETF and a conventional unit trust is therefore that it does not sell units direct to the public.

So what does happen?

ETFs are administered either by index providers or by investment banks. Issuers of ETFs allocate large chunks of the fund – known as *creation units* – to a predetermined list of other investment banks, brokers and large investors. Investment banks then effectively convert the units into shares with a market listing and act as market makers for the ETF.

Creation units are allocated in exchange for a basket of shares that represents the core of the portfolio of the ETF. Investors one tier down can buy and sell the resulting shares freely in the market.

This sounds complicated, so let's forget the jargon. What happens is that the banks and big investors exchange the underlying shares in the index for the units in the ETF, which the banks can then trade, via your broker, with ordinary investors like you and me. Buying and selling between the banks themselves and the issuers keeps the value of the fund on track with the index.

Figure 8.2 – Independent information on ETFs at Trustnet

The pluses and minuses

What are the pluses and minuses of ETFs?

Tracking the index

The most obvious plus is that the ETF's shares track the index. They are a way of getting money into and out of an index quickly. And while you hold them, you have the assurance that you will always perform in line with that index.

Commission charges

For ordinary investors buying and selling the funds in the market, the other key advantage – especially for traditional *buy and hold* investors – is that they have lower dealing charges than a typical tracker fund.

Spreads

You do need to bear in mind one thing, though. On the less actively-traded ETFs in the UK, spreads can be quite wide. There is no doubt that, if you are only looking to buy a small amount, then commission charges can outweigh the saving you might make in management charges over unit trusts. Some brokers have, however, offered commission-free trading of some ETFs if they are placed in an ISA.

Administration charges

Administration charges are generally less than half of one per cent in passively managed ETFs and are paid out of dividend income. Spreads vary but are generally not more than 1%. Bear in mind though that this could be as much as 5p on an ETF priced at 500p. But if the quoted spreads appear wide, some brokers may be able to deal at better prices. ETFs are also free of stamp duty, which cuts the cost of owning them. Some index-tracking unit trusts can match or beat these low costs, but most charge more.

One reason that costs on ETFs can be so low is that the underlying stocks used to assemble the creation units, and in turn the shares in the fund, are transferred back and forth in kind rather than bought or sold in the open market. This means the fund does not undergo any transaction costs or tax penalties when creation units are liquidated. This is in contrast to conventional unit trusts, for example, where performance may suffer as a result of the fund having to sell shares if there is a sharp increase in investors wanting to redeem. In other words, in an ETF, investors are insulated from the adverse effect that trading costs can have on the fund's performance.

Continuous dealing

For many investors, another attraction of ETFs is that dealing is continuous rather than at end-of-day prices, as is the case with conventional unit trusts. If there is a key event in the market and you want to get money in or out quickly, ETFs rather than index-tracking unit trusts are the way to do it. This obviously has a particular attraction to investors when markets are as volatile as they have been in the last few years.

Sector investing

Another key attraction is that ETFs can be used to invest in certain sectors without you having to bear any stock-specific risk.

You might, for example, think that the TMT sector looks attractive but you know that there are stocks in the sector that could issue profit warnings. You don't want to get caught in the wrong stock. By buying a sector ETF you get exposure to all of the stocks in the sector, usually weighted according to their size. If a big stock has a profit warning, that will be reflected in the movement in the sector index and therefore the ETF based on it – but you aren't exposed to that stock alone.

Table 8.1 – UK ETFs versus unit trusts and OEICs

Feature	*ETF*	*UT/OEIC*
Track the index	All	Some
Dealing costs	Broking commission	Initial charge
Spread	Narrow	Can be wide, except for OEIC
Mgt. charges	0.35-0.50%	Similar on trackers, higher on others
Continuous dealing	Yes	No
Sector trackers	No	Very limited choice
Foreign indices	Yes	A few

Where are ETFs quoted?

ETFs are all quoted on mainstream stock exchanges. In London, for example, the LSE set up *extraMark* to be the home for the ETFs and similar securities. extraMark isn't really a separate market. It is simply a subsection of the exchange dedicated to exchange-traded funds.

There are current around 30 equity ETFs currently listed in London. The overwhelming majority of them are issued by iShares, an offshoot of Barclays Global Investors, the world's largest passive investment manager. The range of products on offer has been expanded to include a wide range of overseas market indices, corporate bonds, yield stocks, growth and value segments of the market and a range of UK indices, as well as EFTs based on the gold price and the price of Brent crude oil. Volume has been consistently highest in the FTSE 100 iShare.

The table summarises some of their characteristics.

Table 8.2 – Characteristics of London-listed Equity ETFs

Fund/index tracked	EPIC	Issuer	Currency	AUM(m)	Spread %	TER %	Web address
$ Corporate bond	LQDE	iShares	$	93.4	7.15	0.20	www.ishares.net
$ Govt Bond 1-3	IBTS	iShares	$	102.0		0.20	www.ishares.net
£ Corporate bond	SLXX	iShares	£	155.3	0.38	0.20	www.ishares.net
€ Corporate bond	IBCX	iShares	€	886.2	0.27	0.20	www.ishares.net
€ Govt Bond 1-3	IBGS	iShares	€	104.0		0.20	www.ishares.net
€ Infl. Linked bond	IBCI	iShares	€	122.3	0.47	0.25	www.ishares.net
AEX	IAEX	iShares	€	28.7	0.03	0.30	www.ishares.net
Brent Crude	OILB	Oil Secs.	$	66.0	0.50	1.00	www.oil-etf.com
DJ Asia Pacific Select Dividend	IAPD	iShares	$	10.4		0.59	www.ishares.net
DJ EuroStoxx Growth	IDJG	iShares	€	38.9	0.10	0.40	www.ishares.net
DJ EuroStoxx MidCap	DJMC	iShares	€	145.7	0.23	0.40	www.ishares.net
DJ EuroStoxx Select Dividend	IDVY	iShares	€	111.2	0.19	0.40	www.ishares.net
DJ EuroStoxx SmallCap	DJSC	iShares	€	154.8	0.26	0.40	www.ishares.net
DJ EuroStoxx Value	IDJV	iShares	€	47.2	0.74	0.40	www.ishares.net
DJ EuroStoxx50	EUE	iShares	€	4032.5	0.15	0.15	www.ishares.net
DJ Stoxx50	EUN	iShares	€	871.2	0.28	0.35	www.ishares.net
FTSE Eurofirst 100	IEUT	iShares	€	80.4	0.59	0.40	www.ishares.net
FTSE Eurofirst 80	IEUR	iShares	€	188.5	0.24	0.40	www.ishares.net
FTSE UK Dividend Plus	IUKD	iShares	£	92.3	0.18	0.40	www.ishares.net
FTSE/EPRA Euro Property	IPRP	iShares	€	84.5	0.45	0.40	www.ishares.net
FTSE/Xinhua China 25	FXC	iShares	$	695.7	0.19	0.74	www.ishares.net
FTSE100	ISF	iShares	£	1119.1	0.00	0.40	www.ishares.net
FTSEMid250	MIDD	iShares	£	158.4	0.45	0.40	www.ishares.net
LyxOR Gold Bullion	GBS	LyxOR	$	1546.0	0.74	0.40	www.lyxorgbs.com
MSCI Brazil	IBZL	iShares	$	89.9	1.08	0.74	www.ishares.net
MSCI Eastern Europe	IEER	iShares	$	116.9	0.60	0.74	www.ishares.net
MSCI Emerging Markets	IEEM	iShares	$	229.8	0.57	0.75	www.ishares.net
MSCI Far East (ex-Japan)	IFFF	iShares	$	126.4	0.16	0.74	www.ishares.net
MSCI Japan	IJPN	iShares	$	1951.9	0.24	0.59	www.ishares.net
MSCI Korea	IKOR	iShares	$	47.1	0.12	0.74	www.ishares.net
MSCI North America	INAA	iShares	$	34.4		0.40	www.ishares.net
MSCI Taiwan	ITWN	iShares	$	92.3	0.49	0.74	www.ishares.net
MSCI World	IWRD	iShares	$	208.9	0.92	0.50	www.ishares.net
S&P500	IUSA	iShares	$	2293.6	0.14	0.40	www.ishares.net

Source: iShares, Trustnet

All the ETFs listed in Table 8.2 are issued through iShares (part of BGI), apart from the gold and crude oil ones, which are issued respectively by LyxOr and Oil Securities. An additional 20 or so new commodity based ETFs are expected to have been issued by ETF Securities by the time this edition has been published.

If it seems odd that new equity ETFs are listed relatively infrequently – the list has only expanded from 15 to 30 over the space of three years - it's worth bearing in mind that around 10 sector based ETFs were withdrawn in this period, and also that launching an ETF is appreciably more complicated than launching an index tracker fund. It requires input from and participation by the exchange, the issuer, investment banks, institutional investors, an offshore custodian, market makers, an index provider, a clearing depository and stock market regulators. Each of these players has its own agenda, which may or may not coincide with those of the rest of the group. By comparison, issuing a simple commodity based ETF is simpler.

But regardless of this, let's stress again that –

you can buy and sell ETFs just as you would any other share, through your usual broker.

It is as simple and easy as that.

Why you should consider using ETFs

It should be pretty obvious from all this that ETFs can be of considerable use to you and your portfolio.

Provided you have a reasonable amount to invest, the **charges are low**.

1. They are **easy to deal in** and a good way of getting money into and out of the market quickly. There may be times when you want to do this. You can, of course also do this with futures, spread betting and CFDs – as we've already discovered – but with ETFs, although you have to invest the full amount rather than a down payment, you do not have to worry about expiry dates or gearing. ETFs therefore suit medium-term and long-term investors.

2. **You avoid stock specific risk**. ETFs are not risk-free by any means. If you buy an ETF the market can still go down after you buy it, and if it does you will lose money in the same way you would in an individual share. But you avoid being unduly affected by the problems of any one particular company.

3. You can use ETFs to get **exposure to overseas markets**. The ETFs listed in London include ones based around a wide range of overseas market indices. There is, for example, an ETF listed in London that mimics the S&P 500, one that tracks Chinese shares, and a range of others. See table 8.2 above for details.

4. You can use ETFs to **get exposure to different investment classes,** including corporate bonds, gold and oil, which are difficult and expensive for private investors to deal in individually.

Table 8.3 opposite shows the salient characteristics of the indices on which the various London-listed ETFs are based.

Table 8.3 – Constituents and Beta of London-listed Equity ETFs

Name	Type	EPIC	Index provider	Beta
Gold Bullion Securities	Commodity	GBS	n/a	0.13
iShare $ Investop Corp Bond Fund	Bond	LQDE	GS	0.00
iShare DJ Euro STOXX 50	Non-UK index	EUE	DJ Stoxx	1.02
iShare DJ STOXX 50	Non-UK index	EUN	DJ Stoxx	0.95
iShares AEX	Non-UK index	IAEX	Euronext	0.84
iShares DJ Asia Pacific Select Dividend	Non-UK index	IAPD	DJ Stoxx	n/a
DJ Euro STOXX Growth	Non-UK index	IDJG	DJ Stoxx	0.82
iShares DJEuro STOXX MidCap	Non-UK index	DJMC	DJ Stoxx	0.60
iShares DJEuro STOXX Select	Non-UK index	IDVY	DJ Stoxx	0.75
iShares DJEuro STOXX SmallCap	Non-UK index	DJSC	DJ Stoxx	0.61
iShares DJEuro STOXX Value	Non-UK index	IDJV	DJ Stoxx	0.87
iShares Dollar Govt Bond 1-3	Bond	IBTS	n/a	n/a
iShares Euro Govt Bond 1-3	Bond	IBGS	n/a	n/a
iShares FTSE 250	UK index	MIDD	FTSE	0.60
iShares FTSE EPRA Euro Prop	Non-UK sector	IPRP	FTSE	0.67
iShares FTSE Eurotop 100	Non-UK index	IEUT	FTSE	1.03
iShares FTSE UK Div Plus	UK index	IUKD	FTSE	0.63
iShares FTSE Xinhua China	Non-UK index	FXC	FTSE	0.63
iShares iBoxx Corporate Bond	Bond	SLXX	GS	-0.02
iShares iBoxx € Liquid Corp	Bond	IBCX	GS	-0.01
iShares iFTSE 100	UK index	ISF	FTSE	0.88
iShares MSCI AC Far East ex-Japan	Non-UK index	IFFF	MSCI	0.77
iShares MSCI Brazil	Non-UK index	IBZL	MSCI	1.40
iShares MSCI Eastern Europe	Non-UK index	IEER	MSCI	1.32
iShares MSCI Emerging Markets	Non-UK index	IEEM	MSCI	1.13
iShares MSCI Japan	Non-UK index	IJPN	MSCI	0.68
iShares MSCI Korea	Non-UK index	IKOR	MSCI	1.05
iShares MSCI North America	Non-UK index	INAA	MSCI	n/a
iShares MSCI Taiwan	Non-UK index	ITWN	MSCI	0.76
iShares MSCI World	Non-UK index	IWRD	MSCI	0.60
iShares S&P 500	Non-UK index	IUSA	S&P	0.81
iShares € Inflation Linked Bond	Bond	IBCI	GS	0.06
Oil Securities Ltd	Commodity	OILB	n/a	0.31

Source: iShares; Sharescope

As a footnote to the above table, the beta shows the expected percentage movement for each 1% movement in the market as a whole. A beta of 1.33 means that if the market rises 10%, the likelihood is that the ETF in question will go up 13.3%. And it works the same on the way down.

Betas higher than 1 mean the share in question is more volatile than the market as a whole. Less than 1 means it is less volatile.

One of the other good things about ETFs is that they open up the possibility of trading bonds, commodities and overseas markets as well as UK indices. There are a number of theories and indicators that investors can use to try and pinpoint when a particular market might be at a turning point and some software products that you can use to take advantage of these. We take a closer look at these in Chapter 11.

One regrettable fact about the changes to the ETFs market in the last three years has been the withdrawal of sector ETFs. These used to be a way of playing the well documented patterns of 'sector rotation' (individual sectors coming into and going out of favour in a predictable sequence) with comparative safety, getting exposure to all of the stocks in the sector, rather than undergoing the risk of picking the one that does worse than all the others.

Nonetheless, you can use ETFs to focus on the prospects for a particular market or asset class and back that judgement without going to the bother of analysing individual shares or, in the case of overseas markets, bonds and commodities, having to tackle complicated settlement issues.

Figure 8.3 – the iShares home page, prices of selected issues

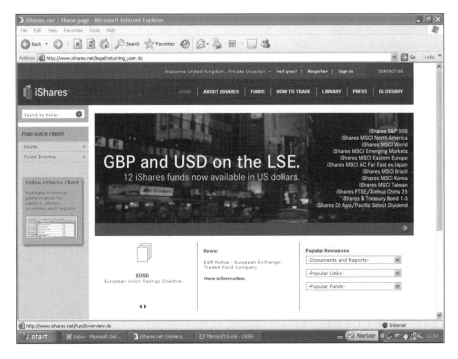

© iShares

Let's summarise the attractions of ETFs:

> ### Why use ETFs?
>
> - Charges are low, dealing is easy
> - There is no expiry date, so this suits medium/long-term view
> - They allow rapid deployment of cash
> - They avoid stock-specific risk
> - You trade equity markets, bonds and commodities, not individual stocks
> - They enable use of market timing software
> - They allow you to focus on a limited number of variables
> - You can use them in conjunction with other derivatives to tailor your market exposure

Although ETFs are best used for gaining medium-term exposure in the market, they can also be used speculatively for the short-term. Some brokers will allow ETFs to be sold short, while shorting an ETF indirectly is always possible through a CFD.

Of more use to many investors is having an ETF as a core holding and using other derivatives to hedge your exposure. A typical strategy might be to have a significant investment in the market via an ETF. If from time to time you feel that the index may drop back, you can hedge your ETF position by selling an index future, buying an index put option, or taking out a down spread bet in the appropriate amount of money. Once you feel the risk has passed, you can then remove the hedge.

By hedging in this way you can avoid having to sell the underlying market exposure that you have via the ETF, on which you may have significant gains that, if you sold, might attract capital gains tax. The example below shows how this works:

Example 8.1 – Simple hedging of an ETF using a spread bet

Problem

*   You hold 10,000 shares of FTSE 100 ETF purchased at 525p. Your holding is currently worth £57,500 and your profit is currently £5,000. You have no unused CGT allowance. The index is currently 5,750

*   You believe the market will fall by 15% in the next three months. You do not want to sell the ETF, because to do so will incur CGT.

Solution

*   Continue to hold ETF. Using spread betting, sell FTSE 100 at 5,750 in £10 a point.

*   Assume the market falls to 5250. ETF holding is now worth £52500, a decrease of £5,000.

*   Close your spread betting position by buying £10 at 5250 *for a profit of £5,000* (500 points x £10).

*   Profit on the spread bet offsets fall in value of holding. The only dealing cost is the spread betting firm's spread (say 10 ticks) multiplied by the stake, or £100 in this example. Selling the ETF would, in this example, have incurred a CGT liability for a 40% taxpayer of £2,000.

This example illustrates how you can use the spread bet to neutralise your exposure to the market for as long as you feel there is a risk present. The flip side is that if you are wrong and the market rises, any gain on the ETF will also be neutralised by a loss on the spread bet.

Non-UK ETFs

In the first edition of this book we looked in brief at ETFs that were available in a range of other markets including the USA, Europe, and Japan. Since then, however, the expansion in the range of markets and asset classes covered by UK listed ETFs makes this largely unnecessary. It is much simpler for UK based investors to use UK listed ETFs to gain exposure to overseas markets and assets like bonds, oil and gold.

Where ETFs go from here

There's no doubt that the volumes traded in ETFs in many European markets and especially in the UK have left a little to be desired, partly because of the availability of other derivatives. I think part of the problem is also education and awareness. These products remain an essential tool in every private investor's locker, but issuers have to keep expenses low, so there is little money left over to promote them actively

Many investors who might be the natural users of the product are sceptical. Some index-tracking unit trusts (although by no means a majority) can be purchased on lower charges than ETFs.

And since they generate low (or no) commissions for advisers, IFAs and others have been generally reluctant to promote them. Ask your IFA what he thinks of them and quiz him as to whether his views are influenced by commission rates.

Fee-based asset managers have a different tale to tell. Some have begun using them actively. And by using ETFs, discretionary investment managers can keep fees to clients down and their own margins up. In addition, the market is opening up for ETFs in the Middle East and Eastern Europe. There is even talk of a Shari'a-compliant ETF to allow Islamic investors the option of investing in this way.

The methods of doing this are straightforward: use ETFs to execute views on specific sectors and markets across the firm's entire client base, minimise stock-specific risk and keep administrative hassles to a minimum. Some fund managers are beginning to take on board what ETFs are and beginning to advise their clients accordingly.

In fact, the selling point for ETFs is much like mundane consumer products. They do exactly what it says on the tin.

9

Dealing

Even if you are experienced at dealing in shares and bonds, you need to read this chapter.

All of the tools we've looked at in the toolbox have their own quirks and idiosyncrasies. Many have a different vocabulary to the one you might use for dealing in shares. Although the differences may be subtle, they are important.

We have ordered this chapter very simply. It looks at the specifics of placing orders in the different products discussed in this book, taking each one in turn. It also looks at the costs involved. Some of these may be hidden from view, so you need to take care. As we'll stress again in the next two chapters, which cover some of the strategies you can employ, you need to examine all of the cost angles before you trade. It's not particularly time-consuming or complicated, but it may save you money.

There are more things to consider than you might think. Many of the products we've looked at can be substitutes for each other in some trades, so the relative cost of trading each one is an important consideration.

Let's take a look at some of the angles.

Ten questions to ask yourself about dealing

1. Do you need a **new broker** to trade the product?
2. Do you have to deposit a **minimum amount** to open an account with the broker?
3. What do you **need to specify** when dealing?
4. What's the lowest **financial commitment** per trade?
5. What are its **margin requirements**?
6. How big is the **bid-offer spread**?
7. What is the **commission** for the size of order you want to do?
8. Is commission a **flat rate or percentage**?
9. Is there **stamp duty** involved?
10. What is the **CGT status** of the product you want to trade?

All of these are important considerations, and almost all of the products we've looked at in this book differ from each other in several respects.

CFDs have tight spreads, and are free of stamp duty, but bear CGT. Spreads on spread betting are wider, but gains are free of CGT. Futures, CFDs, and spread betting involve margin payments, but the percentage margin may differ from product to product. CFD commission is normally a percentage of the underlying consideration, but futures often have commission charged at a flat rate per contract.

Spreads on index futures are narrower than on stock futures. ETFs can be dealt through any normal stockbroker, but only some stockbrokers will deal in covered warrants. Futures and options brokers will deal in futures and options, but not in ETFs or covered warrants. Some CFD brokers also have a spread betting arm, but the chances are you will not be able to switch between the two products in the same account.

ETFs and CFDs have no time limit involved, but futures, almost all spread bets, and options and covered warrants do. The expiry date needs to be specified at the time you trade. Stock futures are available on a limited number of individual stocks, but CFDs and spread bets can be done on a much wider variety. Guaranteed stop-losses are usually available for CFDs and spread bets (though you will probably need a separate account), but may not be from an options broker.

Remember also the ultimate distinction: long-only or short-only positions in futures, spread bets, and CFDs involve gearing in both directions and no limit to profits and losses. ETFs are like shares. They have no time limit. You cannot lose more than you invest and your investment will move precisely in tandem with the index. Options and covered warrants have limited downside risk (you cannot lose more than you invest), but also have gearing both ways, and a time limit. Many certificates function like trackers, but do have expiry dates.

Don't worry about remembering all this now. We'll cover all of these distinctions and more later on in the chapter. The point to remember now is that, when you are using these tools, the detail is important.

Bearing in mind all of these factors, the rest of the chapter takes a look at how the individual products stack up from a dealing perspective.

First of all, though, since you may need to open one or more new broking accounts to take full advantage of all of the products in the toolbox, a brief word on account-opening procedures.

Opening an account

These days there is none of the mumbo jumbo there used to be about getting an introduction to a broker. Brokers will deal with anyone, provided they meet certain financial criteria. The first step is to phone or email for an application form. See the appendix for details of web addresses of brokers.

The broker's application form will ask for the usual personal information, your bank details and also some financial details including your income, and the value of your savings and investments, as well as the equity you own in your own home. This gives the broking firm – whether it's a futures broker, options broker, CFD or spread betting firm – an idea of your financial worth and therefore how good a credit risk you are.

The firm may well wish to know if you have accounts open with other brokers, and also how experienced or otherwise you are at stock market trading in general. Brokers need to make sure that anyone dealing in products like this is fully conversant with the risks involved.

You will have to provide evidence of your assets and also proof of identity. This is designed to thwart would-be money-launderers. You may need to provide proof that you have a certain amount of freely available cash. A good rule of thumb is liquid funds roughly double the account size you are requesting. Some brokers will also ask for proof of extra liquidity if, like me, you are self-employed and your earnings are irregular.

Futures

Futures are in some ways the simplest and most economical products in which to deal, but they may require a minimum financial commitment and gearing level that you don't want to undertake.

Let's start off by looking at how futures stack up on the answers to our earlier questions:

Table 9.1 – Futures dealing specifics

Question	Answer
New Broker?	Yes (but can probably also use to deal in options)
Min. Account size?	Probably
Dealing specifics?	Buy/sell, contract, delivery month
Minimum trade size?	£10 per index pt x margin; 1000 x stock price x margin
Margin % needed?	Varies with volatility of underlying. 5-30%
Spreads?	Tight in index futures; less tight in stock futures
Commission?	Varies but usually £10 per lot, down to £4
Stamp duty?	No
CGT on gains?	Yes

This doesn't quite tell the whole story. For example, the type of product you want to trade and the margin requirements involved will govern the minimum account size you will need. Spreads are a few ticks in actively-traded futures (a tick is the minimum price movement), but stock futures may have spreads that aren't that different from the underlying stock.

Commissions

Commission on futures trades is usually a flat rate and it may depend on the volume of trades you do. A typical private client broker might charge £10 per lot for a stock future, but £7 per lot for an index future, but those trading actively can expect commissions to be as low as £4 per lot. The commission level, as we'll see in the next chapter, makes a big difference to the profitability of some types of trade.

Figure 9.1 – the monitor page in myBroker software, showing assorted indices, futures and options

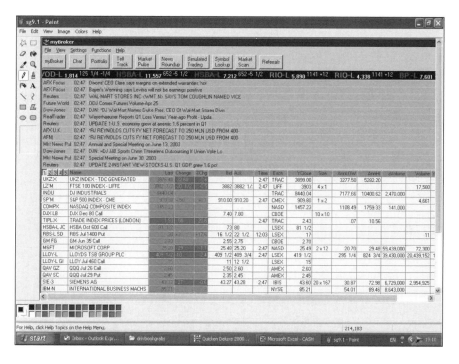

Dealing

Let's take a look at dealing vocabulary and procedure. You need to have a good understanding of this because it's your responsibility, for example, to know how big the contract size is in the stock future you want to deal in, and to make sure you have enough in your account to fund the trade you want to do. Check this out before you contact the dealers. Stock futures on most (but not all) UK shares are based on an underlying 1000 shares.

When you place your order, your broker needs to know:

1.   The **number of contracts** you want to deal in

2.   Whether the order is to **buy or sell**

3.   Whether the order is **opening or closing**

4.   The **expiry month**

5.   Whether the order is a **market order or a limit order**

The simplest type of verbal order would be, for example -

> *"buy to open two lots December short sterling at best"*

In other words, buy two contracts of the December expiry Short Sterling Future at the current market price. The order is to open a trade, not closing out a previous short position.

Obviously the dealing instructions can get more complex if you are carrying out a more complex strategy, say one that involves the simultaneous purchase of one future and the sale of another.

Broker advice

One final point. Many brokers will operate two types of account. These are:

1.   **Execution-only accounts**: you take sole responsibility for initiating the orders.

2.   **Advisory accounts**: the broker provides you with ideas that you may or may not act on.

Some futures and options brokers operate a half-way house whereby the broker will not offer advice on your investment strategies, but will advise on *dealing* and market-related procedures to smooth your trading.

Spread Betting

Spread betting is very akin to trading futures, particularly in terms of the range of products on offer, which typically mimic those available in the futures market. But there are significant differences. Have a look at the answers to our earlier dealing questions in the table below.

Table 9.2 – Spread betting dealing specifics

Question	*Answer*
New Broker?	Yes (but same broker may deal in CFDs)
Min. Account size?	Low
Dealing specifics?	Buy/sell, product, expiry, stake size
Minimum trade size?	Yes, but far from onerous
Margin % needed?	Varies with volatility of underlying – more than futures
Spreads?	Varies with product and firm – less on dailies
Commission?	No
Stamp duty?	No
CGT on gains?	No

Once again we need some clarification here. You will need to open an account with a separate firm. Futures and options brokers do not, on the whole, do spread betting. Many CFD firms also do spread betting, and vice versa, but the chances are you will need separate accounts for spread betting and one for CFDs.

You can generally do spread bets in fairly small sizes, depending on what you want to trade. The margin required for each trade will determine how much you have to have in your account at any one time. Just to recap from our earlier chapter on spread betting, margin is calculated by applying a bet size factor to your stake to work out what spread betting companies call a *notional trading requirement* (or NTR).

You must have at least this amount in your account, plus a bit of headroom in case the trade goes awry. But if you are just spread betting a stock in, say £2 a point, your margin figure will not be that large.

Figure 9.2 – Entering a spread bet electronically on Cantor Index web site

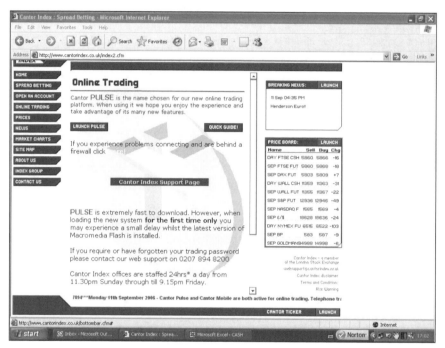

© Cantor Index

What you do need to decide on, however, is which type of account you want. Spread betting firms only operate execution-only accounts, but there are different types of account you can open.

1. **Normal deposit account**. You send a cheque or electronic payment to cover the account size in which you want to trade. Here you keep a certain amount on deposit (earning no interest in some cases). You only get a margin call if your NTR plus any losses mean you breach your account size.

2. **Credit account**. The firm will waive actually charging the NTR until your credit limit is breached. In other words, you don't pay any money up front and

depending on your status the spread betting firm will allow you to trade up to a certain figure without demanding any additional margin.

3. **Separate guaranteed stop-loss account**. You need cleared funds in the account to do this. You can't operate a guaranteed stop-loss on credit. The account has to be separate because, if you want to have a stop-loss in place, the spread you are quoted will be slightly wider, typically by an extra one or two points.

Stop-losses

It's worth recapping on stop-losses.

They are a good thing. You might even say that they are worth their weight in gold. This is particularly true if you don't want to watch the market constantly and you're taking a long-term view. It means that you can limit your losses by placing a stop-loss order at the outset, so that your maximum risk can be defined.

Guaranteed stop-losses operated by CFD brokers or spread betting firms are different to ones with a regular broker. A normal stockbroker has to remember to place your stop-loss order in a share and then wait for the market to execute it. He may not get precisely your stop-loss price. In the case of CFDs and spread bets, the broker *is* the market, and therefore your stop-loss price can be guaranteed.

Dealing

You can deal either by telephone or online. You can, if you wish, just use the internet service to check your account details, although the spread betting firm will send you statements regularly and contract notes when you place a bet.

Margin calls will be communicated to you by phone or letter, or you can arrange for them to be charged to a credit card.

Many spread betting firms and CFD firms offer the opportunity to place bets over the web or by phone. You can phone in an opening bet and close it via the web site, or vice versa.

Depending on the speed of your computer and of your internet connection, however, it may take a few minutes to load the dealing applet, and therefore if the market is moving quickly it may be easier and simpler to simply telephone the dealers.

Remember also that web-based dealing is not offered on all types of spread bet. If, for example, you want to spread bet options or some less actively-traded bets, you may have to ring for a price.

Dealing vocabulary is virtually the same as for futures. You ask for a price in the contract you require, let's say the March footsie. When you receive the price you say –

> *"buy (or sell) £x a point"*

The dealer will repeat the order back to you. You confirm it and the order is dealt. The same processes are mimicked in the online method of dealing, which is password-protected.

Multiple accounts

There's nothing to stop you opening an account with more than one spread betting firm. Their spreads can differ and you may be able to get a better price for a deal you want to do by shopping around.

In addition, different spread betting firms offer slightly different bets. IG has political bets, was at the forefront of launching binary betting and also does spread betting on house prices. Others have a slightly different range of products. For example, most spread betting firms make a market in gold, but some don't make a market in other precious metals.

The problem with having more than one account is simply administrative. You need to be able to fund different accounts and ensure that you are able to meet margin calls they may make. And simply keeping track of the bets you've entered into with each firm could be time consuming, as well as remembering different user names, passwords and account numbers. For beginners, it's best to keep it simple, master the basics of operating one account first and then branch out if you feel it's necessary.

CFDs

I've taken CFDs slightly out of the order they appeared in the earlier chapters, because CFD trading is slightly different to trading futures or spread betting. All three products do, however, share the same basic characteristics of trading on margin and the possibility of unlimited profits or losses.

What's the difference between CFDs and the other two? Spread bets are generally based around futures contracts, with similar expiries and similar (or higher) margin requirements. Futures margin, and therefore spread bet NTRs are largely dictated by the futures exchange and its clearing house, as well as by the broker you use.

With CFDs, the contract is simply between you and the CFD broker. It is not tied to a specific futures product in the way a spread bet may be. The CFD firm may lay off its exposure in the futures market to some degree, but that is an entirely different matter.

It follows from this that CFD brokers can be much more creative in how they operate their business. You can, for example, deal through the night if you so wish. Trading is not confined to prescribed market hours.

Before we look at this in more detail let's home in on our customary list of key questions, by looking at the table overleaf.

Table 9.3 – CFD dealing specifics

Question	*Answer*
New Broker?	Yes (but same broker may do spread bets)
Min. Account size?	Varies but generally higher than for spread betting
Dealing specifics?	Buy/sell, stock/index
Minimum trade size?	Varies but some have no minimum
Margin % needed?	Varies but can be less than futures
Spreads?	Deal at cash market price
Commission?	Commonly 0.25% of consideration – some charge zero
Stamp duty?	No
CGT on gains?	Yes

One of the reasons why I have hedged around some of these answers is that there are marked differences between CFD brokers. Perhaps the best example is CMC Markets (www.Deal4Free.com). As its web address suggests, it does not charge commission on CFD trades.

However, there is no such thing as a free lunch and in this case the *quid pro quo* for commission-free dealing comes in the daily interest that is charged on long CFD positions. You may find that the daily rate of interest charged is slightly greater on long positions, and the interest rate credited slightly less on short positions, compared to other brokers, in order to compensate for the lack of commission.

The big difference between futures and spread betting on the one hand, and CFDs on the other, is that there are no time limits on CFDs, whereas with futures you need to pay attention to delivery dates.

Initial margin may be somewhat lower on a CFD than on a stock future. In the past, for example, CMC has quoted 3% initial margin on Vodafone. This isn't a particularly volatile share these days, so may not be a particularly good benchmark. Many brokers levy margin at around 10% on most equity CFDs, but only around 4% on index CFDs.

As with spread betting, guaranteed stop-loss orders are available as are take-profit orders, and a variety of other types. Clients can stipulate, for example, that if they close a trade, a previously set stop-loss is automatically cancelled.

Account opening requirements are somewhat similar to spread betting in terms of the procedures that need to be completed. However, it is the case that CFD firms generally demand a higher minimum deposit and want clients that are reasonably well-heeled financially. Some CFD firms want clients with accounts of a minimum £20,000, although some only accept those able or willing to commit £50,000.

Dealing procedures are different again from futures and spread bets. Punters deal in numbers of shares, so you might for example put on a buy-to-open CFD in 5000 Vodafone shares, asking the price in the normal way and dealing almost as you would in the underlying shares. The terminology would run something like this:

> *'Buy to open 5,000 Vodafone as a CFD at best'*

In reality you would probably ask for the price 'as a CFD' before you dealt. Some CFD brokers also deal in shares too, so it is important to make this distinction during any conversation with a dealer. Buy to open indicates that you are going 'long' and not buying to 'close' an earlier short sale. Do not indicate which way you plan to trade before you ask the price.

The only real difference between buying a share and buying a CFD comes in the margin and gearing element, and in the fact that interest is charged on a long position and credited on a short.

Options

Dealing in options has an extra layer of complexity compared to trading futures. This is in the nature of the product itself. Let's see why by looking at our original questions:

Table 9.4 – Options dealing specifics

Question	*Answer*
New Broker?	Yes, but many option brokers trade futures too
Min. Account size?	No
Dealing specifics?	Buy or write, stock, put or call, strike, expiry, style
Minimum trade size?	One contract = 1000 shares or £10 per index point
Margin % needed?	Not applicable. Pay 100% of premium
Spreads?	Varies. Often wide on low-priced options
Commission?	Yes, often flat rate plus exchange levy
Stamp duty?	No
CGT on gains?	Yes

The added complexity of options means that when you deal you have to specify the stock, whether you want to deal in a put or call, the strike price, the expiry and – in the case of an index option – the exercise style. The information is easily encapsulated, as in an order to-

> *'Buy to open one Vodafone October 110 call at best'*

Bid-offer spreads

On the face of it this seems quite a simple deal. But you do need to bear one more thing in mind. The percentage gap between the bid and offer price of an option can vary hugely. Options with high prices and a lot of intrinsic value will have a narrow spread in percentage terms. In the case of the example we have chosen here, however, the actual option price is 7p, but the bid-offer spread is 5p bid and 9p offered.

This has a big implication for your trade. The option has to move up by a substantial percentage before you start making money. If, for example, the mid-price of the option moved up to 11p, the same 4p spread would mean the price quote would be 9-13. In other words, it would take a greater than 50% rise in the price of the option for you to escape from the trade without loss even if you completely ignored dealing costs.

Charges

In fact the dealing costs charged by your broker are probably less important than the impact of the spread. Many brokers charge a flat fee per trade. If you are dealing without advice, it might be in the region of £15, for example. Some brokers offer commission rates that include the closing trade (that is when you later sell the option you have bought and take your profit – or loss) free of charge.

Option deals do, however, also bear a standard settlement levy of £1.80 per contract. This can add to your dealing costs if you are buying multiple contracts of low-priced options.

The moral of the story is to **do all these sums before you start dealing**. Calculate what sort of movement in the underlying price you need before you make a profit on the trade after including all of the buying and selling costs, including the spread between the bid and offer price.

Account opening

Account opening procedures are much the same as for any other broker. You can generally choose from execution-only, advisory and managed accounts. Because of the relative complexity of options trading, it may be worth having an advisory account to start with, until you get to know the intricacies of the market.

Writing options

One big point to bear in mind is that some option brokers do not allow private clients to write options. As we'll see in Chapter 11 this is an important component of some of the most desirable options strategies, so it's important to make sure that this is allowed and to determine whether there are any strings attached.

Dealing

Brokers vary in the dealing services they offer. Many option brokers prefer to talk to clients as they are dealing, but some – such as MyBroker (part of ODL Securities) – offer an internet-based trading system that works from software you load into your own PC.

Covered Warrants and Certificates

Covered warrants are the newest market covered in this book and by all accounts it has got off to a rather slow start in the UK. Let's see how covered warrants measure up to the key questions:

Table 9.5 – Covered warrant dealing specifics

Question	*Answer*
New Broker?	Not necessarily
Min. Account size?	No
Dealing specifics?	Buy to open, sell to close a specific warrant
Minimum trade size?	No, can deal in any size
Margin % needed?	Not applicable -pay 100% of premium
Spreads?	Relatively narrow, capped by exchange
Commission?	As for shares – often flat rate per trade
Stamp duty?	No
CGT on gains?	Yes

Not standardised like options

As explained in Chapter 7, covered warrants differ from options in that they are not standardised contracts with a specification dictated by an exchange. They are each subtly different, in the sense of their strike and expiry date and the ratio to the underlying ordinary. As with options, some have American exercise style and some European.

This sounds complicated but in fact many warrants have quite simple terms –

- an **exercise price** that's a round figure, and

- an **expiry date** that is the end of a month, and

- 1:1 **parity** with the ordinary share, (which means, for example, you buy 1,000 warrants where you might have bought a single option contract in the same stock).

- certificates are call warrants with a zero exercise price

Dealing

The order might simply be, for example –

> *'buy 10,000 SF69 at best'*

where SF69 is a call warrant issued by SG in Barclays with a strike of 800 and an expiry date of 21st December 2007. You may need, however, to spell out the terms of the warrant too. Remember that new warrants are issued constantly and you do need to check the precise terms before you deal to avoid any confusion, and to make sure you are buying the best warrant for the purpose you require.

In theory, since warrants are traded on the LSE and settled in CREST, there should be no need to change your broker if you want to deal in these new instruments. However, not all brokers are running with the covered warrant ball at present, so if your broker doesn't offer the service, it is at least worth finding out if they are planning to and, if you want to deal in warrants and they aren't going to, change to one that does.

Online trading in covered warrants got off to a slow start, largely because of problems with regulators. But several brokers now offer both online and telephone trading in warrants.

ETFs

We can deal with trading in ETFs comparatively quickly. As explained earlier these are simply index-tracking shares (actually, technically they are mutual funds) that you deal in through your normal stockbroker.

Figs 9.3(a) and 9.3(b) – Entering an order to buy an ETF through Fastrade

This shot show an order to buy 1,000 shares in the FTSE 100 iShare, and the market response. You can see this is exactly like buying a share in a company.

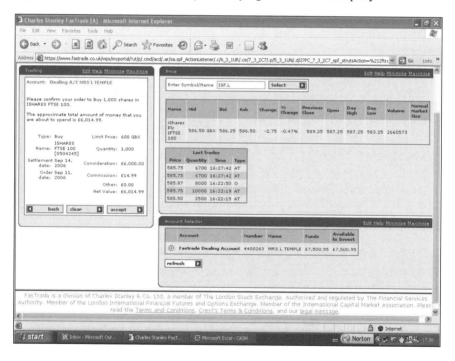

© Charles Stanley

Chapter 8 has details of ticker symbols for UK-listed ETFs. Let's look at how ETFs stack up against our standard list of questions.

Table 9.6 – ETF dealing specifics

Question	Answer
New Broker?	No, trade through your existing broker
Min. Account size?	Not applicable
Dealing specifics?	Buy/sell, product
Minimum trade size?	No
Margin % needed?	Not applicable, you have to put up 100%.
Spreads?	Varies – often possible to deal inside the 'touch'
Commission?	Yes, as for shares
Stamp duty?	No
CGT on gains?	Yes, as for shares

This rather sums it up. You deal in ETFs in exactly the same way you would deal in shares – long only, putting up 100% of the purchase price at the time you deal. Trades are settled through CREST in the normal way, the only difference with shares being the fact that ETFs are free of stamp duty.

Afterword

So that's a flavour of how the dealing system works in each of these new tools in your toolbox. There is no substitute for getting out there and trading them live, but I do recommend that you use one of the web-based simulators to get the hang of trading before committing yourself to real trades. A little practice to get the feel for volatility and the impact of dealing costs is no bad thing.

Simulators are certainly available for index futures, spread betting, CFDs and covered warrants. We highlight some of the sites where these simulators are available in Appendix 2.

10

Trading Strategies I

Futures, CFDs and Spread Betting

This chapter and the one that follows deal with trading strategies using all of the different products we've looked at earlier in the book. You'll learn how you can use the strategies to boost your returns and reduce your risk.

The financial products we've looked at in this book fall neatly into three categories.

The first is exchange-traded funds. These are simply an efficient means of putting money into or taking money out of the market using a product that exactly replicates the movement of the underlying index. Since products like this are exactly like dealing in shares, we won't linger over describing the strategies you can use to trade them. More often than not, it's a simple question of buying or selling.

This is not the case with the remaining two categories of product. Here, there are some distinguishing characteristics that mark them out from normal shares. We can summarise these as follows:

1. **Futures-type products**

    This category includes futures, CFDs, and spread betting. The overriding characteristic here is gearing to movements in the underlying. This is implicit in the fact that the products are traded on margin. If you simply buy or sell short these products as a speculation, you have unlimited geared-up risk.

2. **Option-type products**

    This category includes options and covered warrants. Here the overriding characteristic is that you have products that, if you buy them, have limited downside risk. You can't lose more than you invest even if the underlying price moves against you. You have gearing to the upside if the underlying price moves in your favour. Option-type products are also time-limited, wasting assets, whose value declines progressively sharply as they approach expiry.

This chapter looks at strategies that you can employ using futures-type products. The next chapter looks at the ones you can employ using options-type products.

More than simple speculation

Before starting, I'd like to make one general point. You can use these products simply as geared-up directional investments. In other words, you use them to back your view that a particular market or share will rise (or fall) within a set period of time. In this case you go long (or short) using a future, CFD or spread bet. Or you buy a call option (or a put option).

This is the common way investors think of these products, to use them simply as a means for speculating. But there is more to it than that. The more subtle way to use these products is in combination with each other, or with an existing shareholding, to reduce or control the risks you are running. This is what we really mean by strategies.

Futures strategies

Futures strategies are somewhat simpler than options strategies. They fall into several different headings.

1. Long only / short only for gearing
2. Cash extraction
3. Pairs trading
4. Relative value
5. Hedging a stock or portfolio

All this boils down to two choices. You can use stock futures, CFDs and spread bets to take on higher risk in order to generate a higher return. But you can also use them in different ways to provide risk reduction for a portfolio or in an individual stock. They can, too, be a way of backing your judgement about the relative value of different shares.

Over the rest of this chapter we'll look at how you can use these strategies. I'll talk generally about the strategies by reference to the futures markets. Apart from some minor technicalities, which are covered in earlier chapters, what holds good for futures strategies also holds good for strategies using their close cousins in the CFD and spread bet areas.

1. Long-only or short-only trades

Futures, spread betting and CFDs are ideal if all you want is a cheap way of speculating on a rise or value in the price in an individual share, index, or commodity.

The joy of margin

Let's take the case of shares. You can simply buy a CFD or do a spread bet (both futures type products) rather than buy the individual share. Products like this move, more or less, penny for penny with the underlying share price. The gearing comes from the fact that, as we found out in an earlier chapter, when you buy (or sell) a futures-type product you only have to pay a relatively small initial deposit, called *margin*, to get your exposure to the underlying value of the contract.

To recap this important point, your CFD broker or spread bookmaker will tell you how much margin you need to put up, and it will differ for each individual stock or each different type of contract. Let's say for the sake of argument that you have deposited £5,000 with a spread betting firm and he has said he will allow you to spread bet a range of shares with an underlying value at any one time not exceeding £25,000. In effect this means that, the amount you have to pledge from your account each time you trade, averages out at 20% of the underlying value of the bets you make.

One way of looking at this is that if you normally deal in shares by buying £5,000-worth of stock for each holding, you can get the same amount of exposure with a fifth of the capital. Or you can get five times the exposure you might normally assume for the same amount of capital.

This is an important point. Futures type trades *can* be used to gear up your exposure, but they *don't have to be* used that way. You can simply buy the same amount of exposure you normally take on, but use a fifth of the capital you would normally, and earn interest on the unused amount. We'll return to this point shortly.

Let's now look at an example.

Example 10.1 – Simple futures- type position, Vodafone

Initial parameters

- You're confident about the short-term outlook for Vodafone at 100p.

- The October futures price, as reflected in the spread bet quote is 100-101.

- You bet £100 a point.

- This gives you exposure to 10,000 shares in Vodafone.

- The margin required, via the spread bet NTR is roughly £2,000.

Now let's say that Vodafone shares rise by 10p.

Result

1. If you'd held the underlying shares you would have had £10,000 of capital tied up, and your holding would now be worth £11,000. You'd have made a return of 10%.

2. Holding the future-type position in this way, however, your profit of £1,000 is generated by only £2,000 of capital pledged, giving you a return on the investment of *50%*. (That is, a return on capital *five times greater* than from holding the underlying shares)

Note: in practice, you need to factor in the bid-offer spread as well, both of which reduce your return. In a spread bet the spread might well be wider than in the underlying shares.

Short selling

It's important to remember that you can speculate on a drop in price as easily as on a rise by selling short. In the case of future-type position, for example, this simply means that your opening transaction is a sell order as a CFD or a 'down' spread bet. You make money if the price subsequently goes down. It doesn't matter that you don't own the stock. This is because the CFD or spread bet is a financial contract. The same margin rules apply whether you are long or short. The gearing element is the same, except of course that in the case of short sale, you lose money if the stock rises.

Futures-type products – long-only/short-only speculation

- Buy future/CFD or do 'up' spread bet to speculate on price rise in underlying
- Short future/CFD or do 'down' spread bet to speculate on price fall in underlying
- Price moves penny for penny with underlying
- Gearing comes from margin (probably at least 5:1)
- Trade like this only with stop-losses
- Monitor trade constantly
- Know your market

The danger of gearing

Don't forget one of the big lessons of futures trading: if you are using futures (or CFDs or spread bets) simply to gear up your exposure, the gearing works both ways. If you guess wrong, your losses are magnified in exactly the same way as your profits are when your judgement is correct. Extending the example above, a downward move of 10% in Vodafone would wipe out half of the capital you'd committed to the trade. Dealing costs and the spread would increase the pain.

Stop-losses

You should seriously consider using stop-loss orders to control risk. Stop-losses are placed at the time you execute your initial trade. They are orders that will be executed automatically on your behalf if the price moves the 'wrong way' beyond a certain pre-determined level.

Example 10.2 – Using a stop-loss

Let's say Vodafone is 150p and you want to short it. You hope it's going to go back down to 110p. But if it goes up to 155p it will break a key chart level and might go much higher. You place your initial order to sell at 150p with a stop-loss order (to buy back and close the trade) if it hits 155p. Your maximum loss would be capped at 5p a share.

Guaranteed stop-losses are available for CFDs and spread bets. But you will pay extra in the form of a wider spread or extra commission charges.

There are other ways of controlling your risk. Many traders use futures and futures-type products in ways that neutralise rather than exaggerate the risks they run, either through exploiting differences in relative value or through hedging. These terms might sound complicated but in reality they aren't. We'll look at these trades in more detail later:

2. Cash extraction trades

We saw in the previous section that it is the fact that futures trades, CFDs and spread bets operate on margin that allows investors to gear up their return. But we can turn this idea on its head.

Because you can buy a CFD on, say, 20% margin (sometimes lower with less volatile shares) you can achieve the same exposure to an individual stock with a fifth of the capital. Let's say you have a portfolio of four stocks with £5,000 invested in each. Ideally you would want to have more stocks than this to achieve better diversification, and perhaps free up some cash in case other opportunities come along. Let's assume all your stocks have CFDs available on them.

Your portfolio looks like this:

Table 10.1 – Your share portfolio, *before* cash extraction

Holding	Company	Current price	Value
1,000	Archimedes plc	500p	£5,000
2,000	Brutus plc	250p	£5,000
4,000	Cassius plc	125p	£5,000
1,000	Doric plc	500p	£5,000

Now let's do the cash extraction and see what happens. In simple terms you are substituting CFDs for your shareholdings in the same proportions, and the amount you can extract will depend on the margin requirements. *After cash extraction* your portfolio looks like this:

Table 10.2 – Your CFD portfolio, *after* cash extraction

Shares	Company	Price	Value	Margin %	Cash committed
1000	Archimedes	500	£5,000	20%	£1,000
2000	Brutus	250	£5,000	15%	£750
4000	Cassius	125	£5,000	25%	£1,250
1000	Doric	500	£5,000	10%	£500

Total cash committed £3,500

Cash extracted to keep in reserve or invest elsewhere **£16,500**

This brings up a couple of points. One is that we have ignored dealing costs and interest debits in the example above. The second is to do with the mechanics of margin.

Margin calls

Although you have retained your original economic exposure for a fraction of the capital commitment you had previously, you aren't exactly free to do as you wish with this cash. If any of the stocks go down in price, you will be required to provide additional margin, so you need either to have stop-losses in place to keep the falls to a minimum, or keep plenty of cash in reserve for margin calls.

Let's say you decide to keep some of the cash in reserve, but use the rest to buy an index future and two more CFD contracts. Your portfolio after this operation is now represented by Table 10.3, opposite.

Your total investment here is still only £20,000, of which £11,250 is committed and £8750 is held in reserve in case of margin calls. The difference is striking. Instead of having only four stocks held in the cash market, which is arguably insufficient to ensure effective diversification, you have six stocks and the index future, which should be more than enough to give you diversification.

There is a slight flaw here, of course. It is that unless you take great care to have a very diverse range of stocks, all of the investments may go bad at the same time. You need to watch how closely these stocks' prices have been correlated with one another in the past.

Table 10.3 – Your CFD portfolio after reinvestment

Share/Committed	Company	Price	Value	Margin %	Cash
1000	Archimedes	500	£5,000	20%	£1,000
2000	Brutus	250	£5,000	15%	£750
4000	Cassius	125	£5,000	25%	£1,250
1000	Doric	500	£5,000	10%	£500
2000	Epsilon	250	£5,000	20%	£1,000
1000	Fourier	500	£5,000	15%	£750
4 lots	Mini-FTSE	6,000	£24,000	25%	£6,000

Total cash committed	£11,250
Cash in reserve	**£8,750**

and how volatile they are likely to be for any given movement in the market. We have, however, used this illustration to show how it is possible for even those with limited amounts of capital to use the futures market, mainly via CFDs (or spread bets) to achieve a much more balanced portfolio.

Here's a summary of what we can learn from this.

Cash extraction – key points

- Use cash extraction to **economise on capital**.
- Use cash extraction to **increase diversification**.
- Keep **cash in reserve** for margin calls.
- Use stop-losses on trades to avoid heavy losses.
- Try to find stocks with low correlations to each other.

In the example above, I ignored the impact of dealing costs (though these are quite low in the case of futures but more material in CFDs), the spread, and also the fact that futures prices will probably be at a small premium to the cash market. However, I have also ignored the fact that you can earn interest on the cash extracted.

Since the demise of single stock futures for private investors, most are obliged to do trades like this through the CFD market and through spread betting. Spread betting is straightforward as it replicates the futures markets in most respects, and you simply adjust your stake size to get the correct level of exposure. With CFDs, as we've already noted, the equation is more complicated because you are paying interest on each long CFD. Also, commission is based on a percentage of the underlying contract value.

Now let's have a look at a classic trade you can do using futures-type products – buying an undervalued share and shorting a similar overvalued one.

3. Pairs trading

Hedge funds have exuded a raffish glamour for many years, and this is one way you can do what they do. The strategy is sometimes known as *long/short equity* or *pairs trading*.

The idea is to profit from the narrowing of a disparity in the stock market rating of two similar companies. As an investor, you might, for example, believe that BT is cheap relative to Vodafone. Let's say BT sells on a dividend yield of 5% while Vodafone sells on a yield of less than 4%. You believe that this disparity will even itself out over a period of time.

A relatively low risk way of profiting from this would be to do a matched pairs trade in stock futures, CFDs, or spread bets – shorting Vodafone and going long of BT in equal money amounts.

The argument against this type of trading is that your *dealing costs will be higher*, with two lots of commission in the case of futures and CFDs, and two bid-offer spreads to surmount before you reach profit. In the case of a CFD, the position is mitigated slightly because the financing credit on the short position will partly offset the financing cost of the long position.

The big plus point, however, is that this strategy ought to mean that you are insulated from the ups and downs in the market. In the case of the Vodafone/BT example, if the market as a whole rises, or falls, the effect on your exposure will be neutral. In that event, both stocks should rise or fall in tandem.

What you are interested in here is a change in the relative valuations of the stocks, not their absolute levels. That is how you make money from pairs trading. We'll see *exactly* how in a minute, but first, let's look at the requirements for doing a trade like this.

Figure 10.1 – Vodafone's share price overlaid with BT's (thicker line)

© Sharescope

Pairs trading requirements

We need to have a few conditions in place.

1. You need to check with your CFD broker or financial bookmaker that appropriate **pairs of stocks are actually available**.

2. It's important to remember that the trades must be matched at the outset in terms of their **money value**.

3. You must be happy with the **time limit** on the trade that is implied by the futures expiry date. This applies if you are using spread bets to effect the trade. Although you can roll over futures related spread bet trades to a later delivery date, it is more expensive.

Control of costs is very important

What is important in pairs trading, though, is to make sure your dealing costs are at a minimum. It's unfortunate that individual stock futures are no longer available, because although you can pairs-trade using CFDs rather than futures, this will probably work out to be a more expensive exercise. On the one hand, you get an interest credit on your short side trade, but this will not completely offset the debit on your long side trade because the interest rate used will be higher in the case of the latter. Commission on CFDs is generally higher than on futures trades. Private investors now have no option but to use CFDs for this type of trade.

Spread betting is a viable choice here, too. But bear in mind here that you will need to recoup two lots of bid-offer spread before you are in profit.

Pairs trading isn't without risk. The stock you have bought could bid for the stock you have shorted (about the worst possible combination of events since the ratings will diverge rather than converge if this happens!), but generally risk is minimised. Rather than talk in the abstract, let's have a look at a concrete example.

Example 10.3 – Pairs trading (Vodafone v BT)

Here's the theory.

Say we take our original idea that Vodafone is dear at 120p and BT is cheap at 240p. You think that the market will eventually come round to your way of thinking. By selling double the amount of Vodafone futures for each BT future you buy (to allow for the difference in price between the two), you should be able to profit from the expected adjustment in their market ratings. If the market goes down as a whole, this needn't affect your profit from the trade, because the overvalued stock should drop more, leaving you in pocket.

Let's say, for instance, you buy 1000 BT shares as a CFD and sell 2000 Vodafone as a CFD at, respectively, 240p and 120p. Assume now that the market drops 5%. BT drops from 240p to 230p but Vodafone falls proportionately further from 120p to 105p.

On the basis of the requirement to stump up 20% margin you have to pledge roughly £500 for each side of the trade.

The 15p fall in the price of Vodafone translates into a gain on the short side of the trade of £300.

The 10p drop in BT means that your long position in Vodafone has lost £100.

Because of the change in the relative price of the two stocks, you have a net gain of *£200* even though both stocks have gone down. Return on capital is around 20% (£100 versus margin committed of £1000). However, this excludes the impact of the spread in both cases and the effect of dealing costs. As we can see from the more detailed accounting below, this reduces the return substantially.

Pairs trade summary

Objective: profit from an adjustment in relative prices of Vodafone and BT.

Initial prices

Company	*Cash*	*CFD*
Vodafone	119 – 121	120-122
BT	239– 241	240-242

Action: using CFDs, go short of Vodafone and long of BT.

Opening position

Position	Amount	Type	Stock	Price	Amount	Margin(£)
Sell	2000	CFD	Vodafone	120	2400	480
Buy	1000	CFD	BT	242	2420	484

Market: Vodafone stock falls from 120 to 105; BT stock falls from 240 to 230
Action: Vodafone CFD bought back at 106; BT CFD sold at 230

Profit/loss

	P/L (£)	Calculation
Gain on short Vodafone	240	2 x 14p x 1000
Loss on long BT	-120	1 x 12p x 1000
Stamp duty	-24	0.5% of £4820
Net profit	96	240 - 120 - 24
Return on investment	**10%**	96/964 (964 was the total margin)

The margin element inherent here allows you to profit from quite small changes in the relative value of the two stocks. But you need to keep an eagle eye on dealing costs to make sure you can profit from the trade. In the example above, the impact of the spread and stamp duty halved the theoretical return from the trade. All things considered, spread betting might be an equally (perhaps more) cost-effective route here.

4. Relative value trades

Another lower risk way of trading using stock futures is betting on the relative performance of a stock against the market. Let's say you believe that the market as a whole is overvalued but that defensive stocks, like food companies, are going to do much better than the index over the coming months. Let's use the example of Unilever:

Example 10.4 – Relative value trade (Unilever v FTSE 100)

The way to play this view is to buy a defensive stock, Unilever, and short the index future. This means that you should benefit from the stock's relative strength against the market, irrespective of the size of the fall in the market. You may believe the market is going to crash, but even if it only drops a small amount, this strategy should work, as the example overleaf shows.

One issue here is that individual stock futures tend to be denominated in smaller quantities than stock index futures. The conventional contract is £10 per index point, meaning that the FTSE 100 future has a current underlying value (at the time of writing) of around £37,500. For the purposes of this example, let's assume that we can still use the (now discontinued) FTSE mini-future, which is calculated at £2 per index point. Assuming the FTSE 100 is at 5900 this means the underlying value is £11800 and, assuming margin is 10%, that we can buy or sell one contract for £1180 down.

Figure 10.2 – Unilever share price overlaid with the FTSE 100 (thicker line)

Rather neatly, because it makes the example easy to understand, Unilever is currently (in August 2006) priced around 1190p per share, so that a CFD in 1000 shares is worth £11,900. This more or less matches the value of a FTSE100 mini futures contract. If this weren't the case, and whether you use conventional FTSE 100 contracts or mini ones, the point is that you need to have parity in terms of underlying total contract value for each side of the trade.

In this example we're going to look at what happens if Unilever remains unchanged, but the index falls 250 points - in other words, if Unilever outperforms the index the way you expect it to.

Relative value trade summary

Objective: low-risk profit from appreciation of a defensive stock versus the market

Initial prices

	Cash	*CFD or Future*
Unilever	1190-1192	1192-1194
FTSE 100	5900	5900-5904

Action: go long of Unilever and short of FTSE 100

Opening position

Position	*Amount*	*Inst/Expiry*	*Contract*	*Price*	*Amount*	*Margin(£)*
Buy	1000	CFD	Unilever	1194	11,940	1194
Sell	1	Oct Future	Mini-FTSE 100	5900	11,800	1180

Market: FTSE 100 falls 250 points; Unilever no change

Action: Unilever CFD sold at 1192; FTSE 100 future bought back at 5654

Profit/loss

	P/L (£)	Calculation
Loss on Unilever CFD	-20	1 x 1000 x 2p (spread)
Stamp duty on Unilever	- 11	at 0.5% of consideration
Profit on FTSE future	500	250 x £2
Dealing costs on FTSE futures	-20	2 x £10 per contract
Net profit	449	(-20-11) + (500-20)
Return on investment	**18.91%**	449/2374 (i.e. combined margin)

Trades like this can in principle be done using either CFDs and spread bets, both of which give more flexibility than futures. This is because of the ability to have more precise tailoring of the quantities used in each case. They may, however, attract higher dealing costs, and/or bigger percentage margin requirements. Once again, all of these costs should be carefully checked out ahead of time. They can be a significant drain on the potential profit you can make.

5. Hedging

Another way of using futures is to employ them, quite literally, to hedge your bets.

Hedging is really like insurance. You use a short futures trade, a short CFD or a down spread bet to protect an existing holding in the event of a price fall. This allows you to leave the original holding undisturbed (avoiding a possible capital gains tax bill if you had sold), but make an offsetting profit on the hedge if the underlying price falls. Here's an example.

Example 10.5 – Hedging using CFDs, Vodafone

Background

Let's say that you bought your present holding of 10,000 Vodafone shares when it first spun out of the old Racal Electronics back in the late 1980s. It's a long term holding and you have a big capital gain (let's imagine that the shares are currently 200p). Let's also say that your cost price was 50p and you have no unused CGT allowances and a 40% marginal rate of tax. You might think that the market is overvalued and that Vodafone, in particular, as one of the UK's leading stocks, is likely to come down hard if the market has a setback. Also the company is announcing results in a few day's time and the share price could fall sharply if the results disappoint.

You can take a position in a Vodafone CFD that will neutralise any loss you might suffer if that happens.

Initial parameters

Simply sell 10,000 Vodafone as a CFD. (This matches your exposure to the underlying shares exactly and let's assume, because Vodafone is not very volatile, that it ties up only £1,200 of margin.)

For the sake of argument let's say that Vodafone falls from 120p to 90p.

Result

1. If you had sold your share holding at 120p, you would have had a capital gain of 100p a share, and ended up paying 40p of that amount in capital gains tax.

2. After deducting the tax you would have been, in effect, getting only 80p for your sale at 120p. (You would have been better off if you had not sold at all!)

As it is, using a futures-type trade you recoup your loss without disturbing the underlying holding.

You can use spread betting in much the same way by making a down bet in Vodafone in £100 a point, which equates to the exposure you have in your underlying holding in the shares. Once again, leaving aside the relatively minor cost of the spread itself, your profit on the down spread bet would offset the unrealised loss on the underlying holding, with the advantage in this case that the gain would be free of capital gains tax.

CFDs work in a slightly different way, however. So let's also look in detail at precisely how this hedging strategy works using a CFD, assuming, say, the drop in price is expected to occur over a period of about three months.

Example 10.6 – hedging using CFDs

To recap:

1. You hold 10,000 Vodafone shares bought at 20p a share.
2. The shares are currently priced at 120p.
3. You expect the price to fall to 90p over the next three months.

You want to use a CFD to hedge this position. Here's how it would work if the price fall happens as you expect.

Table 10.5 – Hedging using a CFD

Item	*Hold Shares*	*Short CFD*
Holding	10,000	10,000
Underlying value @ 120p	£12,000	£12,000
Capital employed	£12,000	£2,400 (margin)
Commission (0.25% round trip)	n/a	-£53
Interest @ 4% (90 days)	n/a	£120
Value @90p	£9,000	£9,000
P&L @90p	-£3,000	+£3,067
Net result	+67 (excluding impact of spreads)	

In other words, the loss in the shares has more than been made up for by the gain on the CFD, which also includes interest on the short position. Bear in mind though, that there may be tax to pay on the gain in the CFD (as there would also be on a futures trade).

The influence of tax

Tax considerations can be an important factor. Although in this example the CGT payable on the CFD would be a lot less than it would be if you had sold the shareholding outright (£3,000 at 40% rather than £10,000), it still lessens the impact of your insurance.

Though the spread bet might mean it cost a few pennies more, it would therefore, depending on your capital gains tax position, make more sense to put on the hedge using a down spread bet.

That way, you wouldn't earn interest on your short, but equally you wouldn't pay commission or CGT either.

What happens if you turn out to be wrong, and Vodafone's shares in this example don't fall but continue to rise? Unless you remove the hedge, it works in reverse and deprives you of the benefit of the rise. You don't lose money on a net basis, but you do forgo a gain.

Afterword

Let's have a look at the key points we've learnt in this chapter.

There are several different types of trade you can place: straight long or short; cash extraction; pairs trading; relative value trading; and hedging.

Broadly speaking *futures and spread betting are interchangeable*: the issues that would prompt you to choose one over the other boil down to-

1. **Flexibility** in nominating quantities (which favours spread betting for smaller scale trades), and

2. **Dealing costs** – that's to say the combination of spread and commission in futures versus a (wider) spread in a spread bet. The CGT-free nature of spread betting may favour their use over futures for hedging strategies.

CFDs work well for relative value trades and pairs trading because of the interest earned element on the short side of the trade. Against that, commission may be higher than for futures, although margin might be a little less. Margin percentages are likely to be highest on spread bets and least on futures or possibly CFDs, depending on the firm you use and the stock or stocks involved.

In reality, however, in the case of trades in individual stocks, private investors have little option but to use CFDs or spread bets to effect futures-type trades like this.

Either way, you do need to spend time before you commit to a trade working out exactly what all the costs are and where they will arise. Part of this process is also to analyse price charts to work out realistically the size of the move you can expect in each component of a trade. Then work out what a move like this means for profits and your return on capital after dealing costs and spreads have been taken into account.

Meanwhile, trading options and warrants is somewhat different. This is covered in the next chapter.

11

Trading Strategies II

Options and Warrants

The previous chapter dealt with the strategies you can use to maximise your returns and reduce your risk by using futures, and the other instruments, like spread betting and CFDs, that function in a similar way.

This chapter looks at strategies you can employ using options and option-like products such as covered warrants. If you want a reminder of the basics of options and warrants, look again at Chapters 6 and 7 respectively.

Let's recap on the most basic strategies you can use with both these products.

Geared speculation

We saw in Chapters 6 and 7 that you can buy options and warrants to achieve *gearing*. Unlike futures, spread betting and CFDs, the gearing you get with options and warrants comes with a known and limited downside risk. As an option buyer, you cannot lose more than the initial cost of the option or warrant.

The scale of the gearing involved depends primarily on whether the option or warrant is in or out-of-the-money, in other words whether it has any intrinsic value or not.

1. **In-the-money** options and warrants have *lower gearing*, but also a lower risk of total loss, since the intrinsic value in them acts as a floor on the price.

2. **Out-of-the-money** options have *higher gearing* but more risk of total loss.

Remember that for the gearing to operate in your favour there has to be a movement in the price of the underlying in your favour as soon as possible, and at any event before the option or warrant expires. Warrants typically have *longer expiry dates* than options and may therefore be more useful for some investors. The drawback is that there may not be a warrant that precisely fits your requirements.

Hedging

Put options and put warrants can be used for hedging (or *insurance*). You can hedge individual shares (using individual equity options and equity warrants), or a portfolio of shares or an exchange-traded fund (using index options or index warrants).

There is probably still a bigger choice of individual equity options than of individual equity warrants. Some index warrants have longer expiry dates than LIFFE index options, but may not be available for as many strike prices as the LIFFE products.

The basic procedure for hedging is to buy an at-the-money put option (or warrant) contract or contracts that correspond in value to the portfolio or individual share you want to hedge. Each equity option contract normally represents 1,000 shares. Index options are valued at £10 per index point. In other words one FTSE 100 index option contract in theory insures a portfolio worth in pounds ten times the value of the FTSE 100 at the time.

With warrants, because their terms are not standardised, you need to check the terms of an individual warrant to work out the right quantity to trade in.

You can reduce the cost of your insurance by accepting an excess. This means that instead of buying an at-the-money put option or warrant, you buy one that is out-of-the-money. Your excess is the amount the share or index has to fall before the put option begins to have intrinsic value and your insurance kicks in.

Problem of matching equity option contracts with portfolio value

However, as we noted in the chapter on warrants, you also need to take into account the delta of the option or warrant to make sure that the movement in its price really does provide you with the level of protection you need. In theory you may need to buy a somewhat greater number of contracts than you might need in order to do this. This is a problem specifically with options, because of the *lumpiness* of LIFFE contracts.

In other words, if you own 1,000 shares in Universal Widgets and want to hedge using a put option, but the delta on the option is - 0.75, you are faced with the decision of either buying one put option contract (as you would have if the delta were –1) or two contracts (as you would have if the delta had been –0.5). There's no easy way round this by using options, because you are stuck with the round 1,000-share lot used in LIFFE contracts. Covered warrants are in theory more flexible, but the list of companies covered is at present more limited, and put warrants are also less common than calls, and you might not be able to get the expiry date you want in a warrant.

Writing options

We covered this idea briefly in Chapter 6. It applies solely to options. Investors cannot write covered warrants.

If you write an option you are on the opposite side of the transaction to an option buyer. This means you have the obligation to supply stock and receive cash (or receive stock and pay cash) at the exercise price in the case of a call (or put) – if the option is exercised. If you write an index option the exercise is settled solely in cash.

As a writer you receive the option premium. But in exchange it means you have a cast iron obligation to the option holder that comes into force should he/she decide to exercise the option.

In theory, anyone can write an option. However, some brokers do not allow private investors to write options in any circumstances. Some will only allow it if the investor can prove they have the stock or cash to cover the exercise. Because it is akin to a short sale (or a spread bet), your broker will demand a margin payment from you at the outset, and top-ups if the trade goes the wrong way.

Having said that, option writers have two things going for them-

1. The **passage of time** works against option holders and in option writers' favour.

2. Provided option writers take care only to write options when **volatility is high**, they have a good chance of volatility falling and the option remaining unexercised.

If you write an option you are taking on a wasting liability rather than buying a wasting asset. You are selling volatility rather than buying it.

To recap one final point, as we noted above and explained in Chapter 7, you cannot write a warrant. Therefore the strategies explained below that involve writing apply only to the options market.

Complex strategies

The point about the option and warrant trades we've looked at so far is that they only involve dealing in a single option or warrant: buying a call warrant or buying a put warrant, or writing an option.

But this is only the start of the way in which you can use options and warrants. Most of the option and warrant strategies we'll look at function the way they do because they combine options and warrants in different ways.

So if you have a particular view on the market or an individual share, there is usually a strategy you can use to back your view. Many strategies involve limited risk and limited rewards. Some strategies are more expensive than buying a single option, but some are cheaper.

They often involve buying two options, or buying one option and writing another. Because of this there are *extra dealing costs* associated with them. For the time being we'll ignore this is in the interests of getting the concepts across.

Let's start off by having a look at the different ways in which you can use options and (in some cases) warrants. You can, for example:

1. Buy a call *and* a put option or warrant in the same stock or index.

2. Buy one option, *write* a different option in the same stock or index.

3. Sell (i.e. write) an option on a stock or ETF you hold.

4. Buy a *put* option or warrant in a stock or ETF you hold (i.e. hedge).

That covers some of the basic parameters. But there are also others that come into play by including in the strategy the other attributes of an option or warrant, namely its strike price and expiry date.

If you are buying two different options or warrants, or buying one option and writing another, the options or warrants do not have to have identical terms. So you can, for example:

5. Buy an option or warrant with one expiry date and buy another option or warrant with a different expiry, but with the same strike price.

6. Buy an option or warrant with one strike price and buy another option or warrant with a different strike price, but with the same expiry date.

7. Buy two different options or warrants each of which has a different strike price and a different expiry date.

8. Buy an option with one expiry date and write an option with a different expiry, but with the same strike price.

9. Buy an option with one strike price and write another option with a different strike price, but with the same expiry date.

10. Buy one option and write another where each has a different strike price and a different expiry date.

There are jargon words for each of these different types of strategy but they fall into three broad categories.

Straddle and strangle

This is normally buying a call and a put simultaneously, where both of the options or warrants have the same expiry date and the same (or possibly different) strike prices. If you are just using options, you can also write a straddle or strangle.

Spread

This is buying one option and writing another with either the same expiry and different strike prices, or the same strike price and different expiry dates. Spreads where the options have the same expiry date and different strikes are known as vertical spreads. Spreads where the strike is the same but the expiries differ are known as calendar spreads. Diagonal spreads are where the two options each have different strikes and different expiry dates.

Covered write

This is normally writing an out-of-the-money call option against a stock you hold. This should generate extra portfolio income and is a technique used by many expert option traders

Why all the complexity?

Proponents of the options market suggest that these various permutations simply demonstrate how flexible the options market is. And indeed they do. But it can be daunting to a newcomer. We can, however, easily summarise the reasons why you should use these strategies and the effect they have:

In short you need to ask yourself whether you expect the market or stock to go up down or sideways over the life of the option, and whether you expect its volatility to rise, fall, or stay the same.

If you expect high volatility but are not sure about the direction – that's to say the market could go sharply up or sharply down but you're not sure which way – then buying a *straddle* or *strangle* is in order.

Expectations that volatility will fall and markets remain stable argue for a *covered write*. You will pocket the premium and take advantage of lower option prices and erosion of time value.

Expected fluctuations in price within a defined trading range can be played via a *vertical spread*. Here the effect of writing an option as one side of the trade is to reduce the overall cost of the strategy. Your gains and losses are both limited to defined maximum amounts. Depending on whether you are bullish or bearish will govern which option you buy and which you write. Your expectation of the trend in volatility will govern whether you use options that are in, at or out-of-the-money.

If you expect stable markets and declining volatility for an extended period you can use a *calendar spread* to capture the quicker erosion of time value in an option with a shorter time to go to expiry. Time value erodes very quickly in the last month of an option's life.

Calendar spreads can also be used to express a delayed bullish or bearish view. Writing, say, a one month call option and buying a three month call option is a cheap way of expressing the view that the market will start to rise in a month's time. If it does, the premium received for writing the option will reduce the overall cost of the strategy. Once the written option has expired, you are left with a straight call option with two months to go to expiry. If you expect the market to fall after a month, the same strategy could be performed using put options.

The table opposite the page summarises this:

Table 11.1 – Deciding on a strategy

Market view	Volatility now	Trend in volatility	Strategy
Bullish range	Any	Stable	Bull call spread
Bullish range	Any	Stable	Bull put spread
Bearish range	Any	Stable	Bear call spread
Bearish range	Any	Stable	Bear put spread
Neutral	High	Down	Covered write
Sharp change	Low	Up	Straddle, strangle
Stable	High/medium	Down	Any calendar spread
Delayed bullish	Low/medium	Up	Bull calendar spread
Delayed bearish	Low/medium	Up	Bear calendar spread

There are a couple of other things we need to look at when we are working out the potential profits and losses from strategies like this.

Dealing costs

The first is that dealing costs in options can make a sizeable difference to the profit you make from these complex strategies. Some option investors I know have tended to avoid spreads and straddles, for example, because after dealing costs and the impact of the difference between bid and offer prices has been factored in, it becomes very hard to make money. There are two variables to bear in mind here:

1. Settlement of option trades often involves **flat rate charges** per contract irrespective of the size of the trade in money terms.

2. **Bid-offer spreads** are large in percentage terms for lower-priced options. In other words, an option with a price of around 100p might be quoted 100-103, but an option with a price around 10p might be quoted 10-13. The spread is the same, but in percentage terms it is much larger.

This is a big beef that many traders have with the options market and one reason for using warrants for hedging or for trades like straddles and strangles that just involve *buying* option-type instruments.

However, we can't get around the fact that a straddle or a strangle involves the costs of buying two options (or warrants) at the offer price and closing two options (or warrants) at the bid price. That's to say, two lots of dealing costs and two lots of bid-offer spreads to be absorbed before a profit can be earned.

In a spread strategy, the same applies, but the premium received from the written option reduced the overall cost of the strategy and increases the potential return.

We'll look at dealing costs in a bit more detail in the next chapter.

Option payoff diagrams

Many strategies can be charted using simple diagrams to describe the profit or loss generated at different levels of the underlying price. The underlying price is the horizontal axis and the profit and loss the vertical one.

These give a simple picture of the way the strategy works and can demonstrate intuitively whether or not the strategy is going to work for you. Later in this chapter we'll show several pay-off diagrams for different strategies as we look at each technique in turn. All show not only the position when the trade is instituted but also the (more angular) pattern of profits and losses immediately prior to expiry. Have a flip through the rest of the chapter to look at these charts and you'll see what I mean. Good quality options strategy software will often allow you to draw these charts with ease. They are a good way of grasping exactly what a strategy can do for you.

Let's now have a look at some of these strategies, beginning first with writing covered calls, a good strategy for income-seeking investors with a broad portfolio of stocks.

Writing covered calls

A covered call is call option writing done in conjunction with an equivalent holding in the underlying stock.

Say you have a holding of 2,000 Vodafone. You can write a maximum of two call option contracts against this holding, each contract equating to 1,000 shares. The written call option contracts are *covered* because you have the underlying shares to deliver should they be exercised.

When you are writing calls in this way, you should write out-of-the-money options.

The worst-case scenario, when the option is exercised against you, is that you have to supply the necessary stock from your holding. This will only happen if the price has risen past the exercise price. If exercise happens, in exchange for your holding you will have received the strike price of the call option plus the premium you received for writing the option.

Why would you consider covered writing?

Writers generally write options when *volatility is high but likely to fall*, since high volatility means high option prices. You may also take the view that the price is unlikely to move substantially over the life of the option. In both cases you wish to use the option market to gain additional portfolio income. The extra income derives from the premium received on writing the call. If the option expires unexercised, you have both the premium and your stock intact.

Figure 11.1 – Payoff diagram for a written call option

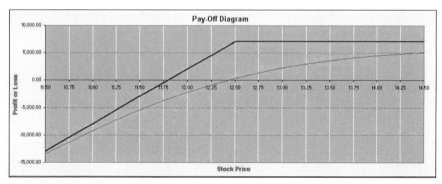

© OptionStrategy

If the option is exercised, you deliver the stock from your holding but receive cash in exchange based on a price significantly higher than the current one. The price you get is, in effect, the strike price of the option you write, plus the premium you get for writing it.

An alternative, but broadly similar, strategy is known as a *buy-write*. Here you buy a stock and immediately write a call with a higher exercise price. The premium from writing the call goes towards reducing the cost of the purchase of the underlying stock. It also establishes your maximum potential profit. This is the exercise price of the call plus the premium received, less the cost of the stock purchase.

Let's look at how the strategies work, using Vodafone as an example.

Example 11.1 – how a covered write works

- You buy (or already hold) 1,000 Vodafone shares. The current price is 100.

- An option with a strike of 110 and three months to run costs 5p. Write one call at 5p.

There are now three things that can happen:

1. The **price rises above 110** in the next three months. The holder exercises the option. After delivering the stock to him or her, you have received 115p (110p strike price + 5p premium) for your 1000 shares.

2. The **price stays between 100 and 110** for the life of the option. The option expires unexercised. You retain your holding. You keep the option premium.

3. The **price falls below 100**. The written option will expire worthless. You retain the holding. You only start to lose money on the shares if they fall below 95p (your buying cost minus the option premium). Even then writing the call option was better than doing nothing.

Strategy return calculations

The benefit derived from covered call writing can be measured in terms of a rate of return calculation which covers the two positive outcomes which you, as the writer, can experience: either the option isn't exercised, or it is exercised.

In the example, this is shown in item 1 and item 2. These are known, respectively, as the *static return* and the *if-called return*.

a) Static return

The static return measures the return you get if the price of the underlying shares remains static. *Static* in this case is defined as staying between the current price and the exercise price over the life of the option. In strict terms, what you receive in this case amounts to the option premium paid plus any dividend paid on the underlying shares during the life of the option. The amount invested, the denominator of the equation, is the capital invested in the holding of the underlying shares less the amount of option premium received for writing the option.

In practice, we can do this calculation quickly, especially if no dividends are paid in the period in question.

- In the example above it is 5/95. This is the option premium (5) divided by the starting price of the shares (100) less the option premium (5).

- However this 5.3% return has been earned over a period of just three months.

- On an annualised basis it is far more. The quick way to annualise it would simply be to multiply 5% by 12/3 and get 20%.

- The correct way to do it is to raise 105.3 to the power four, which equals 122.77, or a return of 22.77%.

b) If-called return

The if-called return works in a slightly different way.

Take our Vodafone example again. Assume now that before expiry the price of the shares rose to 115p. It would now be worth the option holder exercising his option and the shares held by you, as the writer, would be called away at a price of 110p. In this eventuality you would be forced to sell the stock at the exercise price, but you would also make a higher return.

This return would comprise, as before, the option premium plus any dividend (assuming this is received before exercise), but in addition you would also have the benefit of a gain in the underlying shares of 10p from the original buying price to the exercise price.

- If we assume no dividend is paid and the exercise takes place two months from when you first initiate the trade, the denominator remains the same, making the if-called return (10+5)/(100-5) or 15.7%

- This time we need to annualise by raising 100 plus the gain to the power six. So 115.7 to the power six works out at a return of 139.9% on an annualised basis.

Of course this annualising business is pretty notional, but it is also important because it allows you to make a comparison with other strategies that pay off over a different time periods.

Remember too that we need to subtract dealing costs related to writing the option to get the true return. Doing this reduces the numerator and adds to the denominator, thus lowering the return. Say in the example immediately above that dealing costs reduce the premium received from 5 to 4. The 'if called' return is now 14/96, which is 14.58% over two months rather than 15.7%. In other words we need to work with the real amounts we receive or could receive.

Even so, looked at in this way, writing options no longer looks quite as risky as it may at first appear. For those with a neutral view on the market and a list of stocks which they are prepared to hold (if need be) as long term investments irrespective of shorter term market fluctuations, covered call writing makes a lot of sense.

Downside protection versus foregoing upside participation

Looked at another way, covered writing involves a trade-off between the amount of downside protection (or additional portfolio income) offered in exchange for foregoing upside participation in the price beyond a certain level.

There is another aspect too. It relates to the option you write and the degree to which it is out-of-the-money. The deeper out-of-the-money the written option, the lower the level of premium income and downside protection received, but the greater the degree of upside participation before the stock is called away, and the bigger the disparity between the static and if-called returns. Whether you use a low-priced, deeply out-of-the-money option, or something with a strike closer to the current price, depends on how bullish you are.

In the case of our Vodafone example you might only receive 2p for writing a call with a strike of 120. In this case your static return from 100 would only be 102/98 (4%), whereas the if-called return will be a much larger 22/98, or 22.4%.

To do covered writing successfully you need a good sense of the likely limits of the underlying price movements over the life of the option. You should also try to avoid writing options when price volatility is unduly low. How deeply out-of-the-money the written option you choose depends on how bullish you are about prospects for the shares.

There is software available that can help assess the potential profitability of alternative covered writing strategies to help you pick the best one.

Straddles and strangles

If you buy an option or warrant for gearing purposes, or for a hedge, the key point is that the underlying price movement required for it to pay off has to be in a defined direction.

But you can use options or warrants to profit from an expected sharp move in the market in *either direction*. This particularly applies if a known external event (such as a war or an election) could make prices move sharply in either direction within a specific time period.

The flexibility of the options market is such that it is possible to give effect to such a view by a simultaneous purchase of a call and put. In its simplest form, this strategy is known, for obvious reasons, as a *straddle*. Here's a simple example using Vodafone.

Example 11.2 – Straddle, Vodafone

Initial parameters

- Let's say the Vodafone share price is 110.

- An at-the-money call (strike price 110) with three months to run costs 9.5p and the 'at-the-money' put with the same strike price costs the same.

- Dealing costs in each case amount to 1.5p per contract.

Strategy

If we make a simultaneous purchase of a call and put, the deal will cost 22p in total. That's 11p each including dealing costs to buy the call and the put. This means we need the price to move at least 22p in either direction to make money.

In fact we need it to move further than that, because we need to recoup the bid-offer spread and commission when we close out the trade. Let's say for the sake of argument that this adds another 3p to our overall cost, making the total cost of the deal 25p.

Profit/loss forecast

We are only going to be in profit on the trade if the price moves 25p in either direction from the strike price of 110p, either below 85p or above 135p. If neither eventuality materialises during the life of the options, both options will expire and we will lose most of our money. All we will recoup in that instance is the amount by which one or other option is 'in-the-money' at expiry.

Results

1. **Shares move little**

   Say Vodafone *moves narrowly* for the next three months and just before expiry stands at 100p. The put is 10p in-the-money but the call is worthless. So we could sell the put and recoup 10p less dealing costs, but our loss is still going to be sizeable.

2. **Shares move sharply**

   If the underlying *does move sharply* in one direction, however, the picture is different. Let's say a month passes. Vodafone falls to 70p. The call option would be worthless at expiry, but still has two months of time value in the price (let's say 5p). Now we know the direction of the move we can sell the call for 5p. The put price has risen sharply as Vodafone's price has fallen. It has, say, 5p of time value plus 40p of intrinsic value, so we could sell it for 45p. With the 5p we have recouped from selling the redundant call option, we have a potential return of 50p compared to our original outlay and dealing costs totalling 25p – doubling our money.

The example is a classic straddle. Both call and put have the same strike price and the strike prices coincided with the price of the underlying at the time we made the trade.

But there is no need for the call and the put side of the strategy to have the same strike price provided the expiry date is the same. A straddle can therefore be constructed whereby both options are in-the-money, or both out-of-the-money. A straddle where both options are in-the-money is known as a *strangle*. Where both options are out-of-the-money, the strategy is known as a *combination* (or combo).

Figures 11.2 and 11.3 – Payoff diagrams for the buyer of a straddle and a strangle

In this example of a straddle the common strike price of the put and call options is 65, but the strategy only breaks even if the underlying price moves beyond 58 or 72. In the strangle the loss zone is flattened out.

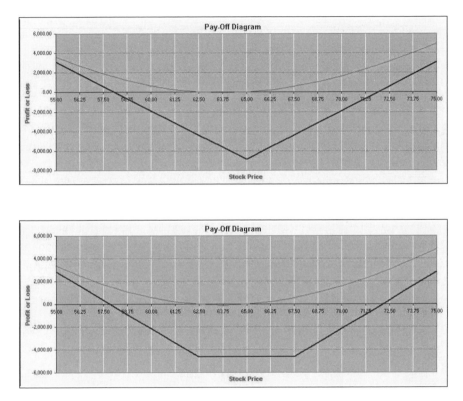

© OptionStrategy

Strangle

The obvious advantage of a strangle is that, although each option will cost more and therefore the break even point will be more distant, if the expected move in the price either up or down does not take place, the transaction will have some residual intrinsic value on expiry. The risk of near total loss is removed.

In the earlier Vodafone example, we could for example have put on a strangle by buying a call with a strike of 100 and a put with a strike of 120. Both options have the same time value and dealing costs to open and close the trade as before, totalling 25p, but there are two lots of 10p intrinsic value to add on too.

The total cost of the trade is 45p, but the risk of losing everything is limited by the fact that each option has a cushion of intrinsic value. If the price moves down, we lose the intrinsic value of the call, but gain an equivalent amount on the intrinsic value of the put. If the price moves up, we lose intrinsic value on the put, but gain an equivalent amount on the call.

To make a positive return we therefore need the underlying price to move significantly in either direction, by an amount at least equivalent to the total cost of the strategy less the combined intrinsic value at the outset.

Combo

In the case of the combo both options are out-of-the-money. In the Vodafone example, you could buy a call with a strike of 120 and a put with a strike of 100. In this case the cost is the same as the original straddle, but you risk losing everything if the shares stay within 100 and 120 for the life of the options, since the time value will erode to zero and there is no intrinsic value to fall back on. This is the riskiest of the three strategies.

You can use either options or covered warrants to produce straddles, strangles or combinations. Covered warrants cannot be used for the next category of options trade, known as spreads, because these involve writing. Covered warrants cannot be written.

Spreads

Spreads are slightly different trades. Their normal characteristics are:

- You buy one option and write another with a **different strike price**.

- They are **cheaper than other strategies** because the premium from the written options offsets the cost of the option you buy.

- You can use **either calls or puts**.

- You have a **known maximum loss or profit**.

- Depending on your view of the markets and the outlook for volatility, you sell and buy in-the-money, at-the-money or out-of-the-money options.

Let's have a look at a simple example involving our old friend Vodafone and options in it that have three months to run.

Example 11.3 – Spread, Vodafone

Initial parameters

- Assume the share price is 120p.

- You think the outlook is mildly bullish.

- You buy an in-the-money call with a strike of 110 (price 23p) and write an out-of-the-money call with a strike of 130 (price 13p).

- The net cost of the strategy is 10p. (For the sake of argument let's ignore dealing costs.)

Objective: essentially what you have done is allowed yourself to participate in any movement in the price between two points.

1. The **lower boundary** is the lower of the two strike prices plus the net cost of the strategy (in this case that's 110p plus 10p, or 120p.)

2. The upper of the two strike prices represents the **higher boundary**.

Payoff profile

With the price currently at 120p, the strategy has a cost of 10p, a maximum loss of 10p (if the shares go down) and a maximum potential profit of 10p.

This is called a *bull call spread*. A good rule of thumb is to have a gap between the two strike prices that is at least double the net cost of the trade.

Figure 11.4 – Payoff diagram for the buyer of a vertical bull spread

The strategy breaks even with the underlying at £10.25. The maximum profit and loss is £3,000 in both cases, respectively reached at £11.00 and £9.50

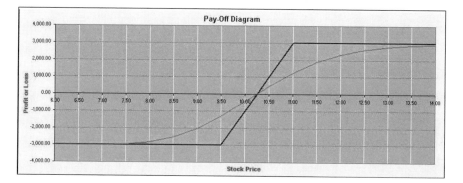

Figure 11.5 – Payoff diagram for a buyer of a vertical bear spread in the index

The strategy breaks even with the index at 5,500. The maximum profit and maximum loss is £2,500 in both cases, reached respectively when the index is 5,000 and 6,000.

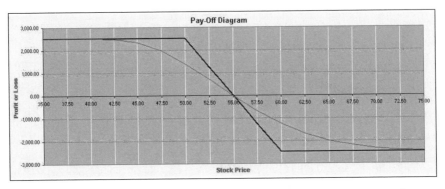

© OptionStrategy

A *bear call spread* works slightly differently. Here you expect the price to fall gently. You buy an out-of-the-money call with a high strike and write an in-the-money call with a lower strike. By doing this you *receive* a net premium at the outset which represents your maximum potential profit.

Let's look at Vodafone again.

- In this instance, assume the prices and parameters are broadly the same, except that you buy the out-of-the-money 130 call for 13p and write the in-the-money 110 call for 23p.

- Your maximum profit is therefore 10p (23p less 13p), which you receive at the outset.

- Your maximum loss is the spread less the net credit on the strategy, once again 20p less 10p, if the shares go up in price.

- You profit on any move between two boundaries, the higher boundary being the higher of the two strikes less the credit on the strategy (120p), and the lower boundary the lower of the two strikes – 110p.

- *Profit profile*: again the maximum loss is 10p and the maximum gain (received at the outset) is 10p.

This is called a bear call spread. A good rule of thumb is to have a gap between the two strike prices that is no more than double the net initial credit from the trade.

Covered writes and spreads are the two techniques that options professionals use most often, because they have known risks and returns and either low outlays or positive revenue from the outset. Bear this in mind when you are next tempted simply to buy an option.

There are many kinds of spreads. Essentially they all work in ways that are similar to one or other of those described above. The chart below shows what type of trade to do given your view on the market and the outlook for volatility.

Table 11.2 – Types of spread

Market view	Volatility view	Spread type	BUY option	WRITE option
Bear	Low	Bear call	OTM	ITM
Bear	Low	Bear put	ITM	OTM
Bull	Low	Bull call	ITM	OTM
Bull	Low	Bull put	OTM	ITM

That's the end of these two chapters on trading strategies. But there is more to learn. To trade successfully you need to have a trading plan and be able to stick to it. This calls for discipline. Trading plans are relatively easy to learn, although some run counter to many investors' intuition. We look at them in detail in the final chapter.

12

Developing Your Plan

So far this book has looked at a range of different ways to boost your investment returns and reduce your risk. We've looked at the basic concepts behind them, how to deal, and at different trading strategies you can use.

But planning is equally important. Futures, spread bets, CFDs, options and warrants are often volatile. They have a time limit. So buying and holding is not a choice you can make here. You need to have a plan of action for your trading, have a method for monitoring it, and a trigger to make you act decisively if it looks as though things are going wrong.

You need to be able to use various software tools, including technical analysis software and option valuation software. These can help you define the likely risks and rewards of the trades you put on. Market timing software can also help.

We'll cover all of these aspects in turn later in this chapter. But first, here are some basic guidelines for your trading.

Trading Rules

The problem of emotion

One of the problems with stock market trading is that emotion gets in the way. And if you let it take hold, it will wreck your chances of making and keeping a decent return.

One way of avoiding being gripped by emotion is a simple one. It is to write down in a notebook, when you make the trade, what your thoughts and the specific reasons for doing it were at the time, and what the financial objectives of the trade are.

Then as events unfold you can return to your notes and act accordingly. Either you cut your losses if things go wrong or circumstances change, or you take your profits if the trade works out as you intended. The last point may seem obvious, but it is not unknown for investors to be overcome by the greed for greater profits and, by holding on, miss the chance to get out. This is particularly important with some of the products we've looked at because of the limited time at your disposal to extract a profit.

Using this method is a simple way of eliminating the emotion that can disrupt your thought processes and lead to losses or missed opportunities. In reality it is just another way of saying that any deal you do should be monitored throughout its life. It's particularly important with investments that can be volatile or which have a time limit. You need to keep your wits about you.

Derivatives are not for 'buy and hold'

One of the great trading rules of the markets is that if anything causes you to doubt the wisdom of holding a particular position, the trade should be closed without delay. In other words, in that famous stock market aphorism –

> *'if in doubt, get out'*

In a derivative that you've bought for a speculation, there is no point, as you might do in a stock, holding on in the hope that better times will eventually come.

Actually there is an exception to this, but it is the only one. It is exchange-traded funds. Funds like this move in line with the market and you do not have gearing or a time limit to worry about. So you can buy and hold in this case, as you might with a share. In fact, exchange-traded funds are particularly suitable for pound cost averaging, whereby you invest a fixed money amount each month. This allows you to smooth out market fluctuations. The fixed money amounts mean you buy relatively fewer units at higher prices and more at lower prices – a good trading plan in itself.

Flexibility

The next cardinal rule is not to stick too dogmatically to a particular stance in the market. I've already said you should try and establish buying and selling points in advance, but don't adhere to them willy-nilly if circumstances look to have changed permanently.

If the outlook for a particular stock appears to have improved (results are better than expected; there are rumours of takeover in the offing; or a bid is announced) it may be wise to abandon a previous profit lock-in point and institute a higher one. The same thing works in reverse if the fundamentals for the company worsen. It pays to be flexible.

Cut losses

For the few trades that go spectacularly right, there will be many that are unexciting. The aim of all trading is to minimise the losses that occur when things go wrong and to maximise the profits of the ones that succeed. Cutting losses relatively quickly is a vital element in this. Equally, don't get too greedy. The legendary financier Bernard Baruch was once asked how he came to be so rich. His answer –

"by always selling too early"

You can learn a lot from studying past losses in detail to work out why they occurred. All investors, even experienced ones, make mistakes. The important point is that, if you study your past mistakes, you can discipline yourself not to repeat them.

KISS

Finally, keep it simple. You might want to have a few different trades open at the same time, but you must remain focused. In order to keep your risk to acceptable levels you might want to make sure that there isn't an obvious correlation between your trades.

There's not much point, for example, having bets in two indices that might move in the same direction at the same time. If you want to speculate on the movement in the NASDAQ market through a spread bet or CFD, it makes sense not to have another trade open in a similar technology-heavy index. In other words, make sure your risks are diversified.

> ### Golden Rules of Trading
>
> 1. Keep a note of your reasons for a trade, and its exit price.
> 2. If in doubt get out.
> 3. Don't let hope get in the way of realism.
> 4. Don't be greedy.
> 5. Be flexible if circumstances change.
> 6. Cut your losses quickly.
> 7. Learn from your mistakes.
> 8. Diversify.

Money management

There are also some basic rules that fall under the heading of what American investors call *money management*. Let's have a look at them and the impact they should have on your trading plan.

Keep losses small

This sounds obvious. But there is a simple mathematical reason why you should do this. Cutting a loss on an investment that has dropped 10% means you only have to have a gain of 11% on a subsequent investment to recoup the loss. If you don't cut your loss until the share has dropped 30%, you need a 43% rise in the next investment to recoup your loss. If the investment halves, your next investment must double to get back the loss. And so on. So have your pain barrier, either in percentage terms or a money amount, and stick to it.

Where you can, use stop-losses

Stop-losses are automatically triggered orders that close out a trade when a certain price is hit. When you speculate using volatile highly-geared investments like futures, spread betting and CFDs you should always trade with stop-loss orders in place. CFD brokers and spread betting firms will guarantee to execute stop-loss orders. It's hard to do this in normal shares. Equally you don't really need stop-losses for conventional options or warrant purchase, because your maximum loss is known at the outset. This doesn't mean you don't sell if you lose money, but because your risk of loss is not unlimited, you can adopt a more informal means of getting out of a losing trade.

Don't risk too much

Accidents happen. Many trades make losses. Don't bet your shirt on a single throw of the dice. Some traders say you should never risk more than 2% of your capital on a single trade. That seems to me to be too restrictive. But certainly the amount in question should be well under 10% of your capital. Divide your total capital by, say, 15 and don't bet more than this on a single deal – even with a stop-loss in place.

Make sure your capital is adequate

Most of the investments discussed in this book entail having a minimum amount of capital invested or collateral available. Make sure if you decide to trade futures, for example, that you have adequate resources to fund the account, that you can pay what's required to trade at least one contract, and that you have plenty left over for margin calls.

Never average down

Averaging down is committing more capital to a losing position to get the average book cost down. It is throwing good money after bad. You are increasing your exposure to a trade that has gone bad. On the other hand, adding to a winning trade can be a good idea.

Know when to sell

This is a hard one. Many investors have great difficulty deciding when to get out. Losses are easy. Cut a loss quickly, when it hits your pain barrier. With trades that are making money, most advocate selling if one of the following happens:

1. If **circumstances generally change**.

2. After a **profit warning**.

3. After an unexpected **management change**.

4. If a **share falls** more than 15% from an all time high.

These rules can apply to spread betting and to futures and CFD trades in individual stocks and markets. With options, a different set of rules applies. Broadly speaking, for futures and futures-type trades, focus on stop-losses. For options and option-type trades, focus on projected volatility and the impact of the passage of time.

Measure your gains and losses

It's worth looking at your performance in a couple of ways. The first is to look at the ratio of profits to losses on your trades. Take all your winning trades and average them. Take all your losing trades and average them. Divide the average profit into the average loss. Then look at how many trades by number are profitable and how many are losers. Divide one number into the other. This is called the accuracy ratio.

These ratios have a simple message. If your accuracy rate is low, you need to improve your trade selection. If your profit-loss ratio is too low, you need to examine whether you are hanging on to losing trades too long, or taking profits too early.

These rules are summarised to the right.

> **Golden Rules of Money Management**
>
> 1. Keep losses small
> 2. Use stop-losses where possible
> 3. Have adequate capital
> 4. Don't play with money you can't afford to lose
> 5. Never average down
> 6. Know when to sell
> 7. Measure your performance

If you follow these rules, you are well along the road to controlling your risks effectively.

Trading tips for specific investment tools

You need to be aware that there are not only general trading and money management rules, but also ones for specific instruments like futures, spread betting, options and warrants.

Futures, spread betting and CFDs

Here are a few pointers on trading that are specific to *futures, spread betting and CFDs*.

In spread betting, avoid the daily index bets, because it will be hard for you to keep pace with the professionals. Use a rolling cash or futures-based bets that can last longer than a day.

If you do have a bet on the daily index, it will be closed out automatically at the closing index value. But aim to be out of the bet before this process starts in the last 30 minutes of trading.

Why is this so? It's simple. End of day book-squaring exercises by professional traders distort share prices and the index value at the close. For the same reason prices set during the first hour of trading may be unrepresentative of the true level that will be established later. Whether you are trading futures, spread bets or CFDs in shares or indices, avoid trading at these times.

Foreign indices, particularly the Dow Jones in the US, affect the way the FTSE 100 index moves in the afternoon UK time. The FTSE 100 index is therefore really only 'its own person' between about 9am and 1.30pm, when US index futures markets begin trading actively.

A stop-loss order is often not automatically cancelled if you close the trade yourself. It's important, when doing a closing trade, to also cancel the stop-loss order at the same time. You need to check the firm's policy on this before you place the trade. This applies to any broking firm, spread betting firm, or CFD provider that offers guaranteed stop-losses.

> ### Trading tips for futures, spread betting and CFDs
>
> 1. Avoid daily index spread bets.
>
> 2. Close daily bets before last hour of trading.
>
> 3. Trade UK index in the morning.
>
> 4. If you close a trade early, cancel stop-loss order too.

Options and warrants

Here are some trading tips that pertain to trading in *options and warrants*.

Buying an option or warrant with some intrinsic value will reduce the gearing element in the price and also reduce your risk of total loss.

The precise date of expiry is important. You should know exactly what date the option or warrant expires, before you buy it.

Don't buy an option (or warrant) with less than a month to go to expiry. Only hold an option (or warrant) with less than a month to go to expiry under exceptional circumstances. You need to remember that time has an important influence on the price of an option. A big move in the underlying is worth more to you if it happens sooner rather than later.

If dealing in an option or warrant where the underlying is an individual share, you should be aware of the timing of any significant announcements, including results, trading statements, AGMs and so on, that might deliver news that has an effect on the price. This applies equally to spread bets on stocks and CFDs on stocks.

Tips for trading options and warrants

1. Options with intrinsic value have lower gearing.

2. Know the precise expiry date.

3. Don't buy with less than a month to go to expiry.

4. Be aware of timing of key announcements.

5. Remember the erosion of time value.

6. Look at strategies other than a straight purchase.

The central point to remember is that time value erodes quickly in the last few weeks of an option's life. Forgetting about time value is probably the biggest reason that many option buyers lose money. Examine your portfolio of stocks and see whether any of the other strategies described in the preceding chapter might be of use to you.

Developing your plan by looking at your assets

How you use return-boosters and risk-reducers like options, warrants, CFDs, spread betting and futures depends on where you are starting from.

In short, the action you take and the instrument you use will depend on the size of your investment portfolio, your requirements for income from those investments, your appetite for risk, the extent to which your assets are already diversified and a number of other factors.

Probably the easiest way of outlining this concept is to look at a number of different scenarios:

Table 12.1 – Return-boosters and risk-reducer scenarios

Scenario	*Solution*
Aunt Agatha – 75 year old investor. Income is a priority. 75% in bonds, 25% in cash.	There is no point Aunt Agatha selling bonds and sacrificing income. If she believes that the market is set for a strong rise in the short term then index futures, spread bets, and CFDs will provide exposure to a rising market at relatively low cost.
John Everyman – 50 year old investor. Broad blue chip portfolio. Wants extra income.	The solution here is covered option writing of stocks in his portfolio. This will yield extra returns and more often than not leave the stock intact.
Justin Large-Bonus – 25 year old City worker. Has just received his first big bonus. Believes the market is rising long term. No investments at present.	Buying a spread of ETFs through a combination of initial lump sum followed by monthly pound cost averaging.
Barry Hedger – 60 year-old investor fully invested in equities, with large blue chip portfolio needed to supplement retirement income. Concerned about possible market falls in the next one or two weeks eroding the value of his nest egg.	The solution here is using index options or warrants to insure the value of the portfolio, perhaps by buying an out-of-the-money put.
Franz Euro – 40 year-old investor, 60% invested in bonds. Wants remaining cash spread in blue chips across several world markets through single broker.	Use stock futures. These allow cost effective investment in a range of more than 100 European and US blue chip stocks through a single LIFFE broker.

Each of these investors is different. And so are so you. So before deciding which, if any, of these tools to use, you need to make a clear and objective assessment of your current portfolio and your aims and objectives in terms of capital growth, income, and risk. Once you have done this, the appropriate strategy and the tools to use to achieve it should become obvious.

Using charts and other software

Whether you are trading in futures, spread bets, CFDs, exchange-traded funds, options or warrants you will need to make a judgement about the likely price movement of the underlying share or index on which they are based. In the case of all except exchange-traded funds there will be some form of time limit involved. Futures and options, and the products based around them, all have expiry dates. With futures, it may be possible simply to roll over your trade to a new expiry month at a modest cost.

With options, however, the time left to expiry is vitally important and affects the value of the options much more significantly than, for example, the passage of time affects the value of a future. It's important for both, but particularly crucial for options.

I'm labouring this point because it does mean that you need to have a reasonably precise idea about the potential magnitude of future rises and falls in the price of the shares, and the speed with which they happen. The only way to determine this with any degree of accuracy (and even here the element of accuracy isn't perfect) is by studying price charts.

This is true of anything you trade. The long term value of anything you trade will ultimately be governed by fundamentals. With shares it might be their profits, balance sheet and growth outlook. For interest rates it might be money supply and GDP growth. And so on. But in both cases judgements about timing need to be made according to the price charts.

Price charts and some of the signals they produce work because traders expect them to work, and because they are part of human nature. If a share price has traded for a long time between 250p and 350p, and it's currently fallen to close to 250p, it's reasonable to suppose that many traders will be looking to buy at that point, and that buying pressure will lift the price. If it then moves up towards 350p, traders will look to sell, depressing the price. This is why many charts move in regular patterns and why technical analysts set so much store by these so-called support and resistance levels.

Technical analysis is a huge subject in itself. There are many books you can read about it that cover all of the main concepts and indicators in some detail. But support and resistance, trend lines, and breaks through moving averages are important for shorter term traders because they can provide predictions of the size and speed of particular movements.

For a flavour of this, the table below describes some key technical analysis signals that can help identify significant points.

Table 12.2 – Some technical indicators and what they mean

Indicator	What happens	Next move in price
Trend channel	Price bounces off bottom	To top of channel
Trend channel	Price bounces off top	To bottom of channel
Support level	Price bounces up	Up to next resistance
Resistance level	Price bounces down	Down to next support
Head & Shoulders	Price falls through 'neckline'	'Neck to head' move down
Reverse H&S	Price rises through 'neckline'	'Neck to head' move up
200D MA	Price breaks up through avg	Up to next resistance
200D MA	Price breaks down through avg	Down to next support
20D and 50D MA	20D crosses 50D, both rising	Bullish
20D and 50D MA	20D crosses 50D, both falling	Bearish

The first of the screen shots opposite shows a long-term chart of the S&P 500 with a logarithmic scale and with a head and shoulders pattern clearly visible between September 1998 and July 2002, with a neckline around the 1000 mark. In percentage terms a fall of around 33% might have been expected once the neckline was broken. The actual fall was just over 20%, showing that rules like this are not precise.

The other chart shows regular trading patterns in AstraZeneca between £18 and £28, for several years both before and after the market peak. In the intervening period £28 became the bottom of a trading range that extended up to around £36. This shows how, once a pattern like this observed and proves reliable, it might be possible to take an option or spread bet position at the top or bottom of the trading range.

This argues for you using a good quality chart software package with daily or even intra-day price updates. I'll describe some of the systems I use myself below.

For option trading in particular, if you know the likely size and probable timing of a price movement as a result of studying a stock's trading range, it is possible to plot fairly precisely how much an option trade could yield. Once again, option pricing software can help in this process. There are several tools available, both in the form of stand-alone software or available in online form. Read on for some illustrations.

For spread betting on indices, trading futures, and buying and selling ETFs, market timing software can be useful. I'll give one excellent example of how this software can work for the US market, which is perfectly accessible to UK investors through the medium of the futures, spread betting and CFD markets.

Figure 12.1 – A chart of the S&P 500 showing head & shoulders formation

© Sharescope

Figure 12.2 – Cyclical trading pattern in AstraZeneca

Key points about software

- You need to be able to read price charts to time your trades properly.

- You must use option valuation software before an option trade.

- Market timing software can help with ETFs, spread bets and futures trades.

- Some software is free.

- Invest in accurate data: successful trades recoup the cost quickly.

- There is extensive literature on how to interpret charts.

Charting software

Software is available that makes use of a broadband internet connection or some other sort of broadcast feed to give constantly updated prices. My own preference is for something simpler – a chart package that uses end-of-day prices (normally sent by email or downloaded from the web). These are available for £100 or so, or for a low monthly fee. Real time prices are much more expensive than end-of-day ones. They are only worth buying if you are happy to make use of them – sat in front of a dealing screen all day.

In the past I have used Updata's *Technical Analyst* package, which is a little more expensive than some, but offers a choice of either end-of-day or real time prices, for a monthly fee range from £29 to £89 plus VAT. Details of the package are available at www.updata.co.uk. This is quite a sophisticated package, which allows easy toggling between different chart types and time periods.

Cheaper options, which I also use regularly, include Sharescope and Winstock's *The Analyst*. Sharescope (www.sharescope.co.uk) is available for a small upfront fee and a monthly fee for data (less than £80 upfront and £14 a month for end-of-day data, or more - ranging up to £85 a month - for real time). Winstock's (www.winstock.co.uk) software costs around £129.95 for the package with end-of-day data delivered free by email. It is very important when buying software like this, particularly if you intend to trade options and warrants, to make sure that the package you choose can chart historic volatility. The Updata and Winstock products certainly do this.

Table 12.3 – What software to use and how

Type	Use	Instrument
Chart	Determining scope of trade	All
Option pricing	'What if' models of price, time, volatility	Options/warrants
Market timing	Timing buys and sells	All US

Option pricing software

Software to perform 'what if' calculations related to pricing options is important if you intend to buy options.

One particularly good package is Peter Hoadley's *OptionStrategy* software, an option strategy evaluation package that works in Excel. This is an excellent piece of work (although perhaps a little complex for first time users to get their heads around). It is free to download and use, part of a range of option strategy tools available at Hoadley's web site at www.hoadley.net/options.

A somewhat simpler package is Nigel Webb's free *Optimum* package at www.warp9.org/nwsoft. Online option calculators are available at www.numa.com and at various other sites. Online software for covered warrants is available at the sites of warrant issuers and at the London Stock Exchange site (www.londonstockex.co.uk). See Appendix 2 and Appendix 5 for warrant issuers' web addresses.

Software like this allows you to work out the theoretical value of an option or warrant for a given price of the underlying and a particular level of volatility. You can change variables like the underlying price, expiry date and volatility to see the effect produced on the option premium or warrant price.

You can't really use this in isolation. You should use it in conjunction with chart patterns in the underlying share or index to work out a likely realistic move on a trade, and identify the best entry and exit points.

For a simple way of getting to the guts of an option's price and its key components and those all important 'what if' calculations –

> *"what if volatility moves up ten points?"*

or

> *"what if the share price moves up 50p in a month's time?"*

and so on, this software is as good as any on the market.

The screen shots overleaf demonstrate this.

Let's assume that a Vodafone three month call option with a strike of 100p is priced at 10.5p. Volatility is 35%. Vodafone itself is priced at 105p.

The Optimum screenshot shows the relevant items filled in for the start of the trade, showing 90 days to expiry, the underlying price, volatility, option premium and so on. You enter these items yourself and click 'calculate' to get price or volatility.

Figure 12.3 – Optimum screenshot showing current option parameters

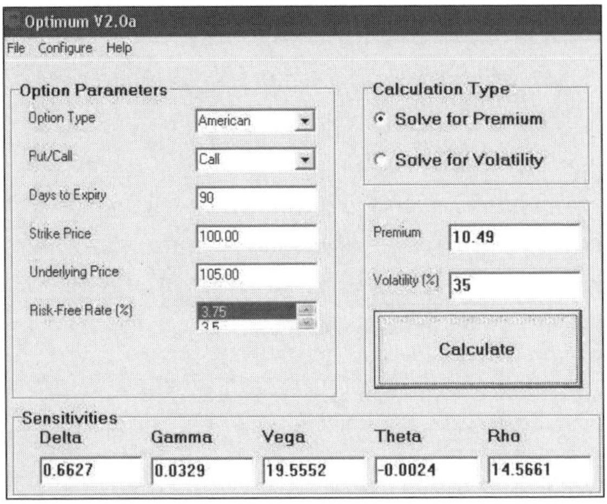

Let's also assume – after looking at Vodafone's chart and studying where the support and resistance levels are – that you think that over the next month volatility could rise to 45% and the price of Vodafone's shares could move to 125p.

Click the button for 'solve for premium' and insert the new parameters – volatility at 45%, 60 days to expiry, underlying price of 125p and click 'calculate'. This shows the new option price assuming your predictions prove correct. This is shown in the screen shot below.

Figure 12.4 – Optimum screenshot showing projected option price after factoring in changes in days to expiry, underlying price and volatility

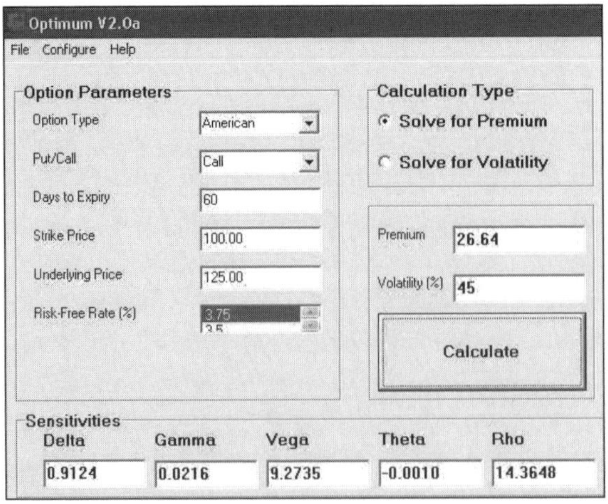

The resulting price increase shows a tempting gain (from 10.5p to 26.6p), but you need to subtract dealing costs and the bid-offer spread before arriving at your real profit. You also need to be totally honest about where you think the price could go. There is no room here for hope or wishful thinking.

The software works equally well for any option, call or put, index or stock, in any options market.

Market timing software

Market timing software takes various forms, but my personal favourite is a package called *Ultra* (www.ultrafs.com), which aggregates the evidence of more than 75 tried and tested technical indicators.

The indicators used fall into several broad categories:

1. Stock market indicators (around 85)

2. Bond market indicators (6)

3. Gold market indicators (7)

4. NASDAQ 100 stock market indicators (13)

Daily data is provided to enable each indicator to be recalculated each day (or week, if the indicator is based on weekly readings) and the current status of the indicator determined. Data is downloaded from a password-protected section of the Ultra web site.

The current status of all indicators is given (*buy*, *short*, or *stay in cash*), and the percentage change in the market since the start of the year is also provided. An overall summary on the stock market indicators page shows what percentage of indicators suggests a buy and what percentage a sell. Basic charts are provided for a range of indices, technical indicators and market and economic data. Historical data on the performance of each indicator and fully referenced information on how it is compiled is also given.

How might this be useful to you? Ultra helps by presenting a consensus view of all of the best historically proven systems. The ones that make the grade are the systems that provide the highest probability of future gain with the minimum level of risk of significant losses – without excessive trading.

Figure 12.5 – Ultra's market timing software for the US market

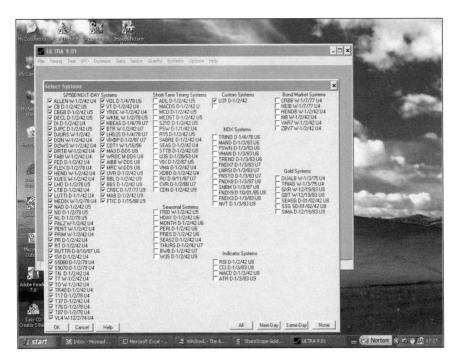

© Ultra Financial Systems

The edge that the Ultra system provides is that each system is tested thoroughly before it is included in the program. About 80% of those investigated are rejected as not being sufficiently durable in all types of market conditions.

The drawback to this system is that no data is available for UK markets. But US markets are easily available through the medium of ETFs, spread bets, futures and options. This system is ideal, for example, for trading S&P or NASDAQ futures and options, or from a longer term standpoint, buying and selling the ETF on the S&P 500.

We're now almost at the end of the book. Read on, though, and have a look at the appendices for more information about web sites and books about these products and techniques, for details of brokers and service providers that can help you get started, and for comparisons that summarise the differences between different derivative products.

Appendices

Appendix 1 – Derivatives Comparison Chart – Dealing Specifics

Question	Futures	Spread Betting	CFDs	ETFs	Options	Covered Warrants
New broker required?	Yes (but can probably use to deal in options)	Yes (but same broker may deal in CFDs)	Yes (but same broker may do spread bets)	No, trade through your existing broker	Yes, but many option brokers trade futures too	Not necessarily
Minimum account size?	Probably	Low	Varies but generally higher than for spread betting	Not applicable	Not necessarily	No
Dealing specifics?	Buy/sell, contract, delivery month	Buy/sell, product, expiry, stake size	Buy/sell, stock/index	Buy/sell, product	Buy or write, stock, put or call, strike, expiry, style	Buy to open, sell to close a specific warrant
Minimum trade size?	£2 per index pt x margin; 1000 x stock price x margin	Yes, but far from onerous	Varies but some have no minimum	No	One contract = 1000 shares or £10 per index point	No, can deal in any size
Margin % needed?	Varies with volatility of underlying. 5-30%	Varies with volatility of underlying – more than futures	Varies but can be less than futures	Not applicable, you have to put up 100%	Not applicable - pay 100% of premium	Not applicable – pay 100% of premium
Spreads?	Tight in index futures, less tight in stock futures	Varies with product and firm – less on dailies	Deal at 'cash' market price	Varies – often possible to deal inside the 'touch'	Varies – often wide on low priced options	Relatively narrow, capped by exchange
Commission?	Varies but usually £10 per lot down to £4	No	Commonly 0.25% of consideration; some charge zero	Yes, as for shares	Yes, often flat rate plus exchange levy	As for shares – often flat rate per trade
Stamp duty?	No	No	No	No	No	No
CGT on gains?	Yes	No	Yes	Yes, as for shares	Yes	Yes

Appendix 2 – Finding the Information

So far in this book we've looked at what these various everyday derivatives tools are, how you trade them, and how you can use them to boost your returns and reduce your risks. But information is power, and you will probably need to read up on the topics in greater depth than I have been able to cover in this book. You also need to know where to find price information and other data.

This appendix looks at web-based sources of information on all of the topics covered in the previous chapters.

Futures

As with options, exchange sites are a good place to start looking for information about futures and futures trading.

LIFFE

LIFFE (www.LIFFEinvestor.com) is a good source of information. The site provides an explanation of the concept of futures plus their potential risks and rewards, how they are priced, how they can be used and a guide to understanding the contract specifications.

Universal Stock Futures are explained by way of interactive education modules for both beginners and more experienced traders, live prices and FAQs. A free information pack is available. A trading simulation game for buying and selling futures is also a useful starting point to realistic trading expectations.

The related site LIFFE Data (www.LIFFE-data.com) provides 15-minute delayed prices for the full LIFFE equity product range in conjunction with Thomson Financial, as well as daily information sheets supplied on a 10-day rolling basis.

Most of the LIFFE-designated brokers previously mentioned in the section on options also trade in futures.

GNITouch

GNI's site (www.gnitouch.com) has information on futures, live prices, screenshots, a demo and software. Research is available on a weekly or daily basis once registered. The daily research features technical analysis of the market and a summary of broker upgrades and downgrades on leading stocks. The weekly research section has the technical outlook for the FTSE100 index and a round-up of Sunday press coverage. Other free research covers: forthcoming new issues; directors' dealings; and additional data on the FTSE.

MyBroker

MyBroker (www.mybroker.com), an offshoot of ODL Securities, has an introduction to Universal Stock Futures courtesy of LIFFE, as well as data and training material from the same source. It offers UK, US and European index futures online.

Man Direct

Man Direct (www.mandirect.com) offers two different online futures trading platforms for individual investors. Mtrade Pro is designed for the electronic futures markets of CME (Globex), Eurex, LIFFE, and CBOT (ACE). Mtrade EP (Electronic and pit) provides access to both electronic and open outcry markets. Apart from the exchanges previously mentioned it also provides access to NYMEX, NYBOT, Mid Am, KCBOT and WCE. The site has guides and demos for both systems. Clients also have access to free specialist research.

Other UK sources

Sucden and Berkeley Futures (both of which are mentioned in more detail in the options section) also deal in futures.

US markets

Information on US futures trading can be found at the Chicago Board of Trade (www.cbot.com). The site features online interactive seminars on a range of topics related to futures trading. The site also contains an interactive tutorial on trading futures. The CBOT offers an online publication *Trading in Futures,* which is both basic and informative.

The 'market data' section of the site has reports, statistics, charts and commentaries to help navigate the markets. Quotes and data are available for products traded on the CBOT site.

In addition to the CBOT, the Chicago Mercantile Exchange (www.cme.com) also trades in futures. The difference is in the products traded. CBOT is home to commodity futures, to US Treasury bond futures contracts and other US Treasury instruments, whilst the CME trades in interest rates, stock indices, foreign exchange and commodities.

Information in trading in all these areas can be found on the site. It also features market data, quotes, historical data, charts and an online trading simulator. The CME offers online courses previously only available at the exchange. These cover areas such as options for beginners, an introduction to futures, understanding forwards and an introduction to technical analysis. The fees for these courses varies from $99-$150.

CFDs

Most information about CFDs comes from the brokers themselves, but there are also some independent sites.

Hargreaves Lansdown

Hargreaves Lansdown's (www.h-l.co.uk) site has an online guide to CFD trading which includes trading strategies, benefits and pitfalls of CFDs and margin trading. Would-be users can order a brochure and apply online to open an account.

CMC Markets

CMC Markets (www.cmcmarkets.co.uk) offers online real-time CFD trading in over 1,000 UK, US, Europe and Pacific Rim products. Information on the site includes an explanation of the concept of CFDs plus a dealing guide and 'marketmaker' trading software. This can be downloaded for a 14-day free trial. The software features real-time prices, news and analysis, and real time charting. The dealing guide covers topics such as opening and closing positions, margin requirements and order types. A worked example of trading in CFDs gives a good insight into the process.

Free seminars are available in London.

IG Index

IG Markets (www.igimarkets.com) offers CFDs on UK stocks over £10m market value, US stocks over $500m and selected Euro-zone stocks It also offers detailed examples of CFD trading and of limited risk trading and a general explanation of CFDs and how they work. The CFD dealing platform has streaming prices and one-click dealing. Dealing is not restricted to the internet.

City Index

City Index (www.cityindex.co.uk) offers live online trading in leading UK, US and European equities as well as major stock indices. Information on the site is detailed and informative. It covers areas such as opening a long/short position and a comparison of conventional stock trading and CFD trading. A downloadable brochure is also available. Market information sheets provide contract specifications for all CFD markets traded by City Index.

Free seminars are held regularly in London.

GNITouch

GNI (www.gnitouch.com) has a guide to CFD trading. A daily CFD morning report and a US and European CFD report can be accessed following registration. Also on offer are recent articles on CFDs and weekly research reports. Trading is either online or traditional.

IFX

IFX (www.ifxmarkets.com) trades in equity and index CFDs online or by telephone. Apart from a product description, the site has detailed worked examples of long/short equity and short index trading. Clients have access to free charting, live prices, news, market commentary and 24 hour support.

Man Direct

Man Direct (www.mandirect.com) trades in UK, US and European markets online or by telephone. The site offers a free online demo of its *MTrade* trading system and other information. Free registration gives access to research reports. Free information can also be received by email.

Spread Betting

Most spread betting information comes courtesy of the spread betting firms themselves, so you may need to take some of it with a grain of salt.

City Index

City Index (www.cityindex.co.uk) has downloadable brochures including market information sheets, spread betting terms and conditions, together with an introduction to the subject as well as the risks involved.

The firm offers bets in shares, FTSE350 sectors, indices, options, interest rates, bonds, commodities and the volatility index. Both online and telephone dealing services are available.

IG Index

IG Index (www.igindex.co.uk) was the first to offer spread betting back in 1978. Its site features a technical guide containing detailed information concerning the bets on offer, with numerous examples.

IG offers spread betting on shares, indices, betting on individual sectors in the FTSE 350, options, interest rates, bonds, commodities and energy, currencies, and house prices.

Online trading is via a browser-based interface which eliminates lengthy downloads and installations. The service also includes automated pricing and dealing, real-time open position valuations and thousands of live dealing prices. There is also a searchable news feed from AFX, historical charts, and real-time tick charts generated from IG's prices, plus technical analysis and research.

Also on offer is a mobile betting service by phone or PDA, with live prices and one-touch betting in most of the markets covered by the main service.

Open evenings for clients and potential clients are held monthly in London.

Cantor Index

Cantor Index (www.cantorindex.com) has an online brochure explaining the ins-and-outs of spread betting. Cantor does concede that spread betting is not for the faint hearted. Accordingly, it offers guaranteed stop-loss facilities and options to allow you to limit potential losses.

Spread betting is offered on shares, indices, interest rates and bonds, commodities, options, and currencies. There are also spreads on sector indices based on the components of the FTSE All-Share Index.

Trading is either real-time online, via the firm's PULSE trading system, or by telephone. The site also features live prices, financial news, interactive charting, a portfolio management system and a trading demo.

Financial Spreads

Financial Spreads (www.finspreads.com) was launched in April 1999. Its site features an online trading demo with interactive examples, plus a guide to spread betting and FAQs. Financial Spreads registers all new clients, free of charge, to an eight-week training course. This explains the fundamentals of spread betting and demonstrates all the different bets on offer.

The firm offers bets in shares, indices, currencies, bonds, interest rates, metals and commodities. Guaranteed stop-loss bets are available, for an extra charge. Credit facilities may be available depending on personal circumstances. Trading is either online or by freephone. An automated phone service is available to account holders 24 hours a day 365 days a year.

CMC

At CMC Spreadbet (www.deal4free.com) there is a dealing guide and general information on spread betting. CMC also majors on commission-free trading of CFDs (see separate entry). Spread betting is available on shares, indices, interest rates and bonds, gold, silver and other commodities, and currencies. Although deal4free is execution-only, dealers are available 24 hours a day to help with any trading queries. Seminars are available around the country on using the firm's *marketmaker* software. There is an online demo of the software on the site.

Spreadex

Spreadex (www.spreadex.co.uk) has an online trading guide with worked examples and live prices. Spreadex offers bets in shares, indices, currencies and interest rates and bonds. Spreadex Radio has a commentary on live sports events.

TradIndex

TradIndex (www.tradindex.com) was launched in April 2002 and is part of Tradition, the UK operating arm of Compagnie Financiere Tradition. The site features a 'learn to trade in five easy steps' section, a good introduction to spread betting. Those new to the spread betting area might also find the trading simulator useful.

Cash management in TradIndex is only via debit cards, which eliminates the necessity for extensive credit checks. It also has the risk-limiting feature of a mandatory stop-loss. Trading is available in indices, commodities, currencies, bonds and single shares.

Options

There is no shortage of information on futures and options, and in both cases the exchanges are a good place to start.

LIFFE

LIFFE's private investor site (www.LIFFEinvestor.com) has much of what you need to understand and develop knowledge about trading equity and index options. It's a great one-stop shop. There are trading examples, information on the potential risks and rewards of options, and explanations about how equity options are priced and how they can be used. Also on the site is information on a range of options, prices to help you to trade, exchange press releases and data and trading tools.

A useful inclusion is a series of interactive education modules ranging from a basic introduction and understanding of options to more detailed learning and information about the more advanced trading techniques.

The LIFFE Market Equity Prices Service contains prices of individual equity options and FTSE 100 index options. These update automatically on a 15-minute delayed basis. The service is free once registered. Also available is information on the underlying shares and an intra-day charting service.

LIFFE made a conscious decision to treat its site partly as an educational tool and partly as a resource for investors and it has succeeded in this aim. As an integrated source of information on options in the UK, the site can hardly be bettered.

Around five years ago, the exchange introduced a Private Investor Broker Access Programme. It aims to work closely with dedicated broker channels through which private investors can access and trade LIFFE's equity futures and options.

ADM Investor Services

ADM Investor Services (www.admworld.com) focuses primarily on FTSE 100 and UK individual equity options. The site offers a brief introduction and outline on the use of options. Also on the site are details of the dealing services and products on offer. ADM offers a full round the clock service, with staff working in shifts.

ODL

ODL (formerly Options Direct) offers online dealing through its MyBroker trading system. The site has a user guide explaining how to execute options trades online and some useful option-related spreadsheets you can download. The firm trades in UK and US equity and index options and offers both an execution-only and advisory service.

The firm's 'Mybroker' software is a complete trading software package. It provides live, continuously updated share prices to account holders and delayed quotes for basic plan users. Access is also provided to many other features such as charts, a trading module and market research data. The 'Market Pulse' section provides over 100 screens containing hundreds of items of technical information such as advances and declines, new highs and lows and so on.

GNItouch Futures

GNItouch Futures (www.gni.co.uk) also offers online options dealing giving access to all leading electronic exchanges on which contracts are available. These include Eurex, LIFFE, CME and CBOT. The trading functions include market orders, limit stops, limit, fill-or-kill and market-if-touched. There is access to a support desk around the clock. Orders can also be placed by telephone. The site also has a downloadable trading demonstration, a quick-start option, and a full user guide.

Rensburg Sheppards

Rensburg (www.rensburgsheppards.co.uk) is a large regional investment management firm. The site has details of its services and charges with a link to LIFFE for information.

ManDirect

ManDirect (www.mandirect.com) has little information concerning options on its site but a booklet is available.

Sucden

Sucden (www.sucden.co.uk) has a useful site offering free online research and analysis material. This includes daily, weekly and monthly research reports, an options calculator and market calendars. It is necessary to register. There is a link to LIFFE for quotes and prices.

Berkeley Futures

Berkeley Futures (www.bfl.co.uk) has an online system for live trading directly into options exchanges. It supports trading in all major options exchanges. Telephone dealing is offered as an alternative to online dealing.

The downloadable trading software enables easy order entry, real-time calculation of profits and losses, and information on open positions and working orders. A free video demo and downloadable user guide is available.

Charles Stanley

Charles Stanley (www.charles-stanley.co.uk) trades in EuronextLIFFE products and all major overseas markets.

Other brokers

In addition to the above LIFFE-recommended brokers there are others who provide access to the exchange's range of options.

- Goy Harris Cartwright (www.ghcl.co.uk), Leicester, plus branches in Bath and London

- Cheviot Capital (www.cheviot.co.uk), London

- Fyshe Horton Finney (www.fyshe.co.uk), Birmingham, Leeds, Northampton, Stamford, Leicester, Huddersfield and London

- The Kyte Group (www.kytegroup.com), London

- James Brearley (www.brearley.co.uk), Blackpool with seven other branches in the NW

- Philip J Milton (www.miltonpj.net), Devon

- Redmayne Bentley (www.redmayne.co.uk), HQ in Leeds with numerous other branches

- Seymour Pierce Bell (www.seymourpierce.com), London and Crawley

- Thomas Grant (www.thomas-grant.com), Leicester

US markets

Elsewhere, the Chicago Board Options Exchange (www.cboe.com) is a good source of information on the US markets. The site features options tutorials and online courses with webcasts. The self-guided tutorials are designed for every level of investor and teach the basics of calls and puts, the intricacies of the market place and the strategies that can be used by individual investors.

The resource centre provides online software, newsletters and strategies plus an options library with a vast collection of CBOE's educational materials in PDF format. In addition there are trading tools such as an options calculator and charts plus market quotes and data. CBOE also has index microsites. These offer additional information specific to selected CBOE products.

Covered Warrants

The new covered warrants market is fairly well served with information. The six (at present) issuers of covered warrants are good sources of information.

Dresdner Kleinwort Wasserstein

Dresdner Kleinwort Wasserstein (www.warrants.dresdner.com) is a particularly good site. There are various pricing tools on offer to calculate gearing, parity ratio and intrinsic value amongst others. A useful feature on the site is an online course in association with Incademy.com. This guides the investor through the ins and outs of covered warrants in some detail.

SG Warrants

SG Warrants (www.warrants.com) covers new SG warrant issues in 'At-the-money', a warrant magazine which also features market trends, trading tips and a series of warrant educational articles. It is available either by email or post. Weekly technical analysis is provided on every stock and index on which SG issues warrants in association with TRADINGcentral. This newsletter can be emailed in PDF form on request. Tools available on the site include warrant calculators and strategy tools, sensitivity analysis and a warrant theory glossary. A range of seminars on the subject is available in London and elsewhere throughout the year.

Goldman Sachs

Goldman Sachs (www.gs-warrants.co.uk) features various tools to help understand and analyse warrant investments. The site also has a downloadable guide containing a variety of information such as pricing and investment strategies.

JP Morgan

JP Morgan (www.jpmorganinvestor.com) features live quotes and a warrants guide.

London Stock Exchange

The London Stock Exchange (www.londonstockexchange.com) has a section on covered warrants that includes a private investor brochure and an introduction to covered warrants (via a link to SG), trading reports and monthly statistics on issuer performance.

Two tools are available; the 3D Warrant Adviser is an interactive tool that allows the investor to simulate different scenarios in real-time, and a turnover analysis tool whereby statistics for trading volumes can be created.

Elsewhere on the LSE site is an e-learning module on covered warrants, taking in both basic and advanced concepts, within the exchange's 'Educational Resources' content.

ADVFN

The LSE sponsors a section on warrants at ADVFN (www.advfn.com). The site has a tutorial by Alpesh Patel. It covers all the main issues relating to covered warrants. Also on the site are warrant prices from the LSE.

The sites of brokers that deal in warrants can be useful sources of information.

TD Waterhouse

TD Waterhouse (www.tdwaterhouse.co.uk) provides detailed information including a section on warrant theory. This covers pricing parameters, sensitivity coefficients, strategies and risks. There are free seminars on warrants in London as part of the firm's wider investor education programme.

Selftrade

Selftrade (www.selftrade.co.uk) has links for prices to SG and DresdnerKleinwort for warrant prices and to the LSE for monthly bulletins, as well as a warrants overview.

Redmayne Bentley

Redmayne Bentley (www.redmayne.co.uk) has a warrant fact sheet plus a glossary of terms.

The McHattie Group

The McHattie Group (www.tipsheets.co.uk) has been publishing advisory newsletters since 1987. The site features a Warrants Documents Library where literature can be downloaded, including a sample copy of Warrants Alert Newsletter. Andrew McHattie can be emailed with a question, the answers to which are posted on the site. The site has a daily email service and '7 steps to success in covered warrants', plus a pricing service in collaboration with Commerzbank.

Exchange Traded Funds

ETFs are relatively new and therefore in the UK at least, there are comparatively few sites with comprehensive information.

iShares

iShares (www.ishares.net) has a comprehensive site containing all you need to know about these instruments. Included in the site is information on the funds, how to trade ishares, news and features, quotes, charts and an index monitor. Further resources include a monthly performance report, an iShares distribution schedule and a description of all the funds together with a glossary of terms. In addition, if you require further information, it is possible to email iShares with a question.

London Stock Exchange

The London Stock Exchange (www.londonstockexchange.com) has a brief introduction to ETFs on its site together with a downloadable brochure.

Trustnet

Trustnet (www.trustnet.com) is a free independent information service for private investors and IFAs. Databases include prices, performance and an A-Z of fund profiles. Risk ratings are updated daily.

NASDAQ

In the USA, where ETFs really took off first, the NASDAQ site (www.nasdaq.com) has a section devoted to ETFs. Why NASDAQ? ETFs were primarily developed in the US by the Amex exchange, which is now part of NASDAQ.

Appendix 3 – Software

We have indicated which of the sites mentioned in previous sections have trading simulators or other valuation tools. It may be, however, that you want to use stand-alone software that can be downloaded to your PC.

Ultra

In the chapter on exchange-traded funds, we mentioned market timing software like *Ultra* (www.ultrafs.com), which is a useful (though US markets-only) aid to trading ETFs and other types of index-tracking products.

Optimum

We strongly recommend using option valuation software to perform 'what if' scenarios before putting on option trades. Option valuation software (and similar products available online for warrants) allow you to project the price of an option or warrant when inputting changes to several different key variables like time to expiry, underlying price, volatility and so on. An easy download is the simple option pricing model called *Optimum*. This is available as a free download from www.warp9.org/nwsoft.

OptionStrategy

An excellent and more detailed option valuation and strategy program, which works in Excel, is OptionStrategy Mk.3. Devised by Peter Hoadley, this is available for download at www.hoadley.net/options. It includes strategy accounting, pay-off diagrams, volatility calculators and a range of other features well worth exploring.

Updata

Updata *Technical Analyst* is an excellent general technical analysis package. Further details of this software can be found at www.updata.co.uk or by contacting the company at:

Updata House
Old York Road
London
SW18 1TG
Tel. 020 8874 4747

Appendix 4 – Further Reading

The following are mini-reviews of a selection of books that will allow you to read more on derivatives in general and the particular categories of product you might wish to deal in. We recommend further reading before you take the plunge.*

Futures

Getting Started in Futures
Todd Lofton
John Wiley, 1997
This is aimed at investors who are new to futures. It is devoid of economic jargon and mathematical formulae with examples being drawn from everyday experience. It explains how the markets work and how profits can be made whilst limiting risk. (Code 22579)

All About Futures - The EasyWay to Get Started
Russell Wasendorf
McGraw-Hill, 2001
This has practical strategies for beginner futures traders. The book includes topics such as developing a trading system, anticipating the direction of futures price movements, the four basic approaches to technical analysis, placing trades and working with a broker. (Code 13640)

Starting out in Futures Trading
Mark Powers
McGraw-Hill, 2001
This is a new edition of the book first published in 1993 and is suitable for both new and experienced traders. It covers the many new influences governing the market such as new rules and regulations and electronic trading and the internet. Also included are the key basics such as choosing a broker, placing an order and the increased importance of stock indices. (Code 13624)

---

*All books listed on these pages are available from the Global-Investor Bookshop:

http://books.global-investor.com

To find the books, go to the url above, and in the Search box type the number which appears in brackets immediately after the description. e.g. for 'Getting Started in Futures', type '14572' in the Search box.

Alternatively, you can order by phone on 01730 233870.

Trading S&P Futures and Options
Humphrey Lloyd
Traders Press, 1997
An introduction to the S&P 500 futures and index option markets. The book provides an overview of the technical indicators used in the futures and options market such as stochastics, Bollinger bands and channel trading amongst others. Charting patterns are also described plus candlestick charting, a favourite of many futures traders. The basics of trading are covered, such as placing an order and the language and techniques involved in trading. (Code 4818)

The Complete Guide to Electronic Futures Trading
Scott Slutsky and Darrell Jobman
McGraw-Hill, 2000
This book aims to help investors with the transition from traditional to online trading. It is a practical guide covering everything from data and software to finding the right broker. (Code 12517)

Outperform the Dow: Using Options, Futures and Portfolio Strategies to Beat the Market.
Gunter Meissner and Randall Folsom
John Wiley, 2000
The book outlines the strategies and techniques that many investors have used to beat this benchmark and make profits. Strategies discussed include last year's winners and smooth risers, semi-monthly analysis, Tuesday opportunities, and covered call writing. (Code 13160)

Understanding and Trading Futures
Carl Luft
Irwin, 1994
This is an insight into the futures markets from basic explanations and principles to more advanced concepts. First published in 1991, the updated edition covers the innovations in the market over the intervening years, Dr Luft uses worksheets to familiarize the reader with futures contracts and the basic trading strategies of hedging, speculating and arbitrage. (Code 3522)

The Four Biggest Mistakes in Futures Trading
Jay Kaeppel
MarketPlace Books, 2000
This book shows how to identify and avoid making four common mistakes that can reduce profits. Topics covered include determining how much money you can afford to risk and learning the ins and outs of leverage and how it can be used to advantage. (Code 13577)

Introduction to Futures and Options
Donald Spence
Woodhead Publishing 1997
This book is a comprehensive guide suitable for all levels of experience. The first part covers the markets, instruments and trading; the second covers regulation and management. (Code 0992)

Winning in the Futures Market (A Money-Making Guide to Trading, Hedging and Speculating)
George Angell
Irwin, 1990
This is suitable both for experienced and novice traders. Basic trading tactics are clearly outlined and the book includes topics such as hedging strategies, moving averages, spread trading, and chart trading techniques. (Code 0657)

Day Trade Futures Online
Larry Williams
John Wiley, 2000
Veteran futures trader Larry Williams explores the many aspects of futures trading online. Topics include winning strategies, using the internet, assessing risk thresholds, and when to get out of your trade. (Code 13212)

A Complete Guide to the Futures Markets (Fundamental Analysis, Technical Analysis, Trading, Spreads and Options)
Jack Schwager
John Wiley, 1984
How to forecast prices and how to incorporate this knowledge into a trading strategy. Written in clear, non-technical language with numerous market examples, charts and tables. (Code 0904)

An Introduction to Derivatives
Reuters Financial Trading Series
John Wiley, 1999
A beginner's guide to derivatives which includes definitions, descriptions, quizzes and examples. Futures, options and swaps are studied from basic concepts through to applications in trading, hedging and arbitrage. (Code 10538)

How the Futures Markets Work
Jake Bernstein
NYIF, 2000
The second edition of this book by a world- renowned trader and author covers the complexities of the futures markets in an easily accessible format .It explores the products, players, mechanisms, procedures, tools and strategies involved in futures trading. (Code 13957)

Single Stock Futures – The Complete Guide
Steven Greenberg
Traders Press, 2002
A guide to every aspect of single stock futures covering all the basics of futures, margin and the mechanics of order placement. (Code 14822)

Options

The Option Traders Guide to Probability, Volatility and Timing
Jay Kaeppel
John Wiley, 2002
This is an introduction to the most important concepts in options, and how to trade in them. The book includes a thorough analysis of both the risk and reward of the various trading strategies and when to use each one. The final section teaches when to take a profit and when to cut losses. The book is written in a clear easy to follow style and is aimed at both those new to the options market and returnees. (Code 16269)

Getting Started in Options
Michael C. Thomsett
John Wiley, 2001

Written by an active options trader, this is a straightforward guide to the options market with explanations of how they work and how to benefit from them. Topics covered include setting up a plan based on individual requirements, reading the market and spotting the specific risks of each type of option and using options as insurance against stock market losses. (Code 22320)

Traded Options – A Private Investor's Guide
Peter Temple
FT Prentice Hall, 2001

The book explains in an easy to read style how traded options work and explores useful strategies and techniques supported by clear worked examples. The various sections include choosing a broker, share price charts, trading rules and objectives and options online. (Code 0434)

Listed Stock Options
Carl Luft and Sheiner
Probus, 1994

This is a hands-on study guide for investors and traders written in a clear concise manner. Included in it are the properties of option pricing, simple call and put option strategies, basic spreads, and advanced option strategies. (Code 0459)

The Options Course
George Fontanills
John Wiley, 1998

This is a complete options trading course based on the author's series of seminars. The basics concepts are covered followed by the various techniques for successful trading. It is designed for investors of all levels of experience. (Code 21024)

Option Pricing (Black-Scholes Made Easy)
Jerry Marlow
John Wiley, 2002

The theory behind option pricing is approached in a straightforward manner by integrating text and interactive computer animations and simulations. The book and accompanying CD-ROM teach the fundamentals of option valuation together with explanations on the practical use and application of the theory. (Code 14741)

Fundamentals of the Options Market
Michael Williams
McGraw-Hill, 2000
A hands-on guide to the options market by an experienced market maker. The book covers topics such as option pricing, the differences between and benefits of listed stock options, index options and LEAPS and the use of technical indicators. Quizzes, checklists, guidelines and examples are used throughout the book as an aid to understanding. (Code 13911)

The Four Biggest Mistakes in Option Trading
Jay Kaeppel
Traders Library, 1998
Kaeppel shows how to avoid the most common pitfalls and explains why they are so common. In an easy-to-read style he breaks down the problems and offers solutions. (Code 9969)

The Compleat Option Player
Kenneth R. Trester
Institute for Options Research 1998
Written by a successful options trader, this book includes worksheets to help traders design strategies easily, plus over 40 option pricing tables to help in deciding on the optimum time for buying and selling. (Code 16743)

Millard on Traded Options
Brian Millard
John Wiley, 1997
Written in a clear concise style the author explores trading strategies from simple to advanced. The book includes sections on buying and writing call and put options, technical indicators, the relationship between share and option prices, and how to use advanced strategies such as spreads, straddles and combinations. Explanations are given on how to take positions that are less risky than shares and how to make profits whether the market rises, falls or stands still. (Code 1424)

All About Options
Thomas McCafferty and Russell Wasendorf
Probus 1998
The book explains in depth the type of options and their use and then moves on to strategies useful for developing a trading plan. The most common mistakes are discussed together with methods of avoiding them. (Code 0489)

Trading Index Options
James B. Bittman
McGraw-Hill, 1998

Written by a leading option educator and trader. There are sections covering the behaviour of option prices, understanding risk and limit exposure and trading psychology. Strategies from basic to complex are covered together with case studies. The book is based on a Windows based software programme. This is included with the book, but according to reviewers this only covers European style options and only allows one install. (Code 9268)

Options Made Easy: Your Guide to Profitable Trading (2nd Edition)
Guy Cohen
FT Prentice Hall, 2002

An interactive guide to options using charts and diagrams. The book covers everything from the basics of trading to advanced strategies with real-life examples throughout. Amongst the topics discussed are fundamental and technical analysis, trading psychology, developing a trading plan and selecting a strategy. (Code 23001)

Conservative Investor's Guide to Trading Options
Leroy Gross
John Wiley, 1999

A balanced approach to options trading including information on reading options quotations in the financial media, entering an options order and negotiating commission discounts. Also discussed are strategies for the moderate risk taker such as buying puts on owned stock to preserve profit and limit risk, and writing straddles. (Code 4108)

Exchange-traded funds

Exchange-Traded Funds
Brad Zigler
McGraw-Hill, 2001
An investor's guide, covering the various types of ETFs, rules and recommendations for trading, strategies for building portfolios and a comparison of ETFs vs mutual funds. (Code 13849)

Exchange-Trade Funds
Jim Wiandt and Will McClatchy
John Wiley, 2001
The authors provide a frank appraisal of the advantages of ETFs including lower capital gains and low management fees. Also covered is the full range of available funds together with help on evaluating the funds' performance and usefulness. Strategies for their use in portfolios and the management of short and long term risk are also discussed. (Code 14485)

All About Exchange-Traded Funds
Archie Riechard
McGraw-Hill, 2002
A practical guide to ETFs covering the basic rules of trading, the various types of ETFs, the difference between ETFs and mutual funds and effective strategies. (Code 14711)

How to Be an Index Investor
Max Isaacman
McGraw-Hill, 2000
Detailed information on investing in listed securities whether as a short-term day trader or a long-term investor. An overview and strategies are covered in part one whilst the second part covers exchange shares. (Code 12947)

Spread betting

How to Win at Financial Spread Betting
Charles Vintcent
FT Prentice Hall, 2001
The first part of the book covers the ins and outs of spread betting such as the characteristics of the various types, instructing a dealer and also using Contracts for Difference. The second half covers the techniques for using spread betting including how to short sell a share or index and the advantages of online dealing facilities. (Code 14024)

Covered warrants

The Investor's Guide to Warrants
Andrew McHattie
FT Prentice Hall, 2000
The book explains the investment process of using warrants, discusses the growth of the warrant market, and the advantages of warrants over shares. The assessment and selection of warrants is outlined plus building a portfolio to suit individual needs. The book is mainly concerned with warrants but covered warrants are also discussed. (Code 12836)

Andrew McHattie on Covered Warrants
Andrew McHattie
Harriman House 2002
The book is intended as a primer for investors new to covered warrants with a focus on the UK. The inevitable jargon is explained throughout the book and in the glossary. The various chapters include the types and terms of covered warrants, pricing and trading, the advantages and disadvantages, strategies and how to analyse covered warrants from beginners level to more advanced. (Code 14709)

General

Derivatives – The Wild Beast of Finance
Alfred Steinherr
John Wiley, 2000
The second edition of a book first published in spring 1998 in which the author predicted a destabilisation of the global market structure if some firm risk management were not exercised in the derivatives market. His predictions became reality and this edition brings the story up to date. The role of derivatives in a developing world economy is discussed at length in a lively and informative manner. The final part of the book looks into the future and predicts the exportation of the American model of finance to the rest of the world. (Code 12533)

Against the Gods
Peter L. Bernstein
John Wiley, 1996
The story of risk from gamblers in ancient Greece to modern chaos theory. The author explains the concepts of probability, sampling, regression, game theory, and rational versus irrational decision making while exploring the role of risk in modern society. Character sketches of world-renowned intellects such as Pascal and Bernoulli and Bayes and Keynes are included as well as the stories of inspired amateurs who influenced modern thinking. The general topic of risk is tied into risk management and thereby to derivatives. (Code 9734)

Derivatives Diary
Richard Folcker
John Wiley, 2001
A guide to professional fund management techniques in diary format. It follows the career of a fictional character as he learns the ropes of the fund management business. (Code 13741)

Fooled by Randomness (The Hidden Role of Chance in the Markets and in Life)
Nassim Nicholas Taleb
Texere, 2001
This is an exploration of how people perceive and deal with luck in business and life. Three major intellectual issues are discussed; the problem of induction, the survivorship biases; and our genetic unfitness to the modern world. Numerous characters who have grasped the significance of chance appear in the book such as George Soros and philosopher Karl Popper. (Code 22346)

Bear Market Investing Strategies
Harry D. Schultz
John Wiley, 2002

The book aims to provide the necessary tools for an investor to survive in a bear market. In addition bear markets are looked at from a historical viewpoint, together with the structure and economic conditions in which they thrive. (Code 14919)

Inventing Money (Long Term Capital Management and the Search for Risk-Free Profits)
Nick Dunbar
John Wiley, 1999

This is an account of the events leading up to the collapse of the hedge fund LTCM. It provides an insight into the world of arbitrage and derivatives. The book tells the story of the individuals and institutions involved and analyses in detail the trades and the reasons they went wrong. (Code 10946)

Appendix 5 – Glossary of Websites

This glossary provides a list of relevant web addresses and the categories of derivative in which they trade. In some cases, particularly private client stockbrokers, it should be noted that many of these firms are primarily dealing in stocks and shares. Inclusion in this glossary indicates that they are also prepared to deal for clients in options, covered warrants and so forth.

A

ADM Investor Services (www.admisi.com): options, futures

ADVFN (www.advfn.com): covered warrants, general

B

Berkeley Futures (www.bfl.co.uk): options, futures

BWD Rensburg (www.bwd-rensburg.co.uk): options

C

Cannon Bridge (www.cannonbridge.co.uk): futures, options, CFDs

Cantor Index (www.cantorindex.com): spread betting

CFD Trading (www.cfdtrading.com): CFDs

Charles Stanley (www.charles-stanley.co.uk): options

Cheviot Capital (www.cheviot.co.uk): options

Chicago Board of Trade (www.cbot.com): futures

Chicago Board options Exchange (www.cboe.com): options

Chicago Mercantile Exchange (www.cme.com): futures

City Index (www.cityindex.co.uk): spread betting, CFDs

CMC Spreadbet (www.deal4free.com): spread betting

comdirect (www.comdirect.co.uk): covered warrants, ETFs, general

Commerzbank (www.warrants.commerzbank.com): covered warrants

D

Deal4Free (www.deal4free.com): CFDs

Dresdner Kleinwort Wasserstein (www.warrants.dresdner.com): covered warrants

Durlacher (www.durlacher.co.uk): covered warrants, CFDs, options

E

Easy2Trade (www.easy2trade.com): futures

F

Financial Spreads (www.finspreads.com): spread betting

Fyshe Horton Finney (www.fyshe.co.uk): options

G

GNI (www.gni.co.uk): futures, CFDs, options

Goldman Sachs (www.gs-warrants.co.uk): covered warrants

Goy Harris Cartwright (www.ghcl.co.uk): options

H

Hargreaves Lansdowne (www.h-l.co.uk): covered warrants, CFDs

Harris Allday (www.harrisallday.c.o.uk): covered warrants

I

iDealing (www.idealing.com): covered warrants, spread betting, CFDs

Ifx (www.ifx.com): CFDs

IG index (www.igindex.co.uk): spread betting, CFDs

Incadamy.com (www.incademy.com): training

Ionic Information (www.sharescope.co.uk): software

iShares (www.ishares.com): ETFs

J

James Brearley (www.brearley.co.uk): options

JP Morgan (www.jpmorganinvestor.com): covered warrants

K

Killik (www.killik.co.uk): covered warrants

Kyte Group (www.kyteclients.com): options, futures

L

LIFFE (www.LIFFEinvestor.com): options, futures

London Stock Exchange (www.londonstockexchange.com): covered warrants, ETFs

M

Man Direct (www.mandirect.com): futures, options,CFDs

MyBroker (www.mybroker.com): options, futures

O

ODL Securities (www.odlsecurities.com): covered warrants, options

Optimum (www.warp9.org/nwsoft): software

Option Strategy (www.hoadley.net/options): software

P

Philip J Milton (www.miltonpj.net): options

R

Redmayne Bentley (www.redmayne.co.uk): covered warrants, options

S

Seymour Pierce Bell (www.seymourpierce.com): options

SG Warrants (www.warrants.com): covered warrants

Spreadex (www.spreadex.co.uk): spread betting

Sucden (www.sucden.co.uk): options, futures, CFDs

T

TD Waterhouse (www.tdwoodhouse.co.uk): covered warrants

The McHattie Group (www.tipsheets.co.uk): covered warrants

Thomas Grant (www.thomas-grant.com): options

TradIndex (www.tradindex.com): spread betting

Trading Lab (www.tradinglab.co.uk): covered warrants

Trustnet (www.trustnet.com): ETFs

U

Ultra (www.ultrafs.com): software

Updata (www.updata.co.uk): software

V

Voltrex options (www.voltrex.net): options, futures

W

Walker, Cripps, Weddle, Beck (www.wcwb.co.uk): covered warrants

Index

B

C

D

G

Gamma – see *The Greeks*

Gearing

> Explanation of 36-37
> On CFD contracts 88
> On futures contracts 54
> with Options 131-133

Greeks, The 127-129

H

Hedging

> Explanation of 38
> of ETFs 174
> Strategies 218-219
> with Options 134-136, 225
> with Warrants 152

Hurdle rate – see *Warrants*

I

IG Index 18

Indexes

> and ETFs 168
> Explanation of 39-40
> Futures contracts 60
> Options on indexes 135, 136

Interest rate futures 64-65

iShares – See *Exchange-traded funds* 279

L

LIFFE

> Development 15
> Equity options 130
> Futures contracts 59
> German Bund 15

R

S

T

U

V

W